STUDIES IN IMPERIALISM

general editor John M. MacKenzie

Established in the belief that imperialism as a cultural
phenomenon had as significant an effect on the dominant
as on the subordinate societies, Studies in Imperialism
seeks to develop the new socio-cultural approach which
has emerged through cross-disciplinary work on popular
culture, media studies, art history, the study of education
and religion, sports history and children's literature.
The cultural emphasis embraces studies of migration and
race, while the older political and constitutional,
economic and military concerns will never be far away.
It incorporates comparative work on European and
American empire-building, with the chronological focus
primarily, though not exclusively, on the nineteenth and
twentieth centuries, when these cultural exchanges were
most powerfully at work.

Gender and imperialism

MANCHESTER
UNIVERSITY PRESS

STUDIES IN IMPERIALISM

Gender
and imperialism

edited by Clare Midgley

MANCHESTER
UNIVERSITY PRESS

Manchester and New York

Distributed exclusively in the USA by
ST. MARTIN'S PRESS

Published by **MANCHESTER UNIVERSITY PRESS**
OXFORD ROAD, MANCHESTER M13 9NR, UK
and ROOM 400, 175 FIFTH AVENUE, NEW YORK, NY 10010, USA

Distributed exclusively in the USA by
ST. MARTIN'S PRESS, INC.
175 FIFTH AVENUE, NEW YORK, NY 10010, USA

Distributed exclusively in Canada by
UBC PRESS, UNIVERSITY OF BRITISH COLUMBIA,
6344 MEMORIAL ROAD, VANCOUVER, BC, CANADA V6T 1Z2

British Library Cataloguing-in-Publication Data
A catalogue record for this book is available from the British Library

Library of Congress Cataloging-in-Publication Data
Gender and imperialism / edited by Clare Midgley.
        p.   cm. — (Studies in imperialism)
    ISBN 0–7190–4819–2 (cloth). — ISBN 0–7190–4820–6 (pbk.)
    1. Imperialism—History.   2. Sex role—History.   3. Feminist
theory.   I. Midgley, Clare, 1955–.   II. Series: Studies in
imperialism (Manchester, England)
JC359.G456   1998
305.3'09—dc21   97–20338

ISBN 0 7190 4819 2 hardback
     0 7190 4820 6 paperback

First published in 1998

01 00 99 98   10 9 8 7 6 5 4 3 2 1

Typeset in Trump Medieval
by Northern Phototypesetting Co Ltd, Bolton
Printed in Great Britain
by Redwood Books, Trowbridge

CONTENTS

GENERAL EDITOR'S INTRODUCTION

Imperialism, as several of the contributors to this volume point out, seemed to be a highly gendered phenomenon. Words like 'manly' and 'effeminate', each of them normatively loaded, were seldom far from the lips of imperial rulers and others involved in the colonial complex. Some shafts of light were cast upon my own dim realisation of this when I surveyed children's literature, plays, exhibition displays and other aspects of popular culture in researching my work *Propaganda and Empire* in the early 1980s. The genderisation of imperialism became even more apparent when I examined the literature of travel and hunting for *The Empire of Nature* a few years later. Social Darwinism seemed to infuse all of these gendered processes: the related activities of hunting and war supposedly defined more highly evolved masculinities, marking off northern Europeans from southern, white from black, male from female, people of the 'manly' mountains from those of the 'effeminate' plains, hardened protein-eating pastoral warriors from the 'softer' carbohydrate-consuming agriculturalists.

It was no accident that pastoral modes tended to emphasise differentiation in gender roles much more than the agricultural. Processes of conquest and domination, including an alleged capacity to penetrate and mould the environment to the will of the 'manly' conqueror, highlighted these gender divisions yet further. Imperial cultures were replete with such social stereotypes, particularly in the socialisation of the young. The atavisms of empire were beautifully conveyed through the privileging of frontier lifestyles to inhabitants of an urban industrialised society, for example through Baden-Powell's creation, the Boy Scouts – and indeed its female response, the Girl Guides.

In unveiling such dominant masculinities, it was all too easy to portray European women as either the victims of or accomplices in the imperial programme, while indigenous women were equally essentialised as objects either of lust or of moral crusades, 'saving brown and black women from brown and black men'. Such crude dichotomies, which have in common the objectivisation of women, have now been banished from serious historical study. A remarkably productive and stimulating wave of women's and gender studies has served to separate propaganda from perceived actuality, the social theory of empire from its practice. Gender relations, interactive and intertwining, responsive and mutually transformatory, have become much clearer in both imperial and indigenous societies. Nowhere is this better illustrated than in the cultural and intellectual dimensions of empires, with their capacity both to reinforce and to weaken, and in the economic roles and powers of resistance of peoples around the world.

This volume makes a major contribution to this new historiography, both in theoretical and empirical forms. By adopting both chronological depth, from the late eighteenth to the mid twentieth centuries, and geographical breadth – including India, Ireland, Australia, the Caribbean and Africa, as well as the so-called metropolitan society – it offers major challenges and profound insights for gender studies. Above all, it reveals the sterility of the monolithic approach. These important essays demonstrate the complex multi-voicing of women in all aspects of the imperial condition.

John M. MacKenzie

ACKNOWLEDGEMENTS

The idea for this book was born when I convened a strand of papers on gender and imperialism for the Anglo-American Conference at the Institute of Historical Research. I am indebted to the Studies in Imperialism series editor, John MacKenzie, who broached the possibility of editing a book on the theme, and who has consistently facilitated its development as I shifted focus from publishing a group of conference papers to the more ambitious project of commissioning a series of thematic essays. I would also like to thank my editors at Manchester University Press: Jane Thorniley-Walker, who commissioned the book, and Vanessa Graham, who saw it through to completion. I benefited from being granted one semester's study leave from Staffordshire University, and I would like to record my gratitude to my history colleagues for covering my teaching and administrative tasks over this period, and to Derek Longhurst, Dean of the School of Arts, for his support. Thanks are also due to Shula Marks and Deborah Gaitskell, for discussions of the original proposal; to members of the colonial/post-colonial study group in the School of Arts at Staffordshire University, whose helpful feedback from a variety of disciplinary perspectives helped to clarify my own approach; and, most importantly, to the book contributors themselves for their collective commitment to the project. Finally I would like to thank Norris Saakwa-Mante for his critical eye, valuable suggestions, encouragement and faith in the value of the book.

Clare Midgley

NOTES ON CONTRIBUTORS

PADMA ANAGOL is Lecturer in History in the School of History and Archaeology at the University of Wales College of Cardiff. She is the author of numerous articles on gender and women's history in India and of a forthcoming book entitled *Beyond the Courtyard: Feminism in Western India, 1850–1920*.

HIMANI BANNERJI was born in India in 1942 and migrated to Canada in 1969. She is currently an Associate Professor in the Department of Sociology at York University, Canada. Her publications include a collection of essays on culture and politics, *The Writing on the Wall*, work seeking to theorise 'race' gender and class relations (*Thinking Through; Unsettling Relations; Returning the Gaze*); feminist historical sociology on colonial and post-colonial India; and a forthcoming collaborative book on bodies and power. Her current research interest is in Canadian state formation and the discourse of multiculturalism. She is also a published poet, novelist and short story writer.

HILARY McD. BECKLES is Professor of Social and Economic History at the Cave Hill Campus of the University of the West Indies. He is the author of several books and articles on Caribbean slavery including *Natural Rebels: A Social History of Enslaved Black Women in Barbados*.

BARBARA BUSH is Principal Lecturer in History in the School of Arts at Staffordshire University and the author of *Slave Women in the British Caribbean, 1650 to 1838*. She has published widely in the area of gender, slavery and resistance and is currently working on a monograph on 'Imperialism, Race and Resistance in Britain and Africa, 1919–1945'.

JANE HAGGIS is a Lecturer in the Sociology Department, Flinders University, Adelaide, South Australia. She has published in the areas of feminist methodology and gender and imperialism. She has just completed a study of British women missionaries and their work in South India and is currently working on a history of women's involvements in the missionary movement in nineteenth-century Britain. She is also undertaking research into the social construction of whiteness in contemporary Australia.

CATHERINE HALL is a Professor in the Department of Sociology at the University of Essex. She is co-author with Leonore Davidoff of *Family Fortunes: Men and Women of the English Middle Class, 1780–1850* and the author of *White, Male and Middle Class: Explorations in Feminism and History*. She is currently completing a book on England and empire in the mid nineteenth century.

MARILYN LAKE holds a Personal Chair in the School of History at La Trobe University, Bundoora, Australia. She has published widely in the history of gender relations in Australia, her most recent books being *Creating a Nation* (with Patricia Grimshaw, Ann McGrath and Marian Quartly) and *Gender and*

War: Australians at War in the Twentieth Century (with Joy Damousi). She is currently writing a history of feminist political thought.

CLARE MIDGLEY is Senior Lecturer in History in the School of Arts at Staffordshire University, and the author of *Women Against Slavery: The British Campaigns, 1780–1870*. She is deputy editor of *Women's History Review*. Her current research is into the relationship between feminism and imperialism.

MARGARET WARD grew up in Belfast, and is currently Research Fellow in History at Bath Spa University College. She has written extensively on women's contribution to the Irish nationalist movement, on the history of Irish suffrage and on contemporary Irish feminism. Publications include *Unmanageable Revolutionaries: Women and Irish Nationalism; Maude Gonne: A Life;* and *'Seeds Beneath the Snow': A Biography of Hanna Sheehy-Skeffington*. Current interests include women and the Irish peace process, and nationalist male responses to female pressures for equality in post-1916 Ireland.

LIST OF ABBREVIATIONS

BCL   British Commonwealth League
CAS   Colonial African Service
CPGB   Communist Party of Great Britain
IAFA   International Association of the Friends of Abyssinia
IASB   International Africa Service Bureau for the Defence of Africans and Peoples of African Descent
ICU   Industrial and Commercial Workers' Union
ILP   Independent Labour Party
LCP   League of Coloured Peoples
LGAA   London Group on African Affairs
LMS   London Missionary Society
SPFEE   Society for the Propagation of Female Education in the East
WEA   Workers' Educational Association

INTRODUCTION

Gender and imperialism: mapping the connections

Clare Midgley

This book brings together two traditionally separate areas of historical literature: writings on women and gender on the one hand, and scholarship on British imperialism and colonialism on the other. The result is not a comfortable marriage, but it is, I believe, a productive one. This introduction traces the course of the engagement between the two fields. It begins by highlighting the separate origins and differing preoccupations of women's/gender history and traditional British Imperial History, and then proceeds to discuss the challenges to traditional Imperial History posed by new 'post-colonial' histories of imperialism. This section provides a background for the survey which follows of existing scholarship on gender and imperialism, which leads in turn to an outline of the arrangement and contents of this new collection of essays.

Gender history and Imperial History: separate developments

In British academia gender history and traditional Imperial History have developed very separately. Gender history has tended to follow the somewhat parochial perspective of much British social history, exploring the interaction of gender and class but ignoring race and ethnicity, claiming to describe Britain while actually talking about England, and rarely attempting to place the history of men and women within Britain in the context of Britain's role as a leading imperial power.[1] Imperial History, on the other hand, has been written as the history of the exploits of male policy-makers, administrators, military commanders, explorers and missionaries, but with no attempt to assess the significance of their masculine gender. The history of women and imperialism has been seen as of marginal significance, as

[1]

a special interest area which can be safely left to female historians. A similar lack of attention has been granted to the gender metaphors which are so central to imperial discourse: to the descriptions of colonial exploration and conquest as the penetration of virgin lands, and to the feminised representations of colonised men – to what Joan Scott describes as the use of gender as 'a primary way of signifying relationships of power'.[2] Even when new topics are tackled, as in Ronald Hyam's study of sexuality and empire, there is resistance to drawing on insights from feminist historians concerning issues of gender and power.[3]

This separation between gender history and Imperial History has its roots in the very contrasting origins of the two sets of scholarship. Gender history has radical, anti-establishment roots in women's history. In Britain, this developed from the early 1970s in response to feminist discontent at the marginalisation of women, and the preoccupation with class to the exclusion of gender, in the writings of labour and social historians. Feminist historians pointed out that one half of the human race was being excluded from accounts which purported to move away from the study of political elites and write the experiences of 'ordinary' people into history.[4] Gender history, however, is more than the recovery of women's pasts and inclusion of female experiences into history. First, it incorporates the study of men as gendered beings – a study of masculinity which has roots in the men's movement and gay politics as well as feminism.[5] Second, as Joan Scott has pointed out, usage of the term 'gender' among British and American feminists developed for three purposes: to stress the social construction, rather than biological determination, of distinctions based on sex; to emphasise the need to study the relationships between men and women rather than simply constructing a separate women's history; and to suggest that the study of women does not simply add new subject matter to history but also involves a rethinking of traditional historical paradigms.[6] Until very recently, however, gender historians have been preoccupied with the rewriting of social history, and have hesitated to challenge the paradigms of Imperial History.

These paradigms derive from Imperial History's roots in the 'high imperial' period of the 1880s to 1914. From the 1880s to the 1940s the desire among leading academic historians to increase scholarly knowledge of the British Empire was closely associated with their desire to foster popular enthusiasm for Britain's role as an imperial nation. University lecture series in Imperial History provided the basis for best-sellers such as Sir John Seeley's *The Expansion of England* (1883), and academics became involved in the production of school textbooks and the provision of adult education in history with a pro-Empire bias.

Imperial History was also closely tied to the practice of imperial rule, with academics themselves acting as advisers on imperial policy and administration, providing education for future members of the Colonial Service, and fostering the development of imperial pressure groups such as the Imperial Federation League and the Round Table. The development of the academic study of Imperial History was encouraged by the financial endowments of the imperial expansionist Cecil Rhodes, who endowed professorial chairs in the field and provided the finance for Rhodes Scholarships, intended to educate potential leaders from the colonies.[7] Such commitments to and involvement in the imperial enterprise affected not only the perspectives and interpretations of historians but also the focus of their study, which was overwhelmingly on colonial policy and administration.

Following the demise of the British Empire with the post-war process of decolonisation, Imperial History lost its original role in forwarding the imperial enterprise and faced challenges to its legitimacy from Britain's former imperial subjects. European historians' perspectives on colonised peoples were condemned as racist and paternalistic and new histories constructed from the viewpoint of the colonised emphasised the negative impact of imperialism on third world economic development, uncovered the rich histories of pre-colonial societies, and developed nationalist perspectives which gave historical legitimacy to newly independent nation states. As the leading Caribbean historian and politician Eric Williams pointed out, the historical field had become a 'battleground on which imperialist politics struggle against nationalist politics'.[8] Liberal nationalist historiography, the dominant alternative to Imperial History, was in turn challenged from the left for remaining trapped in a reactive response to colonial historiography, for presenting a monolithic view of society and for an elitist focus on nationalist leaders.[9] Since the 1980s alternative 'histories from below' have been produced: in India, for example, the Subaltern Studies group has published a series of studies which explore the relationship between mass movements such as peasant uprisings and the development of Indian nationalist politics.[10]

Within Britain itself the separation of Imperial History from the mainstream of British political, economic, social and cultural history has been questioned since the 1970s, and Seeley's assertion of the importance of colonies to the formation of the British nation has been readdressed from a post-colonial perspective.[11] Debates have been initiated over the need to incorporate a critical analysis of empire into the study of history in the national curriculum in schools.[12] Histories of black, Asian and Irish settlers in Britain have shown how the Empire affected the ethnic composition of the metropolis, while studies of the politics of race, immigration and nationality have demonstrated the intersections between imperial and domestic concerns.[13]

Despite these post-war developments, however, Imperial History has succeeded in maintaining itself as a viable and dynamic field of study in Britain, modifying its name to Imperial and Commonwealth History and expanding its subject matter from an original focus on metropolitan policy-making and administration, to give greater attention to interaction with events on the 'periphery', to the economic, social and cultural aspects of empire, and to the impact of empire on British society itself.[14] All these trends are visible in the new *Cambridge Illustrated History of the British Empire* edited by P. J. Marshall. The volume also provides a good example of how Imperial History attempts to diffuse radical challenges to its legitimacy: some space is accorded to non-Western perspectives; these are, however, relegated to the final section of the book – and indeed even within this section only Tapan Raychaudhuri's chapter on British rule in India offers a challenge to the dominant tone of the book. The final words are left to Marshall himself, who sums up this tone in his concluding judgement that 'given the likely alternatives, to have drawn the British ticket in the nineteenth-century lottery of empire may not, on balance, have been an altogether unhappy accident'.[15]

Is it possible, then, to get beyond the impasse of opposed 'first' and 'third' world perspectives on empire existing in parallel, with Imperial Historians acknowledging the existence of alternative viewpoints but relegating them to the margins of their standard accounts of the Empire and continuing to claim for themselves the virtues of greater objectivity and balance? Clearly this is not simply a battle of ideas conducted on a level ground in which the strongest intellectual argument will win. The continuing strength of Imperial History relates to its institutional strength: to its power bases in prestigious British universities and their associated publishing houses at the old heart of empire. There have, however, been important moves to get beyond the impasse at an intellectual level. Imperial History has been challenged not only by the construction of alternative national histories written from the perspective of the colonised, but also by post-colonial theory, developed mainly by literary scholars following in the wake of Edward Said's path-breaking study, *Orientalism* (1978).[16] Post-colonial theory and colonial discourse analysis have been dismissed by many historians of empire as the latest fashionable preoccupations of 'politically correct' literary scholars, and ridiculed for their theoretical obscurantism. Even John MacKenzie, who is sympathetic both to Said's political stance and to his preoccupation with imperial culture, has concluded that his work – and that of his followers and of other colonial discourse analysts – is of little value to historians because, despite claims to historicism, it fails to follow the basic procedures of sound historical scholarship: it does not embed ideas within their shifting economic and social contexts, and thus creates a falsely unidimensional and unchanging picture of Orientalism and the culture of imperialism.[17]

While I am sympathetic to this concern with historical particularity, I believe that MacKenzie's criticisms do not undermine the value of two crucial insights offered by post-colonial theory: that the production of dominant forms of knowledge about the colonised provided an important basis for the exercise of imperial power; and that Imperial History was – and to some extent remains – a key form of colonial discourse. Post-colonial critics have succeeded in exposing what Gyan Prakash has described as the 'leaden understanding of colonialism as History':[18] the representation of European expansion as the motor of historical progress from savagery to civilisation, or of development from static 'traditional' to dynamic 'modern' societies, and of the colonised as passive subjects rather than active agents of historical change.[19] This 'leaden understanding' can be seen manifested in the Whig interpretative framework of much Imperial History, a framework whereby British imperialists are presented as the agents of Britain's gift of freedom and democratic self-government to the peoples of the world: independence is thus represented as the end-result of imperialism rather than as the achievement of the colonised.[20] Imperial History provides the last place within the various sub-disciplines of history in Britain where the Whig approach continues to thrive. The reason for this, I would argue, is ideological: it provides a means of justifying British imperialism.

While post-colonial theory has effectively deconstructed Imperial History as a powerful form of colonial discourse, I would agree with MacKenzie that it has nevertheless provided few tools for reconstructing alternative histories of imperialism. As Dane Kennedy has pointed out, the problem is that post-colonial theorists tend to slide from a critique of Imperial History into hostility to the project of history writing as a whole, to doubts about the possibility of constructing non-Eurocentric historiography, and to assertions of the impossibility of retrieving the voices of the colonised.[21] In challenging Imperial History's claims to scientific objectivity we need to avoid the defeatist trap of such extreme forms of post-modernism, in which history is viewed as no more than one form of fictional discourse. Rather, following the suggestions made by Joyce Appleby, Lynn Hunt and Margaret Jacob, we can construct new histories based on a redefined notion of objectivity 'as an interactive relationship between the inquiring subject and an external object'.[22] Avoiding the trap of relativism, which would allow Imperial History to survive as one legitimate viewpoint among many, we can aspire to tell the truth about the history of imperialism, and to demonstrate that our accounts are more true than the discourse of Imperial History.

New histories of British imperialism will only effectively displace the old Imperial History if we go beyond literary discourse analysis with its exclusive focus on culture to provide new historical perspectives on the economic, social, political, military and administrative facets of imperialism, if we combine the construction of a broad new picture with a sensitivity to regional specifics and chronological shifts, and if we place at the centre the experiences and viewpoints of the colonised. We also need to be wary of unthinking use of the binary categories of coloniser/colonised, recognising that neither were homogeneous groups. In the first place, there were regional complexities: for example, as Marilyn Lake has highlighted, in white settler societies settlers were both coloniser (in relation to indigenous inhabitants) and colonised (in the sense of being under British imperial governance).[23] Second, there were variations within the same geographical area and time span, with gender among the crucial shapers and differentiators of colonial experiences. Feminist historians thus have a key role to play in reconstructing new histories of imperialism, ensuring that both coloniser and colonised are treated as gendered subjects, and that attention is paid to the ways in which imperial involvements and interactions were shaped by gender as well as by race and class.

Gender and imperialism: mapping the connections

This book contributes to this process of revision through building on the existing work in the field of gender and imperialism which has been produced since the 1980s, stimulated both by the growth of women's history and gender history and the development of new histories of imperialism. Increasing scholarly interest in the social and cultural impact of empire in both British and colonial contexts has offered more scope for a consideration of women than did earlier preoccupation with the almost exclusively male domains of policy-making and administration. At the same time the construction of alternative histories from the perspectives of the colonised has opened up possibilities for rendering visible the experiences of colonised women as well as men, while post-colonial theory provides powerful theoretical tools for deconstructing gendered colonial stereotypes of these 'others'.

[6]

What, then, of this existing literature in the field of gender and imperialism? What kinds of topics have been explored, what conceptual frameworks and research agendas have been laid down, and what are some of their strengths and their limitations? Broadly speaking, studies have sought to rectify the exclusion of women from standard histories of imperialism and the exclusion of imperialism from histories of women; they have introduced gender as an analytical concept into the study of empire; and they have drawn attention to the need to study the construction of imperialism as a masculine enterprise. More specifically, six broad areas of scholarship can be identified: white Western women and imperialism; the impact of empire on women in Britain; colonised women's experiences; masculinity and empire; sexuality and empire; and gender and colonial discourse. A brief survey of work in each of these areas will now be provided in order to give an overview of the existing state of scholarship on gender and imperialism.

Studies of white Western women and imperialism focus on India and Africa in the period between the 1860s and the 1940s – from the period of 'high imperialism' characterised by the British Raj and by the 'scramble for Africa', to the beginnings of decolonisation. Work in this area adopts three main approaches. First, work in the 'recovery' mode, much of it aimed at a popular audience, seeks to restore women to Imperial History and demonstrate the scope of women's involvement in the Empire: as the wives of colonial administrators, settlers, explorers, missionaries and nurses.[24] Second, and closely related, are 'recuperative' works which aim to debunk myths of the 'destructive' female whose racial prejudice led to the disruption of 'good' relations between male colonial official and indigenous peoples, and to reassess women's imperial roles in a more positive light.[25] The problems with both the above approaches have been effectively exposed by Jane Haggis's critique of the women-centred approach to writing the history of colonising women. This, she argues, tends to represent white women either as patriarchal victims or as plucky feminist heroines, in both cases ignoring their racial privileges in colonial society, and to render white women visible at the expense of rendering the colonised invisible.[26] Her criticisms are partly met by recent works, which adopt a more critical approach to analysing women's role in shaping colonial societies and the nature of their relationships with indigenous women, and identify female involvement in imperialism ranging from 'complicity' to 'resistance'.[27]

The second major category of works on gender and imperialism are those which explore the impact of imperialism on women within Britain, contributing a gender perspective to the project of bringing together British social and cultural history with Imperial History. These works include studies of women's involvement in the anti-slavery movement,[28] of the relationships between feminism, racism and imperialism,[29] of female colonial emigration,[30] of the impact of state policies focusing on women's roles as mothers of the imperial race,[31] and of the history of black, Asian and Irish women in Britain.[32] Such work is in its early stages but is characterised by a desire to bring a critical consideration of imperial and racial issues into British women's history. But while women's history is certainly being enriched, there is a danger that women will simply become an add-on special interest area whose historical presence fails to disrupt the frameworks of traditional Imperial History unless such scholarship makes explicit the ways in which gender structured the forms of British involvement in empire.

The third key area of research has been into colonised women's experiences. In terms of numbers of women affected, and their immense variety of cultural and social backgrounds, this is a much wider topic than either of the above, and the quantity of research is uneven, reflecting the differential access to resources for research and publication which is one of the legacies of British imperialism. There is a considerable body of literature on women settlers in the 'white settler' colonies but less on the indigenous women whom these colonisers displaced.[33] In the case of India, research has focused on the impact of the British Empire on the dominant Hindu community and on middle-class women, and Kumkum Sangari and Sudesh Vaid point out that 'no anthology or even generalisation about Indian women could hope to be representative'.[34] The impossibility of generalisation is even more true of Africa, and Zenebeworke Tadesse has highlighted both 'the vast potential for the emergence and institutionalisation of women's history in Africa' and the daunting constraints, which are 'not limited to women's history but to African historiography as a whole' and have led to 'the conspicuous absence of the writings of African women from most published and widely circulated materials'.[35]

Despite the large amount of research which remains to be done, an impressively wide variety of topics have begun to be explored. These include: the differential impact of colonialism on men and women; women and resistance, including the involvement of women in nationalist and independence movements, the development of feminisms and women's resistance to colonial slavery; contests over British imperial social reform aimed at women and the impact of such reforms on women; the impact of colonialism on the sexual division of labour and on women's land rights and socio-economic position.[36] Debates have been generated concerning the question of female agency, the relative importance of the pre-colonial and colonial roots of the continuing subordinate status of women in the post-colonial era, and the value of Gramsci's concept of hegemony for an understanding of the balance between coercion and consent in colonial rule.[37] All such scholarship involves an ongoing struggle both against the marginalisation of women in male nationalist historiography and against Western feminist stereotypes of a homogeneous 'third world woman' who is totally subordinated and oppressed.[38]

The newest area of research is into masculinity and empire, and three examples are suggestive of the wide variety of approaches being adopted. Graham Dawson has explored the relationship between changing historical forms of imperial adventure narratives and 'the imagining of masculine subjectivities' in Britain and pinpointed the continuing psychic resonance of the imperial soldier hero as symbol of ideal British masculinity.[39] Catherine Hall has published the preliminary stages of a major project on imperial culture and the construction of Victorian British middle-class masculinity.[40] Mirilinha Sinha, bridging the divide between British and Indian historiography, has explored the simultaneous colonial construction of the 'manly Englishman' and the 'effeminate Bengali'.[41] In addition there is also a growing body of work, particularly relating to India, which explores interactions between indigenous and colonial patriarchal systems.[42]

Work on patriarchy, together with studies of contests over prostitution and the implementation of the Contagious Diseases Acts and the Ilbert Bill in colonial India, also contribute to the fourth major category of scholarship: research into sexuality and empire.[43] From within the fold of Imperial History, Ronald Hyam has delineated the ways in which the Empire acted as an arena of sexual opportunity and adventure for white men. While assembling a mass of fascinating material, he refuses to engage directly with the question of unequal race and gender-based power relations which facilitated and shaped white men's sexual access to colonised peoples.[44] Such questions of power are central to recent analyses of imperialism and sexuality by Anne McClintock and Ann Stoler. McClintock seeks to explore the intersections of discourses of gender, race, class and sexuality within Britain and its Empire through bringing together the approaches of Freudian psychoanalysis and socio-economic history.[45] Anthropologist Ann Stoler connects the development of the European bourgeois order with the colonial management of sexuality through an engagement with Foucault's *History of Sexuality*, throwing new light on the relationship between colonial power and discourses of sexuality.[46]

Foucault's work, as Stoler points out, has been widely influential in post-colonial studies, including the study of gender and colonial discourse. Sara Mills, for example, in her study of women travel writers, is concerned to explore 'the way that Foucault's theories, colonial discourse and feminist theories can interact to produce an analytical framework'.[47] Another set of writings on gender and colonial discourse attempts to rectify the lack of a gender perspective in Edward Said's classic study of Orientalism.[48] Rana Kabbani has explored Western views of Eastern women, highlighting the centrality of images of women in the harem in Western constructions of the Orient.[49] Billie Melman and Reina Lewis respectively examine British women writers' and artists' views of the East, questioning Said's stress on the stability and homogeneity of Orientalism, and Lewis argues that theoretical models of colonial discourse should be reformulated to take into account the marked differences between women's and men's representations of the East. This difference is ascribed to the fact that European women did not have straightforward access to an implicitly male position of Western superiority. As a result they produced representations of the Orientalised 'other' which, while within an imperialist framework, were different from and often less denigrating than men's, and sometimes highlighted similarities rather than differences between themselves and non-Western women.[50] This tendency of British women to draw analogies between their own position and the position of colonised peoples is highlighted in Moira Ferguson's study of British women writers and colonial slavery.[51]

This book's agenda

The collection of essays in this volume builds on this wide-ranging scholarship on gender and imperialism. It discusses both colonising and colonised women and men, as well as women and men in Britain who were affected by empire. It is organised around the conceptual category of gender rather than the subject matter of women and, while the majority of chapters foreground women, all take gender roles and relations as central. Its contributors are academics based in history and sociology departments in Britain, Canada, Australia and the Caribbean, scholars whose own diverse backgrounds and descents reflect patterns of forced and voluntary migration which are part of the legacy of British imperialism, providing the reader with a variety of voices and perspectives.[52]

No collection on the history of British imperialism can hope to be all-encompassing, and this is no exception. The book's chronological focus is on the modern period, between the late eighteenth century and the Second World War. Similarly, the geographical range is uneven and incomplete, but goes beyond the Indian–African axis of much existing imperial history, not excepting work on women and gender, to include the Caribbean, Australia, Ireland and Britain itself.

Contributors were specially commissioned to write on a series of themes. Rather than simply presenting summaries of the existing state of knowledge in the particular area, however, the essays draw on new research, offer new perspectives and make critical interventions into key debates. As a result, it is hoped that all the chapters will be of interest to, and accessible to, students and academics wishing to gain a picture of the current 'state of play' among historians in the field of gender and imperialism.

The book is arranged in three parts. The first two, dealing with 'Impositions and impacts' and 'Reactions and resistances' respectively, focus on colonial contexts, while the third, 'The Empire at home', concentrates on the impact of imperialism within Britain itself. Such a tripartite division may seem problematic, given telling recent critiques of the impact/response model of Imperial History and of the limitations of treating metropole and colony as separate analytic fields.[53] It is retained, however, because it conveniently highlights the differing dominant foci of particular chapters, though most contributors do adopt an interactive model of the relations between coloniser and colonised and between Britain and its Empire.

Part I of the book offers new perspectives on the nature of British imperial power through exploring the gender dimensions of the imposition of British control. Himani Bannerji's study of the age of consent debate contributes to the growing body of scholarship on contesting indigenous and colonial patriarchies in India. Bannerji reveals how the reorganisation of gender relations was central to the establishment of British imperial hegemony in India. This involved increasing interventions in the social and private lives of the colonised in the name of the rule of law and of social reform. Jane Haggis's focus is also on India. Having effectively critiqued earlier work on white women colonisers, Haggis here discusses her attempts to write a 'non-recuperative' history of white women and colonialism. She draws on post-structuralist, anthropological and post-colonial theory to find a way of writing about British women missionaries in India which avoids a simplistic dualism between condemning them as racists or recouping them as benevolent victims of imperialist patriarchy. Instead of creating a unitary account, she tries to bring three histories into relationship: her contemporary perspective on gender and imperialism; missionary women's own accounts of their endeavours; and the story of Indian women.

Part II explores the gender dimensions of a spectrum of reactions to British imperialism. Interestingly, while Haggis is critical of a

[11]

'woman-centred' approach and finds in post-colonial theory fruitful insights for writing about *colonising* women, both Padma Anagol and Margaret Ward critique post-colonial theory for its tendency to deny agency to *colonised* women. Perhaps this difference relates to the need to respond to distinct historiographies: Haggis is concerned to de-centre colonising women following the production of a number of recuperative books on their experiences, whereas Anagol and Ward wish to centre colonised women and stress their agency, so as to combat a tendency to stress the overwhelming power of colonial discourse and indigenous patriarchies to determine their lives. Anagol focuses on the Indian women who were the targets for conversion by the kind of British Christian missionary women discussed by Haggis. She stresses Maharashtrian women's agency in converting from Hinduism to Christianity, their woman-centred approach to religion, their critiques of both Hindu attitudes to women and European missionary racism, and the crystallisation of their feminist consciousness through a selective appropriation of dominant discourses. Ward explores the gendered nature of Irish nationalism, stressing the need to interrogate representations of Irish nationalism, by both discourse theorists and British feminists, as an exclusively masculinist tradition leading to a liberation from Britain which was of little benefit to women. She suggests that male nationalist discourse shifted over time and that some women interpreted nationalist myths in women-centred terms, and she shows that empirical historical work can expose women's efforts to become agents of change in their own right, providing instances of self-assertion as well as self-sacrifice.

The other two chapters in this part on 'Responses and resistances' also foreground female agency in a colonial context. Marilyn Lake argues that the outlook of white Australian feminists in the late nineteenth and early twentieth centuries was 'shaped by the context of an imperial frontier': their position in a pioneer society numerically dominated by the 'marauding white man', and their ascribed colonial role as agents of civilisation and custodians of the race, led them to develop a 'frontier feminism' which stressed the need to protect both white and aboriginal women from sexual exploitation and abuse by white men. Hilary Beckles's chapter moves back in time to the eighteenth and early nineteenth centuries, and shifts the focus from white colonising women to enslaved black women in Britain's West Indian colonies. Like Ward, Beckles stresses that in order to fully appreciate the extent of women's resistance to colonial domination we need to define resistance as far more than violent uprisings. He calls for a gender-aware history which highlights the centrality of black women to the slave system, both as producer and as reproducer, and explores the resulting complexity of their resistances not only to oppression by white men but also to domination by black men and white women. He is particularly concerned to highlight the commodification of the bodies and wombs of slave women and the resultant politicising of child-bearing.

Part III of the book switches from colonial contexts to explore the impact of imperialism within Britain itself. Arranged chronologically, these chapters together suggest the importance of Britain's position as a leading imperial nation to the gendered construction of British and English identities in the period between the 1790s and the 1940s. My own chapter shifts from Beckles's focus on women and anti-slavery within the Caribbean to an examination of British anti-slavery discourses. It presents both the anti-slavery discourse constructed by women anti-slavery campaigners in the 1820s and 1830s and the 'triple discourse' of anti-slavery in early feminist tracts of 1790 to 1869 as marking key roots of the 'imperial feminism' which Antoinette Burton has identified as emerging with the organised women's movement in Britain in the 1860–1914 period, and which is a continuing, if challenged, element of Western feminism today. If empire was constitutive of British feminisms, then Catherine Hall argues that it was also 'constitutive of English masculinities'. Focusing on the famous Victorian novelist Anthony Trollope, Hall shows how in his travel writings he offered to Englishmen 'some of the pleasures and dangers of colonial masculinities and the imagined safeties of an Englishman's identity'. Manliness was a 'quintessentially Anglo-Saxon virtue which could straddle the Empire and find new vigour' in the colonies of white settlement. Such celebrations of Anglo-Saxon brotherhood were linked to assumptions of the inferiority of both women and native peoples and provided an antidote to feminist assertion in the metropolis and violent unrest in the colonies.

In the final chapter Barbara Bush focuses on the inter-war period, exploring the under-researched area of white women's involvement in imperial politics and race issues in a vibrant period which saw both the high point of British imperialism in Africa and the rise of colonial nationalism and black race consciousness, and challenges to Victorian certainties by black activists, socialists and newly enfranchised women within Britain. In contrast to the stance of Victorian 'imperial feminists', Bush identifies a separation between women's feminist interests and their 'African work'. To this they tended to bring a male-defined socialist or liberal perspective, forging political, personal and sometimes sexual links with black men but having little contact with black women.

A number of themes emerge across the chapters. Most basically, the contributors highlight the importance of studying both colonisers and colonised as gendered subjects rather than homogeneous groups: gender shaped the ways in which men and women participated in and were affected by empire, and in turn empire affected the gender identities of both coloniser and colonised. The essays also demonstrate the importance of recognising female agency, both in terms of white women's active role in promoting colonialism, contributing to colonial discourse and using empire as a sphere of opportunity, and in terms of colonised women's active negotiations with and resistances to imperialism and colonialism, and their oppositions to the patriarchal domination by both British colonisers and men in their own communities. Another recurrent and related theme is the way in which the varied forms of feminism in Britain and its Empire were heavily influenced by shifting and differential relations to imperialism and anti-colonial nationalisms. The essays also illuminate questions of masculinity and empire: conflicts between indigenous and colonial patriarchies; the different forms of assertion of control over black women by white men and black men under slavery; the undomesticated frontier masculinity of male white settlers; the construction of white middle-class British male identity in relation to imperial contexts. At a more theoretical level, important interventions are made into the debate on the value to historians of an engagement with postcolonial theory. Overall, it is hoped that the volume forwards the process of meeting Joan Scott's objectives for gender history (laid out near the beginning of this chapter), both by placing the social construction of sex and of relationships between men and women within an imperial context, and by rethinking some of the traditional gender-blind paradigms of Imperial History.

On the basis of the new insights offered in this book, some directions for future research and publication can be suggested. Some aspects of the field merit far more research. The topic of masculinity and imperialism has tremendous scope, with the need to fully explore the implications of the construction of both British imperialism and anti-colonial nationalisms as essentially masculine projects. A fuller study is also needed of the impact of empire on British society itself, economically, politically, socially and culturally, a study which incorporates a gender perspective, and which has the aim of eventually constructing a chronologically-based narrative charting continuities and changes through the early modern and modern periods. In terms of chronology, more work is needed on the period outside the 1880–1914 period of 'high imperialism'. Shifts in emphasis are also needed to expand our understanding: from the present focus on culture, for example, to the material impact of empire in terms of shifts in the family economy and in the sexual division of labour. Work on gender and British imperialism would also benefit from placing within the comparative framework of European imperialism. Finally, the field would profit from a fuller debate on the relationship between post-colonial theory and the writing of new histories of imperialism. This book traces some of the historical connections between gender and imperialism from a variety of perspectives; many more remain to be mapped. It will have achieved its objectives if it encourages the inclusion of gender issues in future histories of imperialism, and the consideration of imperialism in future gender and women's history, and if, in so doing, it contributes to the overturning of traditional Imperial History through the centring of 'another history of agency and knowledge alive in the dead weight of the colonial past'.[54]

Notes

Part of this chapter was presented as the opening paper at the South-West Women's History Network Conference, 'Through Women's Eyes: Perceptions of Travel and Cross-Cultural Encounter', at the University of the West of England, Bristol, 6 July 1996. My thanks to the participants for their fruitful comments.

1 For the importance of widening the scope of British women's history see L. Stanley, 'British feminist histories: an editorial introduction', *Women's Studies International Forum*, 13 (1990), pp. 3–7.

2 J. Scott, 'Gender: a useful category of historical analysis' in Joan Scott (ed.), *Feminism and History* (Oxford, Oxford University Press, 1996), p. 167.

3 R. Hyam, *Empire and Sexuality: The British Experience* (Manchester, Manchester University Press, 1990), Introduction.

4 C. Hall, 'Feminism and feminist history' in *White, Male and Middle Class: Explorations in Feminism and History* (Cambridge, Polity Press, 1992), pp. 1–40.

5 M. Roper and J. Tosh, 'Introduction: historians and the politics of masculinity' in M. Roper and J. Tosh (eds), *Manful Assertions: Masculinities in Britain since 1800* (London, Routledge, 1991).

6 Scott, 'Gender'. See also J. Scott, *Gender and the Politics of History* (New York, Columbia University Press, 1988).

7 R. Aldrich, 'Imperialism in the study and teaching of history' in J. A. Mangan (ed.), *'Benefits Bestowed'? Education and British Imperialism* (Manchester, Manchester University Press, 1988), pp. 23–38; R. Symonds, *Oxford and Empire: The Last Lost Cause?* (Basingstoke, Macmillan, 1986); D. Wormell, *Sir John Seeley and the Uses of History* (Cambridge, Cambridge University Press, 1980), especially chapter 6; P. Burroughs, 'Sir John Seeley and British Imperial History', *The Journal of Imperial and Commonwealth History*, 1:2 (1973), pp. 191–212; B. M. Magubane, *The Round Table Movement: Its Influence on the Historiography of Imperialism* (Harare, Sapes Books, 1994); A. Smith and M. Bull, *Margery Perham and British Rule in Africa* (London, Frank Cass, 1991).

8 E. Williams, *British Historians and the West Indies* (London, André Deutsch, 1966), p. 234. See also E. Williams, *Capitalism and Slavery* (Chapel Hill, University of North Carolina Press, 1944); B. L. Solow and S. L. Engerman, *British Capitalism and Caribbean Slavery: The Legacy of Eric Williams* (Cambridge, Cambridge University Press, 1987).

9 See, for example, A. Temu and B. Swai, *Historians and Africanist History: A Critique* (London, Zed Press, 1981).

10 R. Guha and G. C. Spivak, *Selected Subaltern Studies* (Oxford, Oxford University Press, 1988). See also R. O'Hanlon and D. Washbrook, 'Histories in transition:

approaches to the study of colonialism and culture in India', *History Workshop*, 32 (1991), pp. 110–27.

11 For pioneering explorations of the impact of empire on British society see J. M. MacKenzie, *Propaganda and Empire: The Manipulation of British Public Opinion 1880–1960* (Manchester, Manchester University Press, 1984); J. M. MacKenzie (ed.), *Imperialism and Popular Culture* (Manchester, Manchester University Press, 1986). For recent discussions from a post-colonial perspective see A. Burton, 'Rules of thumb: British history and "imperial culture" in nineteenth- and twentieth-century Britain', *Women's History Review*, 3:4 (1994), pp. 483–500; B. Schwarz (ed.), *The Expansion of England: Race, Ethnicity and Cultural History* (London, Routledge, 1996).

12 S. Marks, 'History, the nation and empire: sniping from the periphery', *History Workshop Journal*, 29 (1990), pp. 111–19; P. Gilroy, 'Nationalism, history and ethnic absolutism', *History Workshop Journal*, 30 (1990), pp. 114–20; J. Bush, 'Moving on – and looking back', *History Workshop Journal*, 36 (1993), pp. 183–94.

13 On settlers from the Empire see, for example: C. Holmes (ed.), *Immigrants and Minorities in British Society* (London, Allen and Unwin, 1978); P. Fryer, *Staying Power: The History of Black People in Britain* (London, Pluto Press, 1984); R. Visram, *Ayahs, Lascars and Princes: Indians in Britain 1700–1947* (London, Pluto Press, 1986); R. Swift and S. Gilley (eds), *The Irish in Britain 1815–1939* (London, Printer, 1989). On the politics of race, immigration and nationality in Britain key recent works include: P. B. Rich, *Race and Empire in British Politics* (Cambridge, Cambridge University Press, 2nd edn, 1990); P. Panayi, *Immigration, Ethnicity and Racism in Britain, 1815–1945* (Manchester, Manchester University Press, 1994); C. Holmes, *John Bull's Island: Immigration and British Society, 1871–1971* (London, Macmillan, 1988); Laura Tabili, *'We Ask for British Justice': Workers and Racial Difference in Late Imperial Britain* (Ithaca, Cornell University Press, 1994).

14 For a useful summary of developments in Imperial History to 1984, see C. C. Eldridge, 'Introduction' in C. C. Eldridge (ed.), *British Imperialism in the Nineteenth Century* (Basingstoke, Macmillan, 1984).

15 P. J. Marshall (ed.), *The Cambridge Illustrated History of the British Empire* (Cambridge, Cambridge University Press, 1996), p. 380.

16 E. Said, *Orientalism* (London, Routledge and Kegan Paul, 1978), and more recently E. Said, *Culture and Imperialism* (New York, Knopf, 1993). Other key post-colonial theorists include Homi Bhabha and Gayatri Spivak.

17 J. MacKenzie, 'Edward Said and the historians', *Nineteenth-Century Contexts*, 18 (1994), pp. 9–25.

18 G. Prakash (ed.), *After Colonialism: Imperial Histories and Postcolonial Displacements* (Princeton, Princeton University Press, 1994), p. 4. See also G. Prakash, 'Writing post-orientalist histories of the third world: perspectives from Indian historiography', *Comparative Studies in Society and History*, 32 (1990), pp. 383–408; D. Chakrabasty, 'Postcoloniality and the artifice of history: who speaks for "Indian" pasts?', *Representations*, 37 (1992), pp. 1–26.

19 J. Fabian, *Time and the Other: How Anthropology Makes Its Object* (New York, Columbia University Press, 1983).

20 This teleological approach is highlighted in Shula Marks's discussion of the 'Whig spirit' which imbued debate on incorporating imperial history into the national curriculum in British schools: see Marks, 'History, the nation and empire', pp. 111–12.

21 Dane Kennedy, 'Imperial history and post-colonial theory', *The Journal of Imperial and Commonwealth History*, 24:3 (Sept. 1996), pp. 345–63. Robert Young in *White Mythologies: Writing History and the West* (London, Routledge, 1990) targets his attack on Marxist historiography, a focus which seems somewhat misplaced, given that Marxism has never provided the dominant theoretical underpinning for Western writings on the history of imperialism, and that Marxian approaches have proved invaluable to scholars such as members of the Subaltern Studies group who aim to rewrite the history of imperialism from the viewpoint of subaltern colonised groups.

22 J. Appleby, L. Hunt and M. Jacob, *Telling the Truth About History* (New York, Norton, 1994), p. 259.

23 See M. Lake, 'Colonised and colonising: the white Australian feminist subject', *Women's History Review*, 2:3 (1993), pp. 377–86.

24 See for example M. MacMillan, *Women of the Raj* (New York, Thames and Hudson, 1988); J. Trollope, *Britannia's Daughters: Women of the British Empire* (London, Random House, 1983).

25 H. Callaway, *Gender, Culture and Empire: European Women in Colonial Nigeria* (Urbana, University of Illinois Press, 1987); C. Knapman, *White Women in Fiji 1835–1930: The Ruin of Empire?* (Sydney, Allen and Unwin, 1986). For a useful outline of 'the myth of the destructive female' see M. Strobel, *European Women and the Second British Empire* (Bloomington, Indiana University Press, 1991), chapter 1.

26 J. Haggis, 'Gendering colonialism or colonising gender? Recent women's studies approaches to white women and the history of British colonialism', *Women's Studies International Forum*, 13 (1990), pp. 105–15.

27 N. Chaudhuri and M. Strobel, *Western Women and Imperialism: Complicity and Resistance* (Bloomington, Indiana University Press, 1992); Kumari Jayawardena, *The White Woman's Other Burden: Western Women and South Asia During British Rule* (London, Routledge, 1995).

28 C. Midgley, *Women Against Slavery: The British Campaigns, 1780–1870* (London, Routledge, 1992).

29 A. Burton, *Burdens of History: British Feminists, Indian Women, and Imperial Culture, 1865–1915* (Chapel Hill, University of North Carolina Press, 1994).

30 J. Bush, '"The right sort of woman": female emigrants and emigration to the British Empire 1890–1910', *Women's History Review*, 3:3 (1994), pp. 385–410.

31 A. Davin, 'Imperialism and motherhood', *History Workshop Journal*, 5 (1978), pp. 9–65.

32 Z. Alexander, 'Let it lie upon the table: the status of black women's biography in the UK', *Gender and History*, 2:1 (1990), pp. 22–33; A. Burton, 'A "pilgrim reformer" at the heart of the Empire: Behramji Malabari in late-Victorian London', *Gender and History*, 8:2 (1996), pp. 175–96; A. Rossitor, 'Bringing the margins into the centre: a review of aspects of Irish women's experience from a British perspective' in A. Smyth (ed.), *Irish Women's Studies Reader* (Dublin, Attic Press, 1993), pp. 177–202. See also C. Midgley, 'Ethnicity, "race" and empire' in J. Purvis (ed.), *Women's History, Britain, 1850–1945: An Introduction* (London, UCL Press, 1995).

33 R. R. Pierson, 'Experience, difference, dominance and voice in the writing of Canadian women's history' in K. Offen, R. R. Pierson and J. Rendall (eds), *Writing Women's History: International Perspectives* (Bloomington, Indiana University Press, 1991), pp. 79–106; P. Grimshaw, 'Writing the history of Australian women' in *ibid.*, pp. 151–70.

34 K. Sangari and S. Vaid, *Recasting Women: Essays in Indian Colonial History* (New Brunswick, Rutgers University Press, 1990 (originally published in India by Kali for Women, 1989)), p. 4.

35 Z. Tadesse, 'Breaking the silence and broadening the frontiers of history: recent studies on African women' in S. J. Kleinberg (ed.), *Retrieving Women's History: Changing Perceptions of the Role of Women in Politics and Society* (Providence and Oxford, Berg, 1992 (first edn 1988)), p. 356. For a sense of developments over the past decade see *Gender and History*, Special Issue: Gendered Colonialisms in African History, 8:3 (Nov. 1996).

36 For articles on aspects of African and Indian women's history see C. Johnson-Odim and M. Strobel, *Expanding the Boundaries of Women's History: Essays on Women in the Third World* (Bloomington, Indiana University Press, 1992); for Indian women see Sangari and Vaid, *Recasting Women*; for women in the Caribbean see V. Shepherd, B. Brereton and B. Bailey, *Engendering History: Caribbean Women in Historical Perspective* (London, James Currey, 1995); for Irish women see M. Luddy and C. Murphy (eds), *Women Surviving: Studies in Irish Women's History in the 19th and 20th Centuries* (Dublin, Poolbeg Press, 1990).

37 G. C. Spivak, 'Can the subaltern speak?' in C. Nelson and L. Grossberg (eds), *Marxism and the Interpretation of Culture* (London, Macmillan, 1988), pp. 271–313; J. Nair, 'On the question of agency in Indian feminist historiography', *Gender and History*, 6:1 (1994), pp. 82–100; D. Engels and S. Marks (eds), *Contesting Colonial Hegemony: State and Society in Africa and India* (London, British Academic Press, 1994).

38 C. T. Mohanty, 'Under western eyes: feminist scholarship and colonial discourse' in C. T. Mohanty, A. Russo and L. Torres (eds), *Third World Women and the Politics of Feminism* (Bloomington, Indiana University Press, 1991), pp. 51–80.

39 G. Dawson, *Soldier Heroes: British Adventure, Empire and the Imagining of Masculinities* (London, Routledge, 1994), quotation from p. 5.

40 Hall, *White, Male and Middle-Class*, chapters 9 and 10.

41 M. Sinha, *Colonial Masculinity: The 'Manly Englishman' and the 'Effeminate Bengali' in the Late Nineteenth Century* (Manchester, Manchester University Press, 1995).

42 See Sangari and Vaid, *Recasting Women*.

43 Burton, *Burdens of History*, chapter 5; M. Sinha, '"Chathams, Pitts, and Gladstones in petticoats": the politics of gender and race in the Ilbert Bill controversy, 1883–1884' in Chaudhuri and Strobel (eds), *Western Women and Imperialism*, pp. 98–118; K. Ballhatchet, *Race, Sex and Class under the Raj: Imperial Attitudes and Policies and their Critics, 1793–1905* (London, Weidenfeld and Nicolson, 1980).

44 Hyam, *The Empire and Sexuality*; for a critique of his approach see M. Berger, 'Imperialism and sexual exploitation: a response to Ronald Hyam's "Empire and sexual opportunity"', *Journal of Imperial and Commonwealth History*, 17:1 (1988), pp. 83–9.

45 A. McClintock, *Imperial Leather: Race, Gender and Sexuality in the Colonial Contest* (London, Routledge, 1995).

46 A. L. Stoler, *Race and the Education of Desire: Foucault's 'History of Sexuality' and the Colonial Order of Things* (Durham, Duke University Press, 1995).

47 S. Mills, *Discourses of Difference: An Analysis of Women's Travel Writing and Colonialism* (London, Routledge, 1991), p. 6.

48 Said, *Orientalism*.

49 R. Kabbani, *Europe's Myths of Orient* (London, Pandora, 1986).

50 B. Melman, *Women's Orients: English Women and the Middle East, 1718–1918: Sexuality, Religion and Work* (Basingstoke, Macmillan, 2nd edn, 1995); Reina Lewis, *Gendering Orientalism: Race, Femininity and Representation* (London, Routledge, 1996).

51 M. Ferguson, *Subject to Others: British Women Writers and Colonial Slavery, 1670–1834* (London, Routledge, 1992).

52 The collection thus differs from Chaudhuri and Strobel, *Western Women and Imperialism*, whose US-based contributors focus on colonising women in Africa and India. It also differs from T. P. Foley, L. Pilkington, S. Ryder and E. Tilley (eds), *Gender and Colonialism* (Galway, Galway University Press, 1995), a collection of short conference papers (presented at the 1992 Gender and Colonialism conference at University College Galway, Ireland) by scholars who come primarily from a literary and cultural studies background and focus on text-based study of colonial discourse.

53 For new approaches see A. L. Stoler and F. Cooper, 'Between metropole and colony: rethinking a research agenda' in F. Cooper and A. L. Stoler (eds), *Tensions of Empire: Colonial Cultures in a Bourgeois World* (Berkeley, University of California Press, forthcoming).

54 Prakash (ed.), *After Colonialism*, p. 5.

[18]

PART I

Impositions and impacts

CHAPTER ONE

Age of consent and hegemonic social reform

Himani Bannerji

Until recently colonialism in general and British colonial hegemony in India in particular has been largely considered in terms of economic exploitation, military repression and direct political administration. This view of hegemony as unequivocally coercive omits consideration of its legitimation-producing aspects. This subtle and complex dimension of hegemony amounts to a reorganisation of the civil society of the colonised which is accomplished through a diffusion of cultural–ideological constructions and moral regulations.[1] Though this legitimation aspect of hegemony is present in most colonial enterprises to varying degrees depending on the nature of the enterprise, it is the case with India that British colonialism sought to legitimise itself through self-characterisation as rule of law and social reform.[2]

Significant legislation pertaining to social reform which sought to penetrate deeply into the everyday life and culture of Indians (in particular of Bengal) marked the passage of British rule in India. This legislation involved such intimate and private aspects of life as marriage, motherhood, women's relationship to their bodies, sex and sexuality and, less intimately, property laws and education. The processes leading up to the enactment of reform legislation entailed the elaboration of colonial cultural constructions and modes of moral regulation. They accomplished the process of colonial state formation in India by ascribing cultural–moral identities to the indigenous population which served in the capacity of ideology for ruling.[3]

In this enterprise patriarchy and the reorganisation of gender relations provided the most crucial elements. Patriarchal colonial moral imperatives came into nineteenth-century Bengal deeply inflected with British/European ideas of 'race' and difference. The laws therefore actually far exceeded their stated legal purpose and in effect provided a set of norms and forms for the society to adhere to.[4] This was particularly effective with the rising Bengali middle classes, who were formed in the terrain of colonial rule. One such law, perhaps the most hegemonically charged, is the Age of Consent Act of 1891. This chapter explores this act's ideologically hegemonic dimensions with respect to the production of identities for Bengali hindu middle-class women. Since these female identities are conceived with reference to their male counterparts, a discussion about them will also be a part of it. These hegemonic identities were not restrained within the boundaries of the act, they continued to texture all manner of social legislation and discussion which surrounded them.

On 9 January 1891, the Viceroy of India, Lord Lansdowne, introduced before the Supreme Legislative Council a bill to amend Section 376 of the Indian Penal Code, which would effect an amendment of Schedule II to the code of criminal procedure of 1882. Drafted and presented at length before the Council by the Honourable Andrew Scobble, circulated for opinion to a large number of colonial administrators, both Indian and British, medical and legal practitioners, including notables among the muslim and hindu communities, the bill was passed with unprecedented speed on 19 March 1891. Entitled 'The Age of Consent', raising the age of legally permissible sex for girls from ten years (the limit set in 1860) to twelve years, this act became the most controversial of reforms legislated by the colonial state.

The objective of this bill, soon to become an act, was a final definition and settlement of the age at which any female of the Indian communities could become the object of male sexual penetration. The violation of this age limit would constitute a criminal offence irrespective of the marital status of the female or the relationship between the female and the male offender in question. This act was crucial in the state's attempt to regulate sex and forms of sexuality among the Indian subjects. It defined legal sex as being heterosexual and penetrative, while equating sexual transactions within and outside of marriage, including prostitution. The same legal provisions would thus hold for rape, statutory rape and illegal solicitation, and implicitly impact on the population growth of the country.[5] This state regulation of the private lives of the colonial subjects also had a profound moral dimension, on the basis of which the reform was proposed and justified. That entailed a negative cultural–moral construction of the local population, which was perceived by the colonial authorities to be in dire need of reform.

The bill created an overwhelming reaction among the indigenous male population at its consultation stage. Huge rallies were organised in protest, especially in Calcutta and Bombay, as well as petitions and signature campaigns. Though some support for the act was also forthcoming, in the main the state faced the accusation of a highhanded imposition.[6] Anticipating this, the colonial state performed various exercises of legitimation. It not only went through motions of public consultation, but also created a viceroy's council which minimally took care of the issue of representation. Of the fifteen members, four were Indians, two each from the hindu and muslim communities. In addition a select committee was appointed to review the objections raised about the bill, and a few minor changes suggested by it were incorporated into the act. Of the two hindu council members, one voted negatively, despite being a loyal legal practitioner. The act in its final state made compromises. A husband's offence, considered non-cognisable, removed for him the penalty of transportation for life, as well as making provision for the case to be tried by the district magistrate (a post reserved for the British), rather than being arrested and investigated by the police.[7]

This large controversy surrounding the age of consent in its bill stage was not a struggle between two homogeneous groups, namely the coloniser and the colonised, embodying the principles of modernity and tradition respectively.[8] As research has shown, preoccupation with social reform and modernity, or social order and tradition, is in no consistent way the project of the British or Indians ranged in oppositional relation. During different phases of colonialism British attention shifted from tradition to modernity or vice versa. The British sought to create a colonial ideological apparatus for ruling just as much on one basis as on the other. Lata Mani, for example, has shown this effectively in terms of invention of tradition in her work on *sati* and colonial representation of Indian women.[9] Colonial rule in nineteenth-century India meandered along a tortuous path between the traditionalism of the Orientalists and the modernising drive of the Utilitarians, all in search of developing a technology for legitimation and social control which would elaborate a hegemonic reorganisation of the indigenous civil society.

The same hegemonic aspirations marked the indigenous male elite, who were also preoccupied with the same issues of social reform and social control.[10] They took opposing stances to proposed colonial legislation, and in some cases constructed other reasons than those of the state's for proposing or demanding laws. Being pro- or anti-reform can not therefore be read as simple signs of being pro- or anti-colonial, that is, of being a colonial loyalist or a nationalist. There were many instances when loyal British subjects disagreed with the proposed Age of Consent Act or the legislation against *sati*.[11] Boundaries to intervention seemed to be drawn by loyalists and nationalists mainly in the matter of domestic life, consisting of legislation regarding women, the control of their bodies and sexuality, marriage and family.[12]

Since neither the issues involved nor the project of social reform as such were unknown and unacceptable to the local male elite, we are left with having to answer why this particular act called for such reaction, rather than the act of 1860 which fixed the age of marriage and sex for girls at ten years. Not even the banning of *satidaha* (1829) nor the introduction of widow remarriage created such an organised protest. Though more research needs to be done in this area, some speculation might be in order. One could begin from the shadow cast over the 1891 act by the death of a ten-year-old girl, Phulmoni Dasi, in 1889. Many, even colonial officials, blamed not only her husband but also the British government for allowing the act of sex with a ten-year-old girl. Reformers of all types found this reprehensible and the state responded to their criticism by raising the age of consent to twelve. This change was considered insufficient by some, while others thought the decision should be left to family members and other guardians. All of these responses were catalysed at the consultation stage of the 1891 bill, probably because it was the second such act[13] to regulate the social morality of the 'natives' related to the issue of control of marriage and sexuality. The state was again posing as the guardian of 'native' morality, claiming to be the protector of Bengali/Indian women, and making charges of immaturity, brutality and incompetence against local males.

This attempt at social and moral interference into the private sphere of Bengali homes and sex lives seems to have unsettled the unofficial trade-off between the local male elite and the state. The 'home and the world split' which has been identified as the base of the national(ist) identity[14] was certainly severely challenged by such a reform proposal, precipitating moral contestation and political turmoil. Interpreted as a virtual assault on indigenous rights to self-definition, objections came not only from *shastric*[15] individuals but also from others asserting the principle of non-interference. If the act of 1860 marked the threshold of local tolerance then that of 1891, following thirty years of deepening anti-colonial politics, created a massive upsurge. To this was added a sense of betrayal, since this act reneged on Queen Victoria's 1858 proclamation of non-interference in indigenous social or private life which she made after the onset of the Great Rebellion in 1857.[16]

It is obvious that debate over the 1891 act involved an extensive dramatis personae, as the project of hegemony involved colonial rulers and their champions and diverse opponents. This chapter, however, does not attempt to cover the full spread. Instead it focuses on one selected group of protagonists and examines their representational discursivities with respect to hegemonic colonial social reform. It is the ideological and cultural premises of the state's proposals and their creation of a body of representation or a 'symbolic cultural constitution'[17] of indigenous women, and relatedly of men, which are under scrutiny here. This focus can be justified on two important grounds. I concentrate on the dominant or the governing group which sets in place a political–cultural agenda which provides the terms for hegemonic contestation. In this agenda patriarchy, organised through a colonial racist perception, projects a site of contestation, a specific and concrete object of rule – namely women, their bodies and familial and sexual conduct.[18] This war of moral and cultural attribution, identity and self-definition is centred on or carried through reform projects that seek to define and organise the lives of local women. This means the regulation of the conduct of families where the control of the conduct of women was to take place. The moot issues are therefore the moral construction and regulation of a 'hindu' culture and a 'hindu' woman, which are equally at stake for the colonial and the local male elite.[19] This is an indelibly patriarchal project for both. But what is central for us is that the cultural–normative terms and regulatory boundaries are initiated by the colonial state: others respond to these even when they create overlapping or oppositional ideological spaces. This chapter concentrates on the discursive–ideological forms arising from the state's proposals and considers them as moments of evolution in the 'ruling discourse' of colonial India. The representations of Bengali/Indian hindu women, their male counterparts and society need to be read in the wider context of British colonial rule as a global project for social/cultural hegemony. My purpose is to focus on these identities and their role as forms of moral regulation and mediation within the textual apparatus for ruling.

Whose consent? At what age? Discursive constructions, ideological interpellations and the colonial state

The reforming impulse of the British colonial state in India had little to do with the protection of women and girls, though initiated in their names. This becomes evident from the fact that the issue of the woman's or the girl's own consent is hardly discussed in the official documents. Nowhere is there a provision in the bill for a direct role to be played by the very people whose bodies are to be the discursive battleground between indigenous men and a patriarchal colonial state. Texts of submissions by and to the state make it apparent that the notion of consent is only a nominal gesture towards women and girls as objects of a legal and social transaction.[20] In actuality they provide the legal guardian (father or custodian) with permission to alienate his (or her) daughter's or ward's body to a male user as husband, client or sexual keeper and also to initiate her pregnancy. Legal penetration and impregnation thus crucially depend on the determination or definition of 'the age' which would provide the state with a fixed and justifiable criterion for consenting to the guardian's consent. It is this definition which was to confer womanhood upon a child or a girl, with or without individual onset of puberty, and thus prevent charges of rape and violent assault against the sexual (ab)user, sparing him, the parents, guardians and pimps the danger of legal prosecution.

The determination of the criterion for 'the age', however, lay with legal, scientific and religious experts as well as community leaders mobilised by the state, and aimed beyond the question of violence against women or children, to an overall definition of an acceptable moral and social order. As this moral order was to be the core of the reform attempted by the state, it needed contrasting points of reference to both an ideal and a degraded type of morality. Thus through a complexly woven set of legal, scientific/medical and moral discourses, marked with inflexions of Christianity and humanism, the state created legislative proposals which served as a social terrain for ruling through the imperatives and models of reform. These legislative practices and their discursive–ideological presentations are simultaneously forms of state regulation and cultural moralisation. At once instruments of legitimation and a penal apparatus, they projected an 'enlightened' self-identity of the colonial power which then sought to rule and reform the colonised 'other' for its own good.

Ascribed identities, put forward as difference produced in a colonial context, have little substantiveness to them, but are rather ideological projections articulated from within the relations of ruling. This type of difference, therefore, is not initially articulated by the population under rule, and as such is not socio-historically intrinsic to their society. Thus, the characterisation of India as an essentially religious/traditional society has less to do with India than with being a marker which is invented to differentiate it from Britain/Europe as rational and secular spaces. This difference is a reforming design which contains a perceived degradation of the 'other' and the enlightened benevolence of the colonial reformer.

The reforming desire of the self-proclaimed moral and rational colonial ruler, the ascribed degraded nature of the object of reform, and the tropes of Indian women's abuse at the hands of Indian men and white men rescuing brown women, in short the entire baggage of the colonial project, stand out in the following quotation from the Honorary Secretary, Public Health Society of Calcutta, summarising reports and submissions from medical practitioners. He reports on the opinion of Dr K. McLeod, brigade-surgeon and professor of medicine at Calcutta

Medical College. This helps us get a sense of the power-driven and complex meaning of reform as encoded in the Age of Consent Act.

> The desired reform is one which will serve to remove a blot from our Indian codes, which will *ameliorate and elevate in a wide and deep reaching manner the condition of the women of India*. It seems to the Council that *it is to the improvement of that condition that the attention of all who seek for well-founded and permanent reform in India should mainly be directed* ... [The] evidence of history goes to show the high status [of women] attained in European countries has proceeded slowly, it may be, but necessarily and surely, ever since the period when the status of women was first elevated, and when she first began to be regarded not as the mere toy and slave of her husband, but as his equal and fellow worker. *Here again the legislature can give a right direction to popular opinion in this country, and can serve an educational purpose, the value of which is almost impossible to overestimate. The evils dealt with in this letter sap national vigour and morality*; and the reform which the Council of the Health Society seek to press on the attention of Supreme Govt., seems to be the natural and necessary corollary of all those beneficent schemes for raising the physical, moral and mental status of the native, and of which the noble institution founded by the Countess of Dufferin is one phase.[21]

This submission from one of the most important members of the colonial medical administration in India attests to an attitude of White Man's Burden endemic to reform projects of this kind. This responsibility for reform encodes the colonial/European self-identity and the difference between them and the constructed 'native other'. Through this reforming gesture the colonising country posed as the universal standard of perfection, as a prescribed social model, upon which to base the moral improvement of the colony. The condition of women is evidently used as an index of both societies, of the perfection of one, and the baseness of the other.[22] The superior agent for change, the colonial state, claims to deserve, and reserve the right of, interpretation and implementation at all times. In keeping with this exalted role, Dr McLeod invests the colonial legislature with the legitimate task of providing the 'right direction to popular opinion in [India]', and serving 'an educational purpose' of uplifting the 'native's' morals. This moral legislator and educator was to eradicate 'evil' practices, particularly so when associated with sexuality, among an uncivilised subject population which was yet to reach a proper adulthood or maturity. The 'native' (always male) was allegedly indulging in sexual activities which 'sap national vigour, and national morality', in particular by cohabiting with 'underage' girls, which spelt 'the degeneration of the Indian race'.[23]

'Native' sexual practices are categorically considered by Dr McLeod as the most important issue before the government, which 'has a wide bearing in a social point of view as regards the native community, and also with reference to the importance of the race'.[24] These references to the race, the nation, and the native community signal a perception of the collective perverse and infantile sexual identity of the other, 'Bengalis in particular', who are 'enervated by this unnatural custom'. The unnatural practice is seen as being pervasive enough to wear away 'the stamina to withstand the baneful effects of malaria and cholera germ'.[25]

In striking contrast to this degenerated 'native' is the morally superior, sexually contained, thus more physically robust European. A submission provided by a Bengali doctor, himself using colonial discourse and working for the medical administration, states: 'After years of observation of the worst epidemic diseases of Bengal the conclusion is reached that placed in an equally unhealthy environment, the European may be said to enjoy an immunity to which the Indian is an utter stranger.'[26] This same European model of socio-sexual morality, consisting of restraint as health, is used by the British administrator who seeks to interpose himself between the 'native' man and 'his' woman, as her rescuer from the 'native's' unnatural sexual appetite. For this he has to legislate against the 'native', but by doing so he accomplishes 'beneficent schemes for raising the physical, moral and mental state' of the whole of the 'native' society. The Age of Consent Act is thus considered the most 'important step towards improvement of the race'. The lofty character of the colonial reform/civilising mission thus expands out into ever widening circles of responsibility and achievement. Thus 'reform is demanded in the interests of the state, of native society, of the Indian peoples, and of humanity ...'.[27] And in this grand scheme of civilisation the European/British man is an embodiment of civilisation, posing as both a teacher and a judge.

The construction of the 'native' as a microcosm of a degraded society is a general colonial practice with a common epistemology, but it is also culturally specific to each colonial situation. In the case of India, the social space itself was declared to be 'traditional' (read backward, superstitious, pagan and so on), while its inhabitants were religiously identified as 'hindu' or 'musulman'. 'The hindu' and its counterpart were then ascribed certain moral and cultural characteristics which were also differentiated in terms of gender. Within the colonial semiotic range 'the hindu' had a special feature – it was an ideological category that allowed an articulation between the colonial project and the local population. Its ideological status is evinced by its homogenising and essentialist character, and its morally regulative function was best displayed by its sexual and reproductive ascriptions to the subject population.[28]

Reform, it was felt by the state, can only come to 'the hindu' from the outside, from the civilised Europeans.[29] In the first instance, 'it is not supposed that a reform of a deep seated custom in the domestic life can be carried out without a persistent opposition.' The state, therefore, must legislate this and 'should not leave it to the growth of improved public opinion'.[30] After all, was not India, as translated and represented by Jones, Colebrook, Wilson and others, a land of traditions? Even if reform, introduced by the British, 'for at least a generation engaged the thoughts of the best men of all of the native communities',[31] 'the hindu' could not be trusted to come through on his own. The state could not, therefore, 'pursue a gentle course of non-interference, especially with regard to something so fundamental yet sensitive, the matter of sexual consummation'.[32] As stated in one submission: 'It [the age of consent] is a question extremely difficult to deal with, because there gather about it the silent but coercive force of traditions, the sanctions of immemorial customs, and the misunderstood [by the hindus, not the British] injunctions of religion.'[33] In fact some of the administrators regretted that there was a certain softness shown by the erstwhile colonial state to the 'Indian tradition' as regards the social life.[34] Nonetheless, the civilising responsibility had to be discharged by any means necessary: 'Reforms introduced from the outside require force as a factor, in their acceptance by the people or communities they may concern, and it may be doubted if they are ever thoroughly assimilated.'[35]

However, the rulers had to be circumspect about this use of force, and seek hegemonic consent from local sources. The Age of Consent Act should not only 'commend itself solely to the Anglo-Indian community', though they did provide the model. The sympathy of the people in Britain, 'and especially of [British] women', was crucial, but the colonial state would need to draw on all that surreptitiously. It would be 'an evil if the impressions were to get abroad that the Government of India in a matter of this sort found the springs of its actions in the sentiments and wishes of the people of England'.[36] One would have to make a show of seeking local assistance, and the loyal part of the hindu subjects, the Westernised reformers, could perhaps be of some assistance. There was, after all, 'a stir, attention in public press in India' brought on by the case of 'the unhappy child Phulmoni Dossee'.[37] The death of a ten-year-old girl, produced legally through marital rape, became an occasion for legitimation, that is expansion of hegemony, of the colonial state.

Discursive construction of 'hindu' sexuality and reproduction

The colonial discourse of racial identity and inferiority which characterised the 'hindu' as a construct was intrinsically patriarchal, with regard to both the men and women of Bengal. To begin with, subjectivity and agency were accorded only to the male, as the 'native' was a masculine construct, and the 'native society' under reform was his and seen as suffused with his cultural characteristics. The British (also referred to by a masculine singular noun) could only conduct business with the male members of 'other' societies. The 'native females' were rendered invisible through a double move of possession and objectification. As 'hindu women' they were seen as the subject of male governance in their own community, and claimed as objects of reform by the British state. At least that much was tacitly agreed upon by both male parties in this hegemonic contestation. But social reform purporting to improve or reorganise the colonial society threatened this equilibrium of power relations. With the Age of Consent Act matters reached a head. As far as the hindus were concerned the colonial state sought now to usurp the authority of the 'native' or 'hindu' male, since he was claimed to be an unfit, brutal governor of women of his community.

The British state argued that 'hindu' women and girls were also to be treated with some consideration as Her Majesty's subjects, since they lived under men full of 'moral abominations'.[38] Their situation was an index of the fundamentally degenerate state of the society and the hindu men they lived with were to be seen as no more than child rapists. The official documents claimed that they were 'subjected to more or less frequent acts of connexion with their husbands',[39] even when below the legal age. Unique to the 'hindu' character was the fact that 'legalized love of child-wives in marriage' was 'represented by lust for female children outside of marriage'.[40] This perversity, if tolerable with prostitutes, when manifested within marriage was to be considered criminal rape, and punishable by life imprisonment and transportation.

This condemnation of the 'hindu' male would have been more than a mere ideological stance had any regard been manifested for actual variations in social practices, and had any consideration been displayed by the state for Indian/Bengali women and girls as legal and social persons by providing them with a real role in debates around the Age of Consent Act. Instead, we find in these colonial legal constructions a deep contempt towards the women themselves. The colonial administrator saw the 'hindu' woman as a partner in the degeneration

[30]

of 'hindu' society, and she was even more of a degraded object for him than the 'hindu' male. Preoccupation with 'the age' rather than consent made the girl/woman little more than a body and a reproductive system to be regulated and investigated. In fact the moralistic stance towards the 'hindu' male and his society hid the instrumental use of the theme of violence against women for the purpose of condemnation of local societies and provided the legitimation of colonial domination. It created for the state a space for conducting research in the areas of sex and reproduction in the name of science and civilisation. The practices and objectives of the colonial medical establishment leading to this act converts the body of the 'native/hindu' woman or girl into an object of scientific penetration and vivisection.[41] The construction and publicisation of the private life of 'hindu society' tore to pieces both the 'hindu' male and the female. The white man condemned the 'hindu' as both weak or effeminate and predatory or brutal, and posed as the ultimate guardian-patriarch who could legally and medically control the 'hindu' woman's sexual and reproductive life.

To appropriate legal control and moral definition of a whole society's sexual and reproductive life, and particularly to create a valid atmosphere of objectification, it had to be proved that the terrible lot of 'hindu' women and girls was due to a moral failure of her own society which sprung from its own intrinsic nature.[42] This essential quality, which distinguished 'hindus' from Europeans, was that of tradition and an identification between being a 'hindu' and being traditional. Everything about 'hindus', according to this view, signalled iron laws of orthodoxy, as opposed to the European rationality and progressivism as well as the morality of christianity. An example offered of this traditionality, presumably peculiar to 'hindus', was their attitude towards marriage. The writer of *Hindu Law*, and an 'expert' on hindu society, Sir Thomas Strange, is quoted by the administrators to characterise the 'hindus' and used to justify the need to reform. According to Strange:

> Marriage, from a Hindu point of view, is a religious duty in the nature of a sacrament invested with sanctions of the highest character, which retain their hold upon the sympathies and customs of the people, because they can be traced back with exceptional freedom from modifications to very early times. Wherever there are Hindus there marriage holds a place it is difficult for other nations to comprehend.[43]

This definition obliterates the christian or any other religion's approach to marriage also as a sacrament and a commitment for life, and provides a directive of difference through the concept of tradition. This relegates the 'hindu' society outside of history and time, and confers on it an opacity or density which puts it outside of European comprehension. In being beyond European comprehension this traditional 'hindu' society becomes the ultimate other of Europe/Britain and beyond the pale of reason or change. The unchanging quality of this society is further reinforced by drawing upon statements of indigenous colonial administrators:

> Girls in our climate could not be left unmarried up to fourteen years, nor would a girl of that age submit to the present system of marriage. ... Unlike *sultanism* [concubinage], marriage is interwoven with the whole texture of our society, especially the Hindu society. You can not seriously alter the marriage system without altering the whole fabric.[44]

The Age of Consent Bill was a peculiar concession to traditionality in so far as the colonial authorities consulted local scriptural experts and claimed to continue non-interference with the age of marriage if not of consummation. Since wives were supposedly indispensable to hindus for religious observances, they would be allowed to marry any time they wanted, and to a girl of any age. Colonial administrators spoke on this matter with the authority and tone of Brahmins when they commented on the 'four orders' [caste] which in 'the hindu view of life ... distinguish the different periods of human life'.[45] They were willing to concede to the 'hindu' belief that marriage 'completes the expiatory ceremonies of sinful taint contracted in the parent's womb', and for women and *sudras* (low caste) this was the only expiatory rite allowed.[46] The British argued, with scriptural quotations, that marriage provided the only important 'obligations to women' and they were equal to 'the ordinances of the vedas'. There were cautionary remarks on 'the difficulty and delicacy of tasks before the government', and how reform must thus 'be moderate in extent and must be as far as possible a return from a deteriorated custom and compliance ...'.[47] A return to what, one might ask, and the answer, curiously, refers to an earlier state of civilisation of the 'hindus' themselves, of being Aryans. For Bengalis in particular, reform would consist of becoming equal to more 'manly races' in India at the present time.[48] Aryans, it seemed, waited to consummate their marriages, or even married at a later age than was the present practice in Bengal. It is noted that marriage 'takes place earlier in Bengal than in the Hindustan provinces, where it may be that among a more purely Aryan population the custom approaches more nearly to the ancient practices'.[49]

This concession to 'traditions of hinduism', as constructed by the British, and especially those regarding marriage, meant little more than a contemptuous tolerance of 'degenerate' practices in keeping with the perceived negative moral characterisation of this

Bengali/Indian society. In fact it is this very concession, with its ascriptions of depravity, which gave the state the reason or excuse to extend its jurisdiction over the sex life of its subjects as a whole and over women's lives in particular. While marriage must be allowed, it was felt that 'the consummatory homebringing of the wife stands upon no such special and peculiar ground; and may be considered in the interest of the people and in these interests be regulated and defined'.[50] This consummatory homebringing, referring to 'the age' at which a girl could be sexually used, brought the British authorities directly into contact with the bodies of Indian/Bengali girls and women. They were perceived as a biological organisation of a certain type of human species, rather than as substantive human beings, or even as objects with any sexual connotation for the white male. Throughout these submissions, the female of the hindu species, unlike the male, was credited with no personality, subjectivity or agency, no matter of what distorted variety. She could only be perceived as a vehicle for 'hindu' (male) sexual perversity and as a breeder for that society. This status as 'the native female' or 'tropical girl/female' determined the ideological discursivities revolving around her.

It is important to note that this pathologisation, in addition to presenting Bengali/Indian women as passive bodies, also has a degraded sexual connotation which is informed by the prevailing racism of European medicine and social anthropology.[51] These disciplines experimented or speculated upon black or dark-skinned people, the inhabitants of the tropics. They were invested with dangerous disease carrying potential and degraded sexual stereotypes.[52] Whether deployed by a local or a British doctor, the discursive composite of 'the native female' or 'tropical woman/girl' contained a passive yet oversexualised connotation. The geographical and sexological homologies between females of the tropics and its warm climate and lush vegetation fantasise an early puberty for the tropical woman (as fruits/vegetation mature quickly in the heat) and an eager sexual readiness.[53] This conflation gave the European Enlightenment's generally patriarchal equation between women and nature a profoundly racist twist. This discourse explains the curious fact in the Age of Consent documents that the doctors, who do not subscribe to the Hindu *shastras*, at the end of their medical-rationalist arguments against them accept the age of twelve as 'the age of consent'. Though they often state the medical fact that puberty does not arrive properly before the ages of fourteen to sixteen either in India or in Britain, they end by concluding that in this country twelve could be acceptable as 'the age'. This racist patriarchal discursive apparatus of difference modifies in the last instance the scientific, charitable or humanitarian concern of the medical man and the scientist.[54]

The central point of these discussions or representations was the girl's or woman's body.[55] There is almost no mention of any personality, volition or moral agency of the girl or the woman. Physicality, paralleled with passivity, is the core of this discursive construction of 'the tropical woman/girl', especially where 'good' women or girls, deserving of protection and charity, are mentioned. A hint of female sexual agency, always conceived as perverse, comes through when older female relatives or older prostitutes are mentioned as engaging in unnatural activities of manipulation of the girl's genitalia in order to facilitate premature coitus.[56] Often this 'evil practice' of child marriage and premature consummation is blamed on older female relatives in the context of the family.[57] A positive female sexuality is utterly inconceivable within this discursive framework. The 'hindu' woman is invariably seen as a sexual object of 'hindu' males, an instrument for his use and a vessel for biological reproduction. It is through this view, either as a wife or a child prostitute, that she constitutes a site for the extension of the state apparatus of criminal and medical jurisprudence and also provides an avenue for the expansion of European/British scientific/medical knowledge.[58]

This degraded identity of the 'hindu' girl or woman is essential to an overarching moral condemnation of the subject. If the colonised male is portrayed as brutal and infantile, with a perverse will and a tradition-enclosed mentality, then the female is the physical substrate of this society. As such, the search for 'the age' operationalises that degrading construction and ascription. It begins with an imperative and assumption of the following kind:

> it is necessary to ascertain the minimum age at which a girl acquires her capacity for sexual intercourse, and the minimum age at which she attains to full maturity for maternity. Such minimum age is, as a rule, lower in a warm country like the plains of India, compared to countries in cold latitudes.[59]

Though some medical practitioners sometimes doubt the geographical dictation of female puberty, more or less the same sentiment extends through the dossier of C. C. Stevens. Scientific experts who are concerned about the effects of climate on 'race' determine in the main the way in which the 'native female' is perceived.

The language of medical submission is an active discursive process of objectification – through physicalisation and pathologisation – of women and girls. The texts are a curious and even macabre mixture of scientific interest and a kind of pity which is generally shown towards an animal. Women and girls are constantly described in terms of their sex and reproductive organs and events of rape, childbirth, mortality and autopsy. Though a protective attitude is put forward regarding them, this is done in terms of moralistic, victim-creating pronouncements, never attributing any active, intelligent, feeling humanity to them. Not only do these women/girls not speak in the texts, but they very rarely even appear with a face or a personality, except as anatomical-biological organs or pathology and a doctor's probe on a dissection table. Except in one or two memos in a large body of submissions, women/girls remain non-humanised, without an outward body or appearance. Even those texts display features of objectification. The following is an example:

> Premature sexual intercourse tells also by its remote effects on Indian wives. Mechanical dilation of the hymen, conical dilation of the vagina, displacements of the uterus, and peculiar hyper-tropical condition of the labiae are its local effects. With an undeveloped pelvis pregnancy entails very often serious consequences, viz. difficult labour, puerperal complications and heavy infantile mortality. Among its constitutional effects I may note down the arrested development of body and mind. A victim of this atrocious practice is known by her girl like face, hands and feet, with the body and figure of an old woman, a description that applies to most Indian women. A mechanical submission to domestic drudgery and tyranny is a sufficient test of her intelligence.[60]

Written by a Bengali doctor, this description, with also its brief reference to the fears and tears of a young girl visiting her husband's home, is the only vaguely humanising reference to women and girls as sentient beings. This may be joined with that of a British doctor who compares the fate of a young girl unfavourably with that of an animal, stating that a female animal has more freedom from sexual and reproductive tyranny than a child wife/mother in Bengal.[61]

The submissions supporting the act, and many against a merely legislative or the present legislative solution, testify to a horrible cruelty against women and girls. Allusions to injuries, rape, pain and blood fill up the pages. However, only a few of the submissions partly call into question the mythology of early sexual maturity of girls in the tropics. Some experts are ready to say that the age of twelve is not satisfactory: 'It is absolutely no test whatever that maturity for the purpose of maternity [for that matter for the act of sex] has been attained.'[62] Some make a distinction between 'puberty' and 'nubility', and deplore the 1860/61 penal code.[63] One states that the law 'instead, almost seems to sanction the infliction of injuries which in many instances prove fatal, and in still more numerous cases seriously affect the future health and wellbeing of native women'.[64] One doctor speaks of 'the terrible strain of premature maternity' and points out that 'at least in 20% of marriages children were born to child wives', between twelve and thirteen years. The injuries are repeatedly detailed: 'difficult and delayed labour, laceration and sloughing of the passage, death of the child, exhaustion, fever, abscesses, contractions, and fistula'.[65] Minority, maternity and mortality are inseparably joined in the reader's mind as he or she progresses through the dossier.

This fleeting awareness of cruelty does not mitigate, but in fact deepens, the pathologisation marked by the typicalities of 'race'. This 'raced' female has no possibility of going beyond matter and nature; she is even more of a physical entity than the European woman.[66] Her pathology then has the anthropology of 'inferior races', and is mainly considered in terms of breeding or reproduction. The life-cycle of this 'hindu/tropical female' falls into two periods: the earlier, briefest period called childhood, which is pre-sexual and pre-reproductive; and most of her life, in which she serves as a male's sex object and reproduces. These two aspects are uniformly collapsed into one. The dividing line between two parts of life – of childhood and womanhood – is the blood line of menstruation, and the only question worth asking about her is 'the aptitude of [her] sexual organs for intercourse with an adult man'.[67] This simultaneously translates out in concerns for her ability to conceive and have a healthy pregnancy, and these are the features which supply the legal formula for 'the age'.

Bodies of women and girls, therefore, were studied in great detail. The entire working apparatus of an extensive colonial medical establishment, also featuring 'native' doctors, launched forth into an in-depth exploration. 'Unanimous in their abhorrence of the present custom',[68] they debated with each other, speculated upon and penetrated these bodies with scalpels in hand, bodies which would show them the secrets of human reproduction in general, but also that of a 'tropical species'. Social statistics, medical and scientific literature from Europe, general studies in anatomy and physiology, all converged on this project. Brigade-Surgeon McLeod, professor of surgery, Calcutta Medical College, and others refer to long-standing research on Indian girls/women and reproduction. He cites 30–35 years of research contained in Dr Allen Webb's *Pathologica Indica* (1850s), Dr Harvey's work, which analyses 127 cases, journals such as *Indian Medical Gazette* and others, and extensively cites his own work, 'Child-wives', in the *Gazette*.[69] As a responsible medical scientist and doctor he discharged his duties solemnly: 'I have brought the whole subject before the Calcutta medical society with a view to eliciting additional facts and ascertaining the opinions of native medical men.'[70] Piece by piece from autopsy reports, surgical dissections, hospital and private cases, police reports and records, a sizeable body of information emerges. Bengal in particular, the seat of the Empire, but also other parts of India, become a vast laboratory of research on reproduction, on the mechanism of copulation, on population and maternal and infant mortality. But along with this incremental increase in scientific knowledge, there is an equally incremental solidification of an ideological moral stance towards this population under rule and tropical others in general. This creates an extension of the medical notion of pathology into moral spheres and a social anthropology, a *Pathologica Indica*, which becomes the colonial perception of India. The old Orientalist discursivities constellated around tradition and civilisation are fed into medical science and jurisprudence and further amplify otherisation and negative difference by connecting with pathology. The 'native' is not only 'traditional' and 'savage', as Jones and Mill would claim respectively, but by the same token pathological and perverted. These traits constitute the essence of 'his' society. The 'hindu female' is not very much more than a cow or any other animal, to be probed into, to be construed as an index of the degradation of the society of which she forms a part, to be an open book on sex and reproduction in the tropics.

Indeed there is an overweening curiosity among various types of experts, bordering on indecency, regarding the gynaecological and obstetric life of the 'native female'. Documents which otherwise exude the coldness of morgues and the precision of autopsies resonate with a righteous scientific wrath at being prevented access into the deepest recesses of their objects' homes, functions and bodies. 'Native' customs of midwifery, as well as gynaecology, are deeply resented and discredited by these experts, as are the practices of 'hindu medicine' or the *ayurveda*. At this point, diverse interpretations of the *shastras* (scriptures) become useful as a tool for discrediting any Indian claim to science and medicine. Not only are 'hindu' medical practices, either of popular or elite variety, condemned, but so also the 'hindu' household which prevents the outsider, especially male (white and indigenous) doctors, from entering into it. *Purdah*, the *zenana* or the *andarmahal* are railed against as obstructions in the way of saving lives, and worse still, for obstructing science.[71] An atmosphere of rumours is created around these homes and what happens within them, including sexual and gynaecological knowledges of older women and midwives that the medical establishment is not privy to. It is also stated that rapes and deaths of women frequently occur there, particularly connected with premature sex and motherhood. As one writer put it: 'The death of Phulmoni has only brought before the public an evil the existence of which is no new development of recent years, and which is far from being co-extensive with the limits of the experience of medical officers, coroners and juries sitting in Presidency towns.'[72] The concept of 'race', which is ubiquitously present in this otherising-identifying discourse, dovetails neatly with European scientific and moral concern with motherhood and breeding which is present both in and out of colonial discourse. In the case of Bengali/Indian, read as 'native/tropical' women, notions of motherhood and breeding are collapsed into the broader discourse of physicality and animality. Fertility, fecundity and population growth, rather than lofty and sentimental notions and images, dominate any consideration of motherhood. If there is any genuine concern for the health of women and girls in the Indian context, it is mainly in terms of eugenics. The central question here is of regulating copulation and reproduction, and in the proper propagation of the 'race'. In fact 'race' and motherhood became functions of each other in this discourse as they constitute each other as signifiers in this situation. Women and girls are to be seen primarily as a race of mothers and as mothers of races. The official concern with the weak masculinity of Bengali males finds its cause in the weakness of the 'race', that is, in premature, overactive sex life and unregulated breeding. Motherhood within this discursive framework is not connected to the socially active verb of mothering, but rather to that of breeding. The importance of this discourse lies in the fact that this approach is shared equally by the 'native' and the European/British doctors, and provides the basic theme which echoes in different ways in different aspects of the controversy surrounding the Age of Consent Act.

Conclusion

This exercise in decoding what the colonial authorities meant by 'hindu' women, men or society makes it evident that the discursive specificity of British colonial cultural politics in India has a global context. Colonial discourse holds a generic sort of quality to it, showing up in other European countries' textual/inscriptional forms of colonial ruling. Though our task here has been to explore a single strand in that repertory, we find similar ascriptions containing comparable forms of moral regulations elaborating from a ground plan of domination.[73] The 'hindu' woman/girl of these documents marks a moment in the overall symbolic cultural constitution, not only of a colonial 'India' but of a global European identity politics, where we see projected binary identities of inferior 'others' *and* of the enlightened self of Europe.

These cultural and moral identities, as the 'hindu' woman/girl for example, were both static and pejorative. As a contrast to European

[38]

idealised identities, this is a form of difference, but of an exclusive and negative nature. The real subject, the European/British male ruler, is however hidden, or spread ubiquitously through the pages of the documents without any necessity for self-naming.[74] The entire discussion emanates from the I/eye of the colonial administrator, his values and relevances produced in the cause and course of rule.

No matter what is its content, colonial discourse is reified and concretised by social relations and cultural forms of power, coded as gender, 'race' and class. In spite of a wide and complex range of constructions it is ultimately a master/slave, black/white, patriarch/woman discourse. The importance of studying this undiluted form of colonial discourse, baring its raw edges, is essential for understanding how totalising power of any kind develops and operates beyond a simple functional project. If there is a colonialism it must have a discourse which is coherent with it and characteristic of it. One cannot help but notice the autonomy and strength of colonial discourse. A world view, a cultural grammar, and a political ideology having a tenacious and unvarying direction have come into being. This does not make it a rigid or monolithic template of concepts and images. It develops at different levels and stages; opposing images and notions constitute its body; but at any given moment, in any shape or form, it remains reificatory – an instance of power/knowledge. It is strong enough to enter not only into middle-class nationalist discourse, but also into discursivities of both European and third world socialist/communist revolutionary and feminist politics.

We should also insist here that all of the European/British political–ideological world is not to be seen as monolithic in discourse and intention. Just as in the colony, the metropole was also divided in ideological and factional disagreements. By the late nineteenth century some British feminists, doctors and missionaries had their disagreements with or evinced some criticism of colonial India. But the purpose of this chapter is not to explore these other discourses of Britain, and perhaps it is worth stressing that these other discourses cannot be wholly disarticulated from colonial discourse, and are often underwritten by colonial christianity – a discourse of charity and civilisation, or a discourse of horror. These critics did not necessarily contradict the state's language and attitude of hegemonic reform and rescue. We cannot therefore either decentre or minimise attempts at negative otherisation such as the one examined here. While similar otherisations were at work at 'home', that is, in Britain, objectifications there took other turns, consequences and contestations. In the case of India, it is still imperative to see what became of these ruling forms of consciousness and modes of reification as they played out their identity games in the heart of the Empire, mobilising 'race' to the purpose of patriarchal class rule.

Notes

1 See P. Corrigan and D. Sayer, *The Great Arch: British State Formation as Cultural Revolution* (Oxford, Basil Blackwell, 1985). See also P. Corrigan, 'On moral regulation: some preliminary remarks', *Sociological Review*, 29:2 (1981), pp. 313–337.

2 See B. Cohn, 'Representing authority in Victorian India' in E. Hobsbawm and T. Ranger (eds), *The Invention of Tradition* (Cambridge, Cambridge University Press, 1983), pp. 165–210; also Cohn, 'The command of language and the language of command' in R. Guha (ed.), *Subaltern Studies 4: Writings on South Asian History and Society* (Delhi, Oxford University Press, 1985), pp. 276–329.

3 See H. Bannerji, 'Beyond the ruling category to what actually happens: notes on James Mill's historiography in *The History of British India*' in M. Campbell and A. Manicom (eds), *Knowledge, Experience and Ruling Relations: Studies in the Social Organization of Knowledge* (Toronto, University of Toronto Press, 1995), pp. 49–64; also Bannerji, 'Writing "India", doing ideology: William Jones' construction of India as an ideological category', *Left History*, 2:2 (Fall 1994), pp. 5–36.

4 On the role played by the creation of difference and 'race' in the course of ruling, see M. Sinha, *Colonial Masculinity: The 'Manly Britishman' and the 'Effeminate Bengali' in the Late Nineteenth Century* (Manchester, Manchester University Press, 1995), pp. 33–68.

5 A Malthusian way of viewing both 'home' and colonial society in terms of 'population growth' was in place by the time the Age of Consent Act was passed. It forms an active part of governance in both spaces, and is also connected with this interest in reproductive biology, eugenics, women and motherhood. See J. Whitehead 'Modernising the motherhood archetype: public health models and the Child Marriage Restraint Act of 1929', *Contributions to Indian Sociology*, 29:1 and 2 (1995), pp. 187–209; see also D. Arnold, *Colonizing the Body: State Medicine and Epidemic Disease in Nineteenth Century India* (Berkeley, University of California Press, 1993).

6 See M. Kosambi, 'Girl-brides and socio-legal change: Age of Consent Bill (1891) controversy', *Economic and Political Weekly* (3–10 Aug. 1991), pp. 1857–1868.

7 A 'non-cognisable' offence was bailable; 'transportation' for life meant a life sentence.

8 See Sinha, *Colonial Masculinity*, Introduction, pp. 1–32, for an extended discussion of this position. See also A. Stoler, 'Rethinking colonial categories: European communities and the boundaries of rule', *Comparative Studies in Society and History*, 31:1 (Jan. 1989), pp. 134–201.

9 See L. Mani, 'Continuous traditions: the debate on *sati* in colonial India' in K. Sangari and S. Vaid (eds), *Recasting Women: Essays in Indian Colonial History* (New Brunswick, New Jersey, Rutgers University Press, 1989), pp. 88–126, for a discussion of *sati* and the deployment of the categories 'tradition' and 'modernity' in the service of patriarchal 'race'-inscribed colonial hegemony. Also see G. Chakravorty Spivak, 'Can the subaltern speak?', in C. Nelson and L. Grossberg (eds), *Marxism and the Interpretations of Culture* (Urbana, University of Illinois Press, 1988), pp. 271–313.

10 H. Bannerji, 'Fashioning a self: educational proposals for and by women in popular magazines in colonial Bengal', *Economic and Political Weekly*, 26:43 (Oct. 1991), pp. 50–62; see also Bannerji, 'Textile prison: discourse on shame (*lajja*) in the attire of the gentlewoman (*bhadramahila*) in colonial Bengal' in M. Valverde (ed.), *Studies in Moral Regulation* (Toronto, Centre of Criminology and Canadian Journal of Sociology, 1994), pp. 145–168.

11 See S. Sarkar, *A Critique of Colonial India* (Calcutta, Papyrus, 1985), pp. 1–17. Sarkar speaks of loyal British subjects, such as Radhakanto Deb, who did not support the anti-*satidaha* stance.

12 See T. Sarkar, 'The Hindu wife and the Hindu nation: domesticity and nationalism in nineteenth century Bengal', *Studies in History*, 8:2 (1992), pp. 213–235; also 'Rhetoric against age of consent: resisting colonial reason and death of a child-wife', *Economic and Political Weekly*, 28:36 (1993), pp. 1869–1878; and 'Nationalist iconography: images of women in nineteenth century Bengali literature', *Economic and Political Weekly*, 22:47 (Nov. 1987), pp. 2011–2015.

13 The first regulation of marriage and consummation was the act of 1860.

14 P. Chatterjee, 'The nationalist resolution of the women's question' in Sangari and Vaid, *Recasting Women*, pp. 233–252; see also *The Nation and its Fragments: Colonial and Postcolonial Histories* (Princeton, Princeton University Press, 1993).

15 *Shastric* refers to individuals who subscribe to the *shastras* or religious/scriptural injunctions of the hindus.

16 The Great Rebellion, or *Mahabidroh*, refers to the armed resistance against British colonialism in 1857. It is also known as the Sepoy Mutiny.

17 R. Inden, *Imagining India* (Oxford, Basil Blackwell, 1990).

18 Sangari and Vaid, 'An introduction', in *Recasting Women*, pp. 1–26.

19 See U. Chakravarti, 'Whatever happened to the Vedic *Dasi*?: Orientalism, nationalism and a script for the past' in Sangari and Vaid, *Recasting Women*, pp. 27–87; also L. Carroll, 'Law, custom and statutory social reform: the Hindu Widows' Remarriage Act of 1856' in J. Krishnamurty (ed.), *Women in Colonial India: Essays on Survival, Work and the State* (New Delhi, Oxford University Press, 1989), pp. 1–26; A. Burton, *Burdens of History: British Feminists, Indian Women and Imperial Culture, 1865–1915* (Chapel Hill, University of North Carolina Press, 1994); and T. Sarkar, 'The Hindu wife and the Hindu nation'.

20 See *Government of India, Legislative Department. Papers (Nos. 4, 11, 12) Relative to The Bill to amend the Indian Penal Code and the Code of Criminal Procedure, 1882* (hereafter: *Papers*), Indian Office Library and Records (IOLR), London, for a full file of the submissions.

21 *Papers*, pp. 419–420, pt. 15, italics mine.

22 The colonial reformers here write within the discursive tradition of using the social status or the 'condition' of women as an index for 'civilisation'. This European Enlightenment measure of self-identity and difference from 'others' is to be found in Mary Wollstonecraft, John Stuart Mill and Friedrich Engels, among others.

23 This construction of the 'native' is complex. It ranges through depictions of an infantile, immature, weak, hypersexed, undersexed, animalistic, decadent and brutal sexuality – leaving no consistent stereotype in view. The element that is consistently present is objectification and denigration, expressing a relation of dominance and its terms, rather than an unvarying body of content. This is clearly brought out in M. L. Pratt, *Imperial Eyes: Travel Writing and Transculturation* (London, Routledge, 1992). R. Hyam describes this phenomenon, though uncritically, in *Empire and Sexuality: The British Experience* (Manchester, Manchester University Press, 1992). Sinha's *Colonial Masculinity* is another critical and rich exposition on this construction of the 'native' (male) as a sexual colonial subject.

24 *Papers*, p. 424, pt. 2.

25 *Ibid.*, p. 426, pt. 5.

26 *Ibid.*

27 *Ibid.*, p. 420, pt. 16. These sentiments of Dr McLeod and his medical colleagues are entirely shared by C. C. Stevens, Chief Secretary to Sir Stewart Bayley, Lieutenant Governor of Bengal, as well as all the other administrators whose opinions he compiles in his file of submissions to the highest colonial authorities. These documents are copy-book exercises of the integrity of discourses on social reform and colonial rule. Their foremost accomplishment is the degraded characterisation of the colonised society in totality, particularly as microcosmically reflected in the character of the 'native'.

28 See Bannerji, 'Writing "India"'. This 'seamlessness', a result of an essentialising epistemology, has been noted by many critics as a characteristic feature of power/knowledge. For the most influential critique of this, see E. Said, *Orientalism*

(New York, Vintage, 1979). For India, see Bannerji, 'Writing "India"' and T. Niranjana, 'Translation, colonialism and the rise of English', *Economic and Political Weekly*, 25:15 (April 1990), pp. 773–779.

The emergence of this category 'hindu', and its identification with 'India', with its own peculiar ideological and cultural baggage, extended over a long period. It was in the making from the era of the Orientalists, of the East India Company's accession to the status of government of Bengal and the post-mutiny (1857) inclusion of India into the Empire (1865). Every stage of legislated social reform, from *satidaha* (burning of widows on their husband's pyre) to widow remarriage, to the Age of Consent, added to the formulation of the notion of 'the hindu' and to the typification of its content. The last in particular was the widest in its scope of debates and discussions, and the culminating step in this process of construction and ascription of a national identity to the ruled, thus finalising the most comprehensive 'difference' between Europeans and Indians. The ideological nature of the category 'hindu', its essentialist, de-historicised and homogenised character, becomes obvious from the way in which the texts produced by colonial administrators, medical and legal experts exorcise it of all its cultural and historical particularities.

29 Thus in the interests of colonial hegemony at different levels colonial administrators and experts, both foreign and local, either suppress facts or contradictions among them, or leave them unaddressed in the text. They adopt a strategy of refusal to draw any logical conclusion from them. Interpreted in this fashion, indigenous reformers are referred to as Europeanised supporters of the state, but ignored as a substantive body of social agents and critical thinkers. At best there is an ambivalence towards them. But even this ambivalent relationship to 'educated men' and to 'a strong and a very intelligent body of public opinion' does not destabilise the ascribed typicality of the notion of 'the hindu'. In fact, these local 'reformers' are depicted as exceptions which prove the rule of orthodoxy and tradition in 'the hindu way of life'. What remains underlined is Stevens's assertion that this 'practice [*garvadhan*] is favoured and enforced by the educated men of the community' (p. 416).

30 *Papers*, p. 416.
31 *Ibid.*, p. 417.
32 *Ibid.*
33 *Ibid.*
34 There was that proclamation by Queen Victoria in 1858 which promised non-interference in religious and daily life, made in fear in the period of the Sepoy Mutiny. As an anti-traditional member of the Council of the Health Society of Calcutta put it, 'the history of British rule and the working of the British courts in India manifest a distinct leaning towards, and non-interference with, the customs and religious observances of the Indian people' (*Papers*, p. 417). The rulers largely agreed that such a stance was obviously no longer needed with the final eradication of armed resistance to British rule and the solidification of the Empire. Besides, as science and civilisation were considered to have progressed apace in Britain and Europe in the meanwhile, the contrast between these enlightened societies and those of the traditional, benighted 'natives' was deemed much sharper than earlier in the century. The earlier Orientalist perception of an ancient Indian civilisation was sought to be replaced by that of James Mill and his intellectual successors, in tandem with the christian missionaries. Assertions of Indian 'savagery', 'rudeness' and 'the perfidy, venality and mendacity' of 'the hindus' abounded in official textual spaces. Now science, medical expertise and medical jurisprudence could be summoned to impose a civilising order upon a barbaric traditional society. Since much of India had been thoroughly colonised economically and militarily by the 1870s, the annexation of the civil society had to be stepped up. The hazards of doing this were also recognised, particularly as 'the hindu' might not be able to morally assimilate this enlightenment, even if he did intellectually comprehend it.

35 *Ibid.*, p. 417.
36 *Ibid.*
37 *Ibid.*

38 *Ibid.*, p. 416.
39 *Ibid.*
40 *Ibid.*, p. 423.
41 See J. Whitehead, 'Modernising the motherhood archetype: public health models and the Child Marriage Restraint Act of 1929', *Contributions to Indian Sociology* (n.s.), 29:1 and 2 (1995), pp. 187–209; also G. Forbes, 'Women and modernity: the issue of child marriage in India', *Women's Studies International Quarterly*, 2 (1979), pp. 407–419.
42 See P. Levin, 'Venereal disease, prostitution, and the politics of Empire: the case of British India', *Journal of the History of Sexuality*, 4:4 (1994), pp. 579–602. This draws on connections with other critiques of moral and social purity stances, on social histories of ruling as implying moral regulation.
43 *Papers*, p. 421.
44 *Ibid.*
45 *Ibid.*, p. 417.
46 *Ibid.*
47 *Ibid.*
48 *Ibid.*
49 *Ibid.*
50 *Ibid.*
51 Other than sources already cited in this context, see S. Gilman, 'Black bodies, white bodies: toward an iconography of female sexuality in late nineteenth-century art, medicine, and literature', in H. L. Gates, Jr (ed.), *'Race', Writing, and Difference* (Chicago, University of Chicago Press, 1985), pp. 223–261; also S. Harding (ed.), *The Racial Economy of Science* (Bloomington, Indiana University Press, 1993), for a comprehensive context to the colonial scientific/medical construction of the colonial subject in India.
52 See P. Levine, 'Venereal disease', on disease carrying potentials as well as on a basically 'abnormal', diseased view of the subject population.
53 For an introjection of climate and geography in creating negative and reifying views of 'others', and in creating racialised forms of difference as an area of critique of colonial and neocolonial discourse, see C. Lutz and J. Collins, *Reading National Geographic* (Chicago, University of Chicago Press, 1993).
54 For a complex view of the medical/scientific experts' approach to the questions of 'the age' (a question which consumes them with a need for facts), a generally committed relationship to the colonial project, and their hippocratic and humanitarian concerns, the entire set of submissions by doctors has to be read. Drs Harvey, McLeod, Webb (author of *Pathologica India*), Chandra, Gupta, Chevers, etc. have to be read carefully. These pages (420–426) of the IOLR file need a clear scrutiny for this. Their stance becomes clearer when we keep an eye on how they speak of girl brides/wives and prostitutes.
55 The archetypal medical description of 'the girl's' body necessary for ascertaining 'the age' comes from a Bengali doctor, Major B. Gupta, whose expertise is developed on the same grounds as that of the British doctors. An MB officiating as a civil surgeon in Hooghly, he gives us the clear clinical view. See *Papers*, p. 426.
56 Allusions to female relatives as evil influences and sadistic participants in 'the girl's' life are made frequently by different functionaries of the state, both British and Bengali. These allusions to older women, who 'prepared' 'the girls' for their use by husbands and male clients, need further research.
57 *Ibid.*
58 The formative conjunction of science and the legal apparatus of the colonial state emerges and evolves as medical jurisprudence. Much of the scientific endeavour is at the service of the development of a legal apparatus. This extends on the one hand into comparative statistics (*ibid.*, p. 426), close physiological and anatomical studies of 'the girl' (pp. 422, 425), and on the other hand into acrimonious, resentful reports of 'secrets' of native child births, closely guarded by midwives and female relatives.

59 *Ibid.*, p. 424.
60 *Ibid.*, p. 426.
61 *Ibid.* p. 425.
62 *Ibid.*, p. 418.
63 *Ibid.*
64 *Ibid.*, pp. 418–419.
65 *Ibid.*, p. 419.
66 G. Lloyd, *The Man of Reason* (London, Methuen, 1984), and M. L. Shanley and C. Pateman (eds), *Feminist Interpretations and Political Theory* (University Park: Pennsylvania State University Press, 1991) in their Introduction, show how establishing a transposable relation between European women and nature contraindicates women's assumption of citizenship. This connection becomes an absolute equation when used towards women of the colonised spaces. See Gilman, 'Black bodies, white bodies', and M. Alloula, *The Colonial Harem* (Minneapolis, University of Minnesota Press, 1986).
67 *Papers*, p. 425.
68 *Ibid.*, p. 422.
69 *Ibid.*, p. 423.
70 *Ibid.*
71 See notes 55 and 56 above, on the resentment against midwives and female relatives and native family relations and daily social life.
72 *Papers*, p. 425.
73 For an interesting reading of colonial identities as sites of domination and resistance, where stereotypically ascribed colonial women subjects take up the project of shaping themselves through lived forms and fantasies, see L. J. Sears (ed.), *Fantasizing the Feminine in Indonesia* (Durham, Duke University Press, 1996).
74 H. Bannerji, 'The passion of naming: identity, difference and politics of class' in *Thinking Through: Essays on Feminism, Marxism and Anti-Racism* (Toronto, Women's Press, 1995), pp. 17–40.

CHAPTER TWO

White women and colonialism: towards a non-recuperative history

Jane Haggis

Only in the last few years has the white woman found a voice in colonial histories. Her voice questions the myth of the ignorant, jealous memsahib who turned the happy Arcadia of early race relations into a bitter segregation. However, almost as soon as she spoke up, the white woman has been told to shut up again. She is told that she speaks from a selective memory; she paints her role in colony-making in the most favourable light; and she refuses to understand the deep-seated class and race oppression which characterises all colonies.[1]

In this quotation from a recent article, Chilla Bulbeck encapsulates the tensions currently felt by many feminist historians working in the specialism of gender and imperialism, particularly those who focus on uncovering and understanding the presences and participations of white women in imperial contexts and colonial locations. A number of studies have convincingly challenged the caricature of the white woman as responsible for the segregations and petty bigotries of colonial societies. These have revealed the gender biases of colonial writers such as Kipling, who helped concoct and popularise the stereotype, and the male historians who have built on and continued the memsahib image, charging the white woman with the ruin and loss of empire.[2] However, as Bulbeck's somewhat bitter words indicate, some of these studies have received a sharply critical response from other feminist writers and historians, myself included, who have criticised the new histories for not being new enough, and for continuing the colonising and Eurocentric discourses of mainstream colonial and imperial histories in their narration of white women's stories.[3] In her response, Bulbeck draws on her account of the experiences of expatriate women in Papua New Guinea to charge that such criticisms result from adopting questions 'produced by male colonisers and male colonial historians', in effect importing a 'non-feminist' discourse into feminist history by relegating 'gender' to a subsidiary analytical role.[4]

This sharp exchange of views is informed by a broader debate over the nature of the feminist historical project.[5] Is the task primarily to restore women's presences to the past and the historical account, or is it a broader endeavour to draw on the conceptual absence of women and gender to fundamentally challenge and reinscribe history writing and our accounts of the past? Joan Scott has summarised this wider debate as that between historians of women and historians of gender.[6]

Historians of women take the category of 'women' as their primary conceptual focus and seek to uncover women's 'voices' and 'experiences', placing them within a past presumed knowable and transparently reconstructed in the historian's narrative. Scott identifies several variants within this approach, not all of which see themselves or would be identified as feminist. The feminist variant sees a specific women's history as distinct from and parallel to the men's history of mainstream history, constructing a separate sphere of historical endeavour, distinct in its subject, themes and causal frameworks.

Gender history, in Scott's typology, is influenced by post-structuralist literary theory, and focuses on meaning and discourse rather than experience and voice. The categories 'woman' and 'man' are not viewed as fixed identities or natural entities, but as constructions of gender with variable meanings across culture and time. Gender itself is analytically conceived as an aspect of social organisation constructed through discourses of power and knowledge which ascribe historically and culturally contingent meanings to sexual difference. Within this schema, the gender historian's praxis is a reflexive art of constructing narratives which are relative, partial and fundamentally contemporary in their resonance. Thus, bringing gender (and women) into historical narrative involves challenging the taken-for-granted assumptions of positivist history, going beyond a recuperative exercise to embrace a new theoretical and methodological agenda for the writing of history, an agenda overtly political in its feminist intent to make explicit, and to challenge, the 'ways in which hierarchies of differences – inclusions and exclusions – have been constituted'.[7]

For many women's history practitioners, Scott's agenda is threatening to, rather than enabling of, a specific feminist history. A focus on a relativist conception of gender, fractured by multiple aspects of difference, seems to erode the visibility of women as specific historical agents just as their presence is being written into our accounts of the past. A core tenet of feminism – the historic and continuing subjugation of women by a dominant patriarchy – appears undermined, even dismissed, when attention is focused on other relations of power, such as class and race, which undercut the commonality of women's subordination. As Stanley and Birkett and Wheelwright comment, the awareness of women's absence from the historical stage has often fuelled a desire to find 'the perfect feminist heroines for us to admire, feel close to, inspired by and even imitate'[8] and encouraged a tendency to 'romanticise'[9] or explain away 'unpalatable facts'.[10] Birkett and Wheelwright suggest that the way to guard against such dangers is to allow 'these historical figures to live within their context' rather than '[t]o rewrite history to conform more exactly with current received notions'.[11] From this perspective, then, concerns of the present should not impinge on the recovery of the past. Issues of difference which might fracture or question the restoration of women to the historical account can thus be seen as contemporary distractions, their place in history writing limited to a contextual preamble for today's readership rather than as thematic aspects of the past, integral to the historical narrative. Such a view of the feminist historical project, however, has some problematic implications when applied to the history of empire.

The recuperative drive to place women in the history of colonialism and imperialism takes the texts and reminiscences of white women as literal accounts of their experiences, authentic and significant in their meaning – a meaning directly available to the historian and providing a readily comprehensible and valid, if partial, account of the past. Retrieving the voice and experience of white women in colonial settings, these histories place it alongside the existing 'male' narrative as an autonomous account of the past, while the histories of the colonised – male and female – are presumed to be another, different project, by implication awaiting the attentions of 'native' historians themselves.

A kind of pluralism is implicit in this approach. 'History' consists of a series of distinct strands, each largely independent of each other. The respective accounts are given their priority by the historians, from their defined historical goals. Thus, to paraphrase Bulbeck, for a feminist historian of white women (as against a male or 'third world' one) the task is to privilege gender, understood as the voice of the white female subject, as the primary analytical perspective. The singular perspective of the white woman and her prior exclusion from the existing male account becomes the connection between the different strands: the white woman's authenticity is confirmed by her taken-for-granted status as subordinate to, indeed outside of, the male-defined world of colonialism.

This exteriority, buttressed by an unexamined assumption of a shared woman-ness with her colonised counterparts, permits a double recuperation of the white woman. She is restored to the account of the past in her own authenticity, refuting a male-constructed invisibility and presumed irrelevance, while giving the lie to the fitful male inclusion of the negative memsahib. The white woman, by her own account, is rendered irresponsible, a victim of the white male colonising adventure, who, through this exclusion, is uniquely positioned, nevertheless, to forge a different, more benevolent, colonial relation with her 'native' sisters in the interstices of the masculine project, by virtue of her shared experience of being a woman in a male world. Where such benevolence and positive interaction is not borne out in the words and actions of the white woman, it is, again, not her responsibility, but a logical outcome of the constraints of the roles accorded her in a patriarchal world – a world where the clash between being a good mother and a dutiful wife in the midst of the masculine adventure of the colonial frontier led many women to negative appraisals of their colonial surroundings and an understandable desire to isolate themselves and their children from the dangers of an alien and 'uncivilised' environment.[12]

I have pointed out elsewhere how such recuperative histories of white women risk colonising gender for white men and women rather than gendering colonialism as a historical process.[13] Centring a singular female subjectivity fosters an inability to deal with the power relations of colonialism, privileging the White Woman as benevolent victim of the imperialist White Man. The colonised are relegated to an ungendered background against which the white genders act out their historical roles. Race, class and the asymmetry of colonial domination cannot be addressed without risking the fragmentation of the subject 'woman'. Bulbeck's assertion that these other dimensions of power are 'non-feminist' discourses, external to a cohesive category of gender, ignores the subtleties of colonial social relations, reducing the ambivalences of the peculiar location of white women in the colonial hierarchy, where, 'although race and class might intersect to accumulate her power, her sex did not'.[14] Focusing on gender to the exclusion of race or class does little to capture the nature of relations between women across the colonial divide, while white women's own historical agency is limited by her all-encompassing status as patriarchal victim.

Segregating gender and race as either/or categories ignores the ways in which the two aspects of social organisation are imbricated with each other. Framed as a dichotomy, an implicit ranking exercise is imposed on the analysis such that one or other of the two categories must be prioritised in any given context. A reductionism results, whereby gender is captured only in the veracity accorded white women's voice and experience. Race is reduced to behaviour and the accusatory issue of whether the historical subjects were guilty of racism or not. Hence Bulbeck's response to the critics of the new histories of white women is to charge them with silencing her historical subjects. The dualism informing her recuperative model provides only two positions for the white woman to assume in the feminist historical record: a vocality likely to leave her vulnerable to a new version of the negative stereotypes of mainstream, male, history, or a guilty silence, repentant in its compliance with the norms of a contemporary feminist political correctness.

Presenting the voices of white women in a singular authenticity reduces the historical narrative to a series of parallel tracks essentially unrelated to each other. In an attempt to retheorise the politics of difference in women's history away from such a recuperative framework, Elsa Barkley Brown uses a musical analogy particularly apt in capturing the dilemmas of writing a history of white women and colonisation. She contrasts the 'classical score' of much Western knowledge, which demands 'surrounding silence – of the audience, of all the instruments not singled out as the performers in this section',[15] with the 'gumbo ya-ya' of African–Americans' ways of conversing and recounting their stories to each other: 'They do this simultaneously because, in fact, their histories are joined – occurring simultaneously, in connection, in dialogue with each other. To relate their tales separately would be to obliterate that connection.'[16] Instead of a classical singularity the 'gumbo ya-ya' echoes the democratic individualism of Afro-American jazz music – 'the various voices in a piece of music may go their own ways but still be held together by their relationship to each other'.[17] Thus, history becomes, by analogy, expressive of difference and inter-relatedness, 'everybody talking at once, multiple rhythms being played simultaneously',[18] but held together, in a particular narrative, by the explicit awareness of inter-relatedness.

This awareness of inter-relatedness is crucial in going beyond paying lip service to difference within feminist discourses, where, as Barkley Brown observes, the tendency is either to acknowledge differences between women and then proceed to ignore them, or to see differences as pertaining to 'otherness' such that – to take white women and colonialism – race is something pertaining to colonised people and not an inherent part of the identity of the white woman (despite the racial marker of colour identifying her specificity).[19] Difference thus remains a mark of deviance from the norm, rather than a concept disrupting the complacent authority of the dominant discursive presence.

Writing a feminist history of white women and colonialism sensitive to issues of difference involves more than capturing the complex qualities of hierarchy embedded in past narratives. As Spivak and Said have demonstrated, even where texts of the past are not overtly about

empire, the power dynamics of imperialism form an underlying structure of reference, forming an essential, taken-for-granted part of the
fabric of metropolitan life and its imaginative representations.[20] Any
non-recuperative history of white women and colonialism must also
engage with the hierarchies of the present or risk producing a discourse which, as post-colonial critics of contemporary Western academic discourses have revealed, continues colonising the non-Western
'other' even where the express intention is to challenge such oppressions and exploitations.[21]

Such arguments indicate the dual nature of the problems raised in
writing feminist histories of colonialism and imperialism. On the one
hand there are the issues associated with how to deal with the remnants and records of the past, in their incompleteness and partialities,
and on the other are the related issues of writing history in a late-
twentieth-century context of post-coloniality. How does one try to
write a non-recuperative history that confronts the contemporary
challenges of acknowledging difference and attempts to construct a
'gumbo ya-ya' of gender and imperialism while nevertheless trying to
avoid the problem identified by Birkett and Wheelwright, of rewriting
history to conform to the present rather than the past? In the remainder of this chapter I want to draw on my own experiences of researching and writing about British women missionaries in South India
during the nineteenth century to suggest the kinds of issues and
strategies which might form part of such an endeavour.

As yet no comprehensive history of women's involvements in the
British foreign missionary movement that emerged out of the evangelical revival of the late eighteenth century has been written. Drawing on the work done by feminist and other historians on American
missionary women,[22] I was interested in exploring the British context
to see how missionary women were located as actors within both the
metropolitan gender order and the arena of empire and colonialism,
and what the connections were between the two. Based on a study of
the publications and archival records of the major British Protestant
missionary societies active in India during the nineteenth century, I
undertook a detailed investigation of one such society, the London
Missionary Society (LMS). Drawing on the official archive of the LMS,
I traced the involvement of women in the Society from the national
organisation in Britain through to the workings of a particular mission
district, South Travancore, in South India.[23] Writing this history in a
way which addresses both the integrity of the past as it emerges from
a partial and incomplete historical record, and my contemporary
awareness of the feminist and post-colonial politics of difference,
has involved questions of power, authority and voice. At least three

histories are imbricated in this particular process of history writing: my story of gender and imperialism; the missionaries' account of their endeavours; and the story of Indian women. In the remainder of this chapter I make explicit the discursive procedure by which I brought these three histories into an uneasy and unequal relationship in an attempt to write a feminist, post-colonial history of British women missionaries.

Labours of love

Though missionary work was originally conceived of as purely a male endeavour, by 1899 it was estimated that women missionaries out-numbered men in the 'foreign field' by over a thousand.[24] This numer-ical ascendancy reflected the recruitment of single women as missionaries by the major missionary societies during the last three decades of the century. One writer calculated that in 1879 there were no more than 400 single women serving in the entire foreign mission field (covering the Protestant missions from Britain, the USA and Europe),[25] yet in the seven years 1887–1894, the Church Missionary Society alone sent 214 women overseas as 'lady missionaries'.[26]

This chronology of the feminisation of the missionary endeavour parallels that trajectory revealed by historians looking at middle-class women's entry into formal education and paid employment in the second half of the nineteenth century – a trajectory intimately caught in the emergence of Victorian feminism as an initiator of and vocal participant in a rapidly changing social context. The single lady mis-sionary, as she was known, assumes a position analogous to that of her sisters entering the sphere of paid employment as office workers, teachers, nurses and even medical doctors,[27] forming part of that shift feminist historians have charted 'out of the garden, out of idleness, out of ignorance, and into wisdom, service and adventure',[28] leaving behind 'the confining domestic world of married women'.[29]

However, a closer inspection of the missionary archive reveals a more nuanced, more subtle and lengthier process of female involve-ment in the missionary movement. This was an agency that turned less on the activism of single women in breaching the walls of a patri-archal domesticity, than on the efforts of missionary wives to carve out a separate sphere of 'women's work', as it was called, within the boundaries of conventional ideologies of gender. It was this women's work, initiated, developed and promoted by the wives of missionaries, which instigated the recruitment of single women, eventually in num-bers sufficient to displace the male missionary's numerical ascen-dancy. As Davidoff and Hall have noted, there was a degree of ambiguity in evangelical notions of appropriate male and female roles: '[b]etween the recognition of influence and the marking out of a female sphere there was contested ground'.[30] It was precisely this 'contested ground' upon which women argued for their inclusion within the missionary movement. As one anonymous woman wrote in 1797, 'Why are females alone excluded from ... these labours of love? ... Nor let it be argued that their own familiar and domestic concerns afford the only sphere of their exertions. Here, indeed they ought undoubtedly to begin, but they are not called upon to stop there.'[31]

Her plea was a response to the exclusion of women from membership of the new societies. Women's role was to be limited to being 'the Mothers of the Missionaries', as one sermon put it.[32] However, by the 1820s missionary wives, most notably in India, were pushing the boundaries of female involvement well beyond the role of mother, carving out a separate sphere of women's work in female education. Wherever there was a missionary wife a school for girls was established.[33] To a degree the activism of missionary wives was appropriate to their role within the missionary marriage – a role the husband, wife and missionary society assumed would extend beyond that of simply intimate companion and domestic keeper to their spouse.[34] However, the endorsement by the missionary societies stopped short of according a separate status to wives' efforts at missionary work. Their labours were assumed to be part of their husbands' work and, as such, had no claim on the funds and resources raised for missionary work, understood as the work of the ordained in converting men.

In a way, a division of labour emerged in the field which the ideology of the missionary marriage as a single labour did not acknowledge. It was against this background that the need for female education began to be articulated by wives and their supporters as a distinct aspect of the mission – as an appeal for funds, supporters and workers over and above those being devoted to the labours of the (male) missionaries, and outside the official concerns of the missionary societies. With no direct claims on society funds, wives established their own links to sources of material support amongst their friends and sympathisers in Britain and India.

This separate sphere of female endeavour assumed distinctive organisational form in 1834 with the founding of the Society for the Propagation of Female Education in the East (SPFEE) in London, which had the aim of supporting the efforts of wives both financially and by recruiting single women as teachers to go to India and other fields to further female education. It was the first systematic British initiative to send single women abroad as part of the general missionary endeavour. The justification for such an innovation was argued on the grounds of the 'Asiatic' practice of secluding women, which meant only 'ladies' had any chance of 'being welcomed to their seclusion, and can win upon their confiding affection'.[35] Without this specific female effort, moreover, 'the great work' of 'our revered fathers and brethren' to evangelise the world would be at risk: 'What help would a young Christian receive from an ignorant, idolatrous wife?'[36] The aim of female education was thus to produce the good wives and mothers deemed essential if the converts of the male missionaries were to establish solid Christian families and communities as the critical bulwark against 'heathenism'.

The idea of sending single women out as teachers to the 'East' does not seem to have come as a shock or generated much opposition,[37] in part because the groundwork had already been laid. The work of wives in the mission field had developed and fleshed out the need of a separate sphere of women's work, while married and single women were continuing to expand and organise their religious philanthropy in Britain.[38] Evangelical doctrine and the Woman Question were coming together in new formulations of the most appropriate roles for women and men, which, even at their most prescriptive, condoned an active Christian engagement for women that could extend well beyond the home.

Another reason for the acceptance of the initiative to send single women abroad also seems to lie in the ideology of separate spheres which informed the establishment of the SPFEE and the way it went about its purpose. The historian of the SPFEE explained the reasons behind the Society's formation thus: 'as a Committee of gentlemen would be manifestly incompetent to select [female teachers] and superintend their preparatory training, it followed of course that a Ladies Society could alone meet the emergency. Their discernment and discrimination are thus most usefully brought to bear upon a matter of serious responsibility.' Even if the existing missionary societies were prepared to finance and manage the endeavour 'it would still be advisable to adopt the principle ... of a division of labour with a specific female society'.[39]

The missionary societies were not prepared to take the responsibility anyway. Missionary wives had petitioned the societies to sponsor single women teachers but, while the need was acknowledged, propriety prevented any action.[40] The SPFEE dealt with such issues in several ways. Candidates for 'lady teachers' were carefully vetted in an exhaustive selection process which placed considerable emphasis on character as well as education and training.[41] The Society was also careful to act, and be seen to act, as a facilitator rather than an initiator of women's work, limiting itself to responding to requests from wives in the field rather than instituting new arenas of work. Its teachers were represented as helpers to missionary wives rather than as autonomous workers. To the SPFEE and its supporters, if single women could be attached in some way, their presence in the foreign field was less contentious or open to the husband-hunting charge.[42] The link with the missionary couple served as a respectable alternative to fatherly or brotherly protection. At the same time, however, the missionary wives, the Society and their supporters made a virtue of the unmarried state. Only single women were able to bring to bear the 'distinct agency' capable of carrying the work forward. In the words of the Society's historian: '[T]he great design of the Society is to maintain a distinct agency for a specific purpose, which shall be undistracted by relative interests, and at full liberty to devote its whole time and its undivided energy to the work assigned it.'[43] Thus by 1847 the SPFEE had sent out fifty single women as teachers to India, Africa and Southeast Asia, and associated organisations had been established in Scotland, Basle, Geneva and Berlin, while in England Committee members 'wrote letters, and encouraged candidates, ... took some journeys ... held drawing-room meetings, and formed associations in aid of the Society'.[44] Women in the mission field had established a separate organisation for the conduct of a female mission – the women's work of educating the female 'heathen'. The ambiguities between wife and lady worker were resolved by portraying the missionary wife as the critical grass-roots actor, defining, initiating and overseeing the work, thus conforming to the proprieties of gender. This portrayal was predicated on the existence of women's work as a separate sphere of organisation and endeavour which allowed the female agency, married or single, to operate outside the immediate structures of a masculine world.

By the 1870s, however, the role of the SPFEE in providing an organisational form for 'women's work' in the foreign field was largely redundant as the major missionary societies moved to recruit single women as foreign missionaries. The directors of the LMS announced their decision in 1875, giving a range of reasons, including a huge expansion of openings for work with women in 'the East' beyond the scope of missionary wives to fill; the increasing availability of suitable lady candidates; and the willingness of the public at home to finance such an effort.[45] The directors' resolutions reflect profound social changes occurring during this period both at home and in India, particularly the circumstances of British middle-class women, often lacking the support, fiscal and otherwise, of husband, father or brother presumed in the Victorian gender ideology of domesticity and the 'angel in the house'. In India, the assumption of direct imperial authority by the

Crown in 1857 provided the missionary movement with a more secure and legitimate base for their endeavours, endeavours which elicited a somewhat unexpected and often disconcerting response, as whole communities of low caste people converted *en masse* to Christianity, particularly in South India. To the chagrin of many in the missionary movement, access to, influence over and conversion of the upper caste elites of India remained frustratingly limited. It was these poor and lowly converts who made up the bulk of the pupils in the schools run by missionary wives and the lady teachers recruited by the SPFEE. During the 1860s, however, a new agency was developed by mission-ary women – *zenana* visitation – intended to side-step the strictures of seclusion and caste which often prevented easy contact with high caste women, by taking Christian teaching and influence into any high caste homes they could gain access to. Thus by the 1870s new demands were being placed on women's work in terms of finance, organisation and personnel, while the relative success of *zenana* visitation in gaining access to, if not converts from, upper caste homes, and the need to 'civilise' the masses of low caste converts, brought women's work more centrally into the concerns of the mainstream missionary soci-eties. It was now no longer seen as a useful adjunct to the main mis-sion of converting men, but rather as a potentially powerful way to achieve precisely that end.

The recruitment of single women as lady missionaries by the major missionary societies marked the beginning of a process of incorpora-tion and professionalisation of women's work. It signals a shift in gender protocols as single women no longer risked breaking the 'pro-prieties' by being cast, and casting themselves, as active agents and initiators in missionary work. There is more than a tinge of irony in this shift, however, as missionary wives, in a reversal of the earlier imagery and role, are increasingly portrayed as helpers to the lady mis-sionaries. However, the separate sphere of women's work was not immediately dismantled with the shift into the mainstream, but was initially reconstituted within the boundaries of the male society.

In the LMS the 1875 decision to recruit women as missionaries involved the setting up of a Ladies Committee of well-known women drawn from the Congregational circles from which the LMS drew its closest supporters and affiliations. The Committee was to oversee all aspects of women's work, including fund-raising, recruitment and training of suitable candidates, and all matters pertaining to the employment of lady missionaries in the field.[46] This organisational form for women's work continued until 1890, when the Ladies Com-mittee threatened to break with the Society and form an independent *zenana* society if it was not accorded representation on the board.[47]

The board responded to this demand without much ado, reconstituting the Committee as the Ladies Examination Committee, which, unlike its predecessor, was formally integrated into the structure of the Society as one of seven Standing Committees, another of which was the Male Examination Committee, with its nine female members given seats on the Board of Directors.

While this reorganisation satisfied the demand for representation, the new committee was only a shadow of its former self, responsible only for the examination and selection of lady candidates, while its proceedings were now conducted by the Home Secretary of the LMS. All other issues to do with lady missionaries and women's work were now dealt with in the same organisational manner and structure as the work and employment of male missionaries.[48] The separate sphere of women's work appears to have been dissolved into the general mission, except in terms of a narrow division of labour and mark of difference between male and female candidates. In 1907 the male and ladies committees were amalgamated into a single Examination Committee, completing the image of incorporation.

The period during which the Ladies Committee was responsible for the application and selection process of lady missionaries, from 1875 to 1890, negotiates the transition and transformation of women's work from a labour of love carried out by missionary wives on the basis of their influence as 'good Christian women' to a professional and paid employment of single women, predicated as much on education and training as it was on Christian and feminine influence. The minute books and other records of the Ladies Committee depict a kind of balancing act in the application and selection process established for the post of lady missionary. On the one hand, the Committee maintained determined and exhaustive expectations of education and training, formal and vocational, for the work, a work now extending beyond teaching to embrace nursing, medicine and industrial work (the term used for the embroidery, lace and other money-making ventures which were set up to train and employ poor low caste women in 'respectable' occupations while at the same time generating useful funds for the work). On the other hand, the Committee was rigorous in ascertaining that the quality of being a 'lady' pertained to all candidates deemed suitable, regardless of an individual's otherwise exemplary training, experience, religiosity and sense of mission.

Being a lady meant demonstrating the qualities of respectable femininity – culture, civility and manners – in the milieu of the home (usually by invitation to tea at a Committee member's house), qualities deemed intrinsic to the exercise of that specifically female influence women's work was predicated upon.[49] The image of the true lady not only negotiated the complexities of class; it also ensured that the lady missionary, despite all the emphasis on training, experience and work, remained cast within a rubric of femininity rooted in the ideology of the private sphere of domesticity where home was the heart of culture and the powerful underpinning of female influence. Thus the proprieties of gender were still at work, interlaced with class, in constituting the lady missionary, although in a somewhat different configuration from those the SPFEE negotiated in the 1840s and 1850s. In the missionary archive and literature this transformation is articulated and accorded a legitimacy through the discursive construction of a 'mission of sisterhood', a process I explore below. For now, I want to briefly turn to the conduct of women's work in the field, where gender and class are reworked in a colonial patterning of this process of professionalisation.

I have argued in this section that over the course of the nineteenth century women's work shifted from being a labour of love carried out by missionary wives to a professional employment for single female missionaries. However, the impact of this shift on the ways in which women's work was actually conducted in the mission field was minimal. In effect, the lady missionary largely continued the pattern of work already established by wives in the preceding decades. The primary role undertaken by both wives and lady missionaries in the field was that of superintendence of the work, their responsibilities and activism portrayed as organisational and inspirational, as they managed and supervised a work largely carried out by a labour force of Indian Christian women, overwhelmingly drawn from the ranks of the lowest communities in the Indian caste hierarchy. It was these women who, by the last quarter of the century, actually did most of the teaching, nursing and training being carried out under the rubric of women's work.[50]

Ironically, whereas the single lady missionary was displacing the missionary wife as the principal actor, these Indian Christian women were overwhelmingly married or widowed, many apparently with dependent children still requiring care.[51] Another irony lay in the fact that it was primarily their credentials as 'good Christian women' which first accorded evangelical women, as wives of missionaries, the sense of mission and influence which instigated a specific female sphere of women's work in the mission field. It was this same essence of good woman that the single woman had to retain as lady in order to be considered effective as a missionary, her influence of superior Christian womanhood thus assured. This essence of goodness was closely connected, as I stated earlier, to the idealised versions of femininity dominant in Victorian gender ideologies, which connected the good woman so closely with home and hearth. The inversions threatened in the missionary wives' activisms and the lady missionaries' flight from home are contained by the religious rubric: a call from, and service to, God. Yet in their efforts at women's work, to produce 'good Christian wives and mothers', it is the Bible women who are actually produced, as working women earning a wage, not evangelical philanthropists – more in the image of the lady missionary than the domestic ideal of the angel in the house. At the same time, the very appellation 'Bible women' denotes the ways in which discourses of class and race as well as gender intersect the relational configurations of women's work in the field. However much the Bible women of South India come to resemble the lady missionary in qualification, effort and dedication, they are never accorded the title 'lady' while their attributes as teachers, trainers, evangelists or nurses are always prefaced by the qualifying 'native'.[52] 'Lady', as a designation of Indian femininity, is reserved for the upper caste women of the *zenanas*, although even their assumed superior class qualities remain confined by the racial signifier – as 'native ladies'.

The history I have recounted here documents how women's work in the mission field shifted in meaning and identity from being a service and duty carried out largely by the wives of male missionaries, to an occupation and relation of employment conducted by single missionary women by the turn of the century. In effect, I document another aspect of the emancipation of Victorian single middle-class women from the bounds of domesticity and economic dependency on men – one that demonstrates a broader and more ambiguous chronology of female agency and escape 'out of the garden' than that charted in the available feminist historiography of middle-class women's entry into the world of education, employment and profession. Moreover, the lady missionary negotiates her way out of the garden along a path of convention rather than a path of rebellion, as a religious rubric couches the aspirations of the missionary women in an idiom compatible with the conventionalities of Victorian ideals of gender. It is, moreover, a path firmly caught within the intricate web of race, class and gender that underpinned the age of empire. This is a very different story from that depicted in the missionary texts themselves. In the following section I will briefly outline their portrayal of women's work, before returning to the methodological issues of power and authority raised in the initial part of the chapter.

The mission of sisterhood

The missionary movement in Britain was prolific in its production of texts to advertise, promote and celebrate its efforts. A vast publishing effort, of books, tracts and periodicals ranging from serious treatises on the theological basis of the mission impulse through to Sunday school texts for children, has, along with the extensive archival collections, left a rich source for the historian trying to track the movement and its understandings of itself. A significant subsection of this textual record was devoted specifically to proselytising and recording the needs, activities and achievements of women's work. Taken together, the missionary literature evinces a remarkable degree of consistency in its portrayal of the work over the course of the century.

In the missionary text a mission of sisterhood was constructed, in which British women were cast as the saviours of Indian women, liberating them from the degradation of a vindictive Hindu culture and religion. As one missionary wife put it: 'The daughters of India are unwelcomed at their birth, untaught in childhood, enslaved when married, accursed as widows, and unlamented at their death.'[53] Indian women were portrayed as innocent and passive victims of a merciless system which used and abused them as daughters and as wives. In contrast, British women are portrayed as having the virtues and responsibilities of their free-born and independent situation. Not for them the walls of a domestic prison; rather they are portrayed as intelligent, respected agents in their own right, as well as help-meets in male endeavours, secure in their own sphere of usefulness and purpose: women's work. It is in the setting up of this opposition of stereotypes that the 'mission' of English women to their Indian counterparts is constructed, and in emotional, graphic language they are urged to respond: 'Hear the wail of India's women! Millions, millions, to us cry, They to us for aid appealing ... "Come to us!" with hands uplifted And with streaming eyes they plead.'[54]

These two contrasting stereotypes – the passive, pitiable Indian woman and the active, independent British lady missionary – were nevertheless brought together in a very close relation indeed. For it is as sisters that British ladies are urged to respond to India's call. The argument as to why British women should assume responsibility for this mission of enlightenment and rescue to Indian women started from a common basis. Both Indian and British women, by virtue of being women, are seen alike as innately religious, spiritual and moral, in ways that men (by implication and regardless of race) are not. However, at the same time as sisterhood is constructed on a shared womanly identity, a set of differences around axes of class, religion and race-nation were drawn, which break down this assumed identity into constituent parts, in keeping with the dichotomised stereotypes described above. British ladies were also accorded a superior gendered authority, as better women. The endeavour women missionaries are involved in becomes not one simply to convert, educate or enlighten, but to impose/introduce a very specific set of gender roles and models belonging to Victorian middle-class culture. In the specific milieu of South India this meant transforming Indian women into good wives and mothers as well as active Christian workers, much in the image of their missionary teachers.

This ambition was reinforced by the explicit linkage made between the religious aims of the missionary movement and British imperial rule: 'This great empire has ... been delivered into our hands ... not, surely to gratify us, but to use our influence in elevating and enlightening the vast myriads of her people.'[55] In particular, 'It is to alleviate that misery as God may enable us and bless our efforts, and to deliver our sisters out of it, that we English women are called and selected in the providence of God – a wondrous honour [and] responsibility of the deepest solemnity.'[56]

Problems of representation

The portrayal of this mission of sisterhood in the missionary texts confronted me with a number of dilemmas over issues of representation and discursive practice. Put simply, I did not believe the missionary account of women's work in the mission field. From the perspective of feminist history, Victorian women are not seen as liberated and free, but constrained by the boundaries of a patriarchal gender order. Also, to the contemporary eye of someone in the 1990s, the colonising and imperialist nature of the missionary discourse and construction of the mission of sisterhood is obvious, particularly in the stereotype of the *zenana* victim. Both contemporary stances thus question the emancipation offered to Indian women by the claim of sisterhood and the energies of women's work in the mission field.

One way of dealing with my disbelief would be to dismiss the missionary view, deconstructing the mission of sisterhood as a colonising artifice. This would reveal the missionary women as racist agents of an imperial state. At the same time, they would appear as gullible victims of a patriarchal fiction, with a false consciousness of themselves as free women, flying in the face of the historical 'fact' of their subordinate and unfree status in the Victorian social order. But where would this leave their representations of Indian women as pitiful victims of a domesticity cruel and relentless in its captivity? Not to say of Indian culture at large. By dismissing the mission of sisterhood did I leave their depiction of India intact?

The problem was exaggerated by the limits of the historical sources I had to rely upon. As yet no substantive history of Indian women or gender transformation in South India exists and documentary resources are few. The chronicle of the missionary texts was the primary available story of the missionary endeavours in the indigenous locale. In these texts Indian voices, male or female, were few and embedded within the missionary narrative. There was no easily available Indian story to replace or set against the mission of sisterhood.

Moreover, I had a growing respect for the integrity of my historical subjects – the missionary women – and the sense they clearly made of their world. This was a sense which often challenged the stereotypes I held of them as subordinate to Victorian patriarchy. Yet I was unwilling to accept or simply re-present their views of themselves and their Indian sisters. My dilemma was threefold. While I sought to present the authenticity of the past, I also felt compelled to respect my own scepticism, a scepticism which rested on my secular location in the post-colonial world of the late twentieth century. I sought to address, with some degree of equivalence, three distinct interests: my subjects – the missionaries; their Indian subjects; and my own purpose: a feminist post-colonial history.

Facts and fictions

In seeking a way to address these three interests I have drawn on the work of Hayden White, Talal Asad and Edward Said. Influenced by post-structuralist and post-colonial critical theory, these three writers treat with issues of authority, power and voice in ways which usefully extend the feminist critiques of recuperative history discussed at the outset of this chapter. By developing the notion of translation variously addressed by White, Asad and Said, I am able to construct a discursive framework for writing my history.

In *Tropics of Discourse* White has argued that, put simply, there is no 'real' history of events beyond the historian's text – no 'true story' that historians discern – to uncover 'what must have been'. Rather, White argues, the historian translates facts into 'fictions' – culturally familiar story forms, thus rendering the strange and exotic past comprehensible to the contemporary reader. Even these 'facts', the grounding of the historian's translation, are not to be treated as given, but as *constructed* 'by the kinds of questions which the investigator asks of the phenomena'.[57] In White's analysis, therefore, the 'single correct view' is replaced by 'many correct views'. The basis of judgement is no longer that of correspondence to 'fact' but effective choice of metaphor and mode of representation.

There is a seductive quality about White's analysis, offering, as it seems to do, the individual writer of history a free choice (within the bounds of culture) to 'translate' and 'encode' her/his 'fiction'. But doubts persist. If history as knowing the past becomes a series of culturally specific but varied stories from the present, all equally true as representations and translations of historical remnants, what are the implications for feminist and post-colonial histories? To be one among a plurality of true stories might take more than it seems to give. Are all interpretations, regardless of form, accorded equivalent authority as true stories? The effects of White's dismantling of a positivist singularity risks flattening out 'history'. If there is no one 'true story' neither is there, it seems, any disparity between them in effect or authority; all are portrayed as equally recognised and available as a construction of the past.

Social anthropologists, from whom White borrows his methodological model, have, however, begun to cast a critical eye over the notion of 'translation' in ways which challenge White's straightforward co-option of the term for historical method. Talal Asad has argued that 'the process of cultural "translation" is inevitably enmeshed in conditions of power – professional, national, international'.[58] Within anthropology, Asad argues, the method of translation is based on the privilege accorded the anthropologist to ascertain the real meaning of what his informants say. The ethnographer becomes author, not translator, a displacement of authority which takes particular effect in the institutional context of the anthropological exercise. The 'real' meaning discerned by the anthropologist is not simply an alternative or parallel text to that produced by its ethnographic subjects. Rather the anthropologist's translation is accorded a privileged authority which threatens to undermine the self-knowledge of her/his informants, given the global circumstances of its production. At no stage of the translation process does a dialogical relationship exist between the two sets of meanings: '[I]n the long run ... it is not the personal authority of the ethnographer, but the social authority of his ethnography that matters. And that authority is inscribed in the institutionalised forces of industrial capitalist society which are constantly *tending* to push the meanings of various Third World countries in a single direction.'[59]

Asad's critique of anthropological translations raises a number of points relevant to White's historical method. Clearly, the historian can never hope to construct a dialogue between her/his 'translation' and an authentic original – they (usually) being dead and we dealing with textual remnants. This does not, however, exonerate historians from dealing with the issues of power and authority Asad raises.

White's identification of the multiple meanings and fictional nature of historical narrative and method fails to acknowledge precisely the wider contexts within which the historian's story takes effect. His critique appears to be addressed primarily to fellow practitioners of history in contemporary North America and Europe. Revealing the fictional qualities of their discourse does not dislodge the authoritative status accorded their texts by the broader society – as history it is *their* stories which inscribe meaning in the past as part of the metropolitan canon of knowing its others. Even within the academy, the struggles for recognition fought by those writing histories from the perspective of a subordinate gender, class or race demonstrate the different authority lent some stories over others. No less than the anthropologist's ethnography, the historian's history is a powerful invention beyond any aspirations of the author her/himself.

It is not only the worldliness of the historian's discursive products that White fails to address, but also that of the historical texts which form the basis of his/her translations. White rightly challenges the positivist claim to discern a real history beyond the limits of the textual evidence, a claim similar to the anthropologist's search for an implicit meaning in its assumption of objective perspicacity. In the process, however, he conceives of the historical text as a disembodied entity whose potential meanings are entirely constructed by the reader/historian. White's historical methodology therefore obtains a doubly fictive character, the historian as translator effectively mediating between two free-floating texts anchored only by the disciplinary location of their author.

Edward Said, however, cogently argues that this fails to acknowledge that: '[T]exts are worldly, to some degree they are events, ... a part of the social world, human life, and of course the historical moments in which they are located and interpreted.'[60] Taking as his example Macaulay's Minute of 1835 on Indian education and the English language, Said argues that the text cannot be viewed as an opinion of Macaulay's nor as simply an instance of ethnocentrism: 'For it is that and more. Macaulay's was an ethnocentric opinion with ascertainable results. He was speaking from a position of power where he could translate his opinions into the decision to make an entire subcontinent of natives submit to studying in a language not their own.'[61] Macaulay's Minute does not simply form part of a powerful administrative nexus however. It is representative of nineteenth-century thought more generally. As Said points out, no European writer, however critical of the status quo, could avoid, at that time, expressing a hierarchy which positioned themselves 'above' and 'interior' to those others 'below' and 'exterior'.[62] It was the discourse providing the culturally available means of ordering and representing their thought. More than this, in a context of European imperialism and colonial domination, the nineteenth-century corpus contributed to a powerful cultural hegemony which effectively imposed this discourse on colonised societies to the extent that even oppositional anti-colonial

thought could be caught within the parameters of this Eurocentric discourse.[63]

Said's intervention complicates rather than denies White's claim that
there is no historical reality beyond the text for the historian to discern.
Acknowledging the worldly nature of a historical document does not
overcome the distance of the past, or facilitate some kind of authentic
reconstruction of what it must have been. What it does, surely, is to
provide a potential limitation on the historian's choice of enplotment
for her/his translated narrative. To continue Said's nineteenth-century
example, failure to take into account the imperialist discourse within
which such texts were constructed risks re-presenting material whose
complicity in past relations of domination assumes a contemporary relevance in the global context of Western economic and political domination, precisely the warning Asad directs to social anthropologists.

Such an awareness is, of course, thoroughly contemporary to the
1990s. In this sense, White's depiction of historical writing as fictional
remains an accurate and important qualifier to the issues of power and
meaning raised by Asad and Said. The ability to problematise the hierarchies of race and culture present in Macaulay's text is a consequence
of late-twentieth-century sensibilities and politics reinforced by a particular knowledge of the consequences his Minute helped engender.
To explicate Macaulay's words from such a position is to create a 'fiction' in terms of any relationship to the original meanings the Minute
might have held for its author or those implicated in its application,
while establishing a truism for the contemporary readership.

So where does this leave me and my writing of the mission of sisterhood? The comparative frame I bring White, Asad and Said within provides me with a discursive methodology which holds out the potential
to address the twin tasks of contextualising the subject while avoiding
the pitfalls of a singular, exclusive focus. By utilising White's depiction
of history as fiction and narrative I am able to juxtapose the missionary
chronicle of the mission of sisterhood and my own *translation* of that
representation in ways which facilitate precisely the acknowledgement
of power and context both Asad and Said, in different ways, insist upon.
In doing so I am thus able to avoid the dichotomies of good and bad
women which structure a woman-centred historiography, whilst
making difference a central axis of my history.

Different stories

The missionary texts recount a story about Indian women and the
efforts of British 'ladies' to emancipate them from the bounds of both
culture and religion. Women's work in the mission field is the *mechanism* through which this liberation is attempted.

The mission of sisterhood turns on a comparison between the unfree Indian woman and her free British counterpart, portrayed most starkly in the contrast between the confining Indian household or *zenana* and the freedoms of the British home, drawn as a harmony of companionate marriage. Such a picture assumes an artificial gloss in the light of the contemporary feminist understanding of the nineteenth-century middle-class home and family to be a place of confinement and site of rebellion for many Victorian women, an image more nearly like that of the *zenana* of missionary imagination than the suburban ideal of the British home portrayed in the missionary literature.

Across the distance of time, the image of the Indian woman seems more an artifice with which the narrative of women's work in the mission field is able to negotiate the boundaries of a Victorian gender order rather than a rendition of Indian circumstances – a point of view reinforced by the knowledge that strict female seclusion and *zenanas* were a phenomenon specific to time, place, caste and class in India. By constructing the gap of culture and religion represented by the image of the *zenana* victim, the need and legitimation for women's work in the foreign field is established within a conventional frame of feminine action and agency. Yet despite the rhetoric of making good wives and mothers of the *zenana* inmates, the interventions of women's work do not produce images of domesticity or of freedom from the *zenana*. Rather, the images are of intellectual development and occupational industry by the Bible women – the low caste and low class women who, in the circumstances of South India, never were inhabitants of the *zenana*. The missionary women write of themselves engaged in educating their pupils for posts as – good Christian – teachers and nurses, and even, by the end of the century, for university entrance. It is a picture that most nearly captures the agency of the missionary women themselves, hardly the good wives and mothers of the stereotypical 'home', embroiled as they were in the demands of the work, demands which, as the century progressed, often precluded marriage.

The story I tell reverses the configuration of character and agency which in the missionary texts situates women's work as the means of emancipating Indian women. In my narrative, women's work takes centre stage as the means of emancipating not Indian women, but the missionary women themselves, albeit in ultimately ambiguous ways. The key aspect in my documentation of the professionalisation of missionary women's work is how the colonial context played a vital role in articulating these changes in the configuration of gender and work. My analysis turns on the ways in which the representation of Indian women, the ostensible subjects of women's work, mediates the participation of British women in the mission of sisterhood.

[65]

The missionary discourse of women's work is revealed, I argue, as a process of 'othering' which constructs Indian women as the converse of their free and active British sisters through the image of the *zenana* victim. The point of reference is precisely the measure of difference between the 'lady' and the 'Indian sister', forming the space in which women's work takes shape. The effect, however, is contrary. It is not the other of the *zenana* who is 'made' in this process, but her British sister, as the professional, and single, lady missionary. The *zenana* inmate remains a stereotype, the representation around which the agency of the missionary woman obtains its feasibility. In my translation Indian women are no longer the subjects of the narrative, but the textual device around which the missionary story turns. The difference between my narrative and that of the mission of sisterhood thus raises those issues of fact, fiction and translation dealt with by White, Asad and Said. The basis of my 'translation' turns on my stance in the late twentieth century and the 'knowledge' this distance of time gives me about the missionary past, in a sense, constructing a prism through which I represent the missionaries.

The key to the missionary texts' representation of the missionary women as free, emancipated, devoted workers, while nevertheless archetypes of conventional Christian womanhood, lay in the religious rubric in which it was couched. It was the higher call of God which legitimated the efforts and ambitions of the missionary women and the conduct of women's work. This call was not simply an injunction to carry out scriptural commands to spread the word, but a call to assume fully the particular role allocated to Christian women, a role perceived of as equivalent to, though not the same as, that of their male counterparts, and fully documented from the annals of biblical history. It was a role which could overcome bounds of familial obligation, sending daughters thousands of miles from parental care, and casting the role of missionary wife as 'an independent sphere of labour and responsibility', both nevertheless expressed in terms of selflessness, duty and obedience – to God.[64] It is, however, precisely this religious rubric which sets off the missionary narrative from my own.

From the more secular viewpoint of the 1990s, nineteenth-century Britain is not caught in a trajectory of Christian mission and selflessness, as the missionary literature assumes. Rather, it is the chronicle of the development of capitalism and a secular individualism, conceived of as a cultural and psychological as well as an economic and social configuration. It is this secular history which provides the prism within which I am able to make sense, for myself, of the missionary literature and through which I discern an alternative story based not on duty, selflessness and service to God but independence, individual aspiration and material transformations.

It is through this play-off between the religious perspective of the missionaries and my own secular reading of these texts that I am able to document the transformation in the meanings of women's work around which my analysis turns. Precisely because of the place allocated the nineteenth century in the development of contemporary capitalist society, the missionary narrative of women's work provides both evidence and point of departure for my argument. I document the transition from their meaning of women's work, of work as duty and service, to one closer to the contemporary meanings of my own culture and time, as individual ambition and waged employment. Thus, despite the limitations of my prism, I do accord the missionary view of work a validity as fact as well as fiction in the shift from a labour of love for God to a professional employment relation.

Further, it is not just the racial hierarchies explicit in the idioms and images of the missionary narrative which make these texts 'worldly' in the context of empire and colonialism, but also the circumstances of their production. As I mentioned earlier, Indian contributions to these texts are caught firmly within the purview of the missionary narrative, forming part of a literature which stood alone in its powerful authority to represent both itself and its subjects to a British audience increasingly engaged with the ideals of empire. The missionary account of India and its women was, if not the main, then undoubtedly a primary contributor to the public perceptions of India as an appropriate subject of British imperial rule.[65]

A failure to 'translate' the mission of sisterhood into our contemporary discourses of post-colonialism would risk, therefore, contributing to precisely those global relations of power Talal Asad is concerned to take account of in anthropological ethnography, rather than to an ethical integrity towards the past. My dilemma thus becomes the reverse of Asad's, however, for it is only by imposing my translation on the historical chronicle that I can attempt to avoid contributing to our contemporary inequalities.

The last word

Acknowledging the fictional quality of my narrative and the ways in which I am constrained in my treatment of the missionary sources does not overcome the problems of translation identified by Asad. The historical, rather than contemporary ethnographic, relationship reverses but does not avoid the dilemmas of imposition and allocation of meaning. I am unable to believe or simply reproduce the missionary narrative of the mission of sisterhood but, rather than dismissing that

[67]

account entirely, I have tried to present both narratives – the missionaries' and my own – rather than simply my translation; marking the missionary language as distinct from my own and making explicit the points at which the translation occurs, in an attempt to represent both as contingently available versions of the historical events.

But of course, this does not solve the problem. My 'distant primitives' – the missionaries – are given a relevance and integrity within their own time and culture, but there is no dialogical relationship established between the two narratives. I tell a story about the ways in which a group of Victorian middle-class women experienced the transformation to a professional employment relationship and the ways, from my point of view, a colonial subject facilitated this process. It is not a story of the mission of sisterhood and labours of love designed to emancipate Indian women.

The duality of my text is artificial, reserving for my narrative the authority of determining meaning – the last word. At best, by making explicit the ways in which the two narratives meet, I am able to indicate the ways in which the missionary view of women's work had a sense which not only differs from, but in some ways is both inaccessible and unacceptable to, my own.

There is one other narrative implicit in this historical chronicle, that of Indian women. By showing how the image of the *zenana* victim acted as a literary device and artifice of the missionary women's *self-representation* to their home audience, as professional workers who, by virtue of the contrast with a colonial other, maintain a conventional quality of good women despite their independence and unmarried state, I am able to suggest the fictional quality of the missionary portrayal of Indian women. By revealing how their subject status operated as device for the story of women's work, however, I risk duplicating the emancipatory efforts of the mission of sisterhood. I have tried to avoid this possibility by purposely refusing to tell a story of Indian women. Instead, I have attempted to place them as outside either the liberation effort of women's work or my agenda of professional 'ladies'. I have sought to suggest that, buried in the as yet inaccessible past, lies yet another account of emancipation but one which turned on very different axes to those of the missionaries or myself.

The principal Indian voices to come through in the missionary texts are the Bible women, Christian converts who, in South India, assisted the missionary women by actually doing the work of reaching the 'heathen women'. They are present in fragments of their work diaries, submitted to the missionary women who supervised their work. These reports were translated into English and edited by the missionaries for inclusion in missionary reports and articles. Hence, they are very far from any 'authentic voice'. However, what at first glance seems a complicit reflection of the mission of sisterhood's emancipatory aims, takes on another sheen when read against the backdrop of the emerging history of colonial South India – a history conceived of from within an indigenous milieu, rather than from a stance which assumes a universalising presence for the forces of colonialism.[66] While the story is far from complete yet, even within the constraints of the Bible women's fragments, one can discern a struggle in which the missionary women's efforts at education and emancipation assume a secondary role as a resource mobilised by Indian women to wage their own struggles about issues of class and caste.[67]

Conclusion

My approach to the missionary discourse on women's work was dictated by my scepticism of their representation of the mission of sisterhood as an effort to emancipate Indian women. A contemporary post-colonial sensibility ensured I was unwilling to simply reproduce the missionary account. This was reinforced by a secular understanding of the nineteenth century as a chronicle of developing capitalism rather than of true religion. Thus, I translate the mission of sisterhood into a narrative of the emancipation of British 'ladies'[68] – an emancipation achieved, in the missionary texts, through the discursive mechanism of the colonial other: Indian women.

However, I have tried to avoid simply dismissing the missionary account as indicative of either false consciousness or of propaganda, by presenting it as a contingently available version of the historical events. Thus, while I have resolutely located the mission of sisterhood within an imperialist context of colonial domination based on distinctions of both class and race, I have refrained from labelling these professional ladies and working wives either 'good' or 'bad' women, to parody the various approaches to white women and colonialism in the literature. Issues of imperialism and race, as a politics of post-colonialism, are explicitly located within my contemporary 'fiction' of the past, their salience one of the 1990s rather than the 1890s.

My ability to construct a dual (though not a dialogical) text rests in large part on the distance I assume between the 'exotic' past and the mundane present, the former conceived of as beyond the semantic knowing of the latter. In particular, it is the religious idioms and images of the missionary discourse which allow me to articulate this difference and make my translations explicit. I am able, therefore, to portray the coherence of the self-representations of the missionary women.

Despite the distance I assume between my present and the Victorian

[69]

past, it is an assumption based on the knowledge that this distance nevertheless forms part of a continuum, one I have labelled the development of a capitalist social formation. However, I cannot assume a similar continuum between my present and the past of the Indian women who, in the fragmented voices of the Bible women, occasionally impinge on the missionary record. While India, over the same time-span, has also experienced the development of capitalism, it has done so as part of a very different context, one which cannot be assumed to fit the framework of secular individualism which underpins my counterpoint to the missionary chronicle of true religion.

Yet this same distance and sense of difference which reveals the internal integrity of women's work uncovers another, profoundly disturbing, continuity. I have also laid bare the origins of another contemporary relationship. The mission of sisterhood and its trope of emancipation bear an uncanny resemblance to the contemporary relationship drawn between 'Western' feminism and 'third world' women. Replacing the images of veiled Islamic women or the brides of arranged marriages in some contemporary Western feminist texts with that of the *zenana* inmate is an unnerving experience. The legacy is surely made explicit in that claim to universal sisterhood which galvanised second-wave feminism as much as it appears to have done the Victorian women of my study. While the slogan is currently much the worse for wear, its sentiment continues to resonate.

To return to the debates over women's and gender history with which I began this chapter, have I succeeded in my aim of constructing a 'gumbo-ya-ya' rather than a 'symphonic' history? Not entirely. The limitations of historical sources, particularly the lack of an Indian narrative, mean I am only able to suggest the space such a story would fill. As well, the over-riding authority given my 'translation' precludes the kind of democracy Barkley Brown seems to claim for 'gumbo-ya-ya'.[69] However, by adopting a post-structuralist discursive method, I am able to overcome the dualisms of a recuperative history in a way which does not tell white women – either of the past or the present – to 'shut up'. By making explicit the ways in which I 'translate' the missionary narrative I am able to avoid either dismissing or apologising for the missionary women's accounts of their presences and actions. Instead, it is revealed as a historically contingent and coherent version of events. My lady missionaries may not emerge as feminist heroines, but neither are they caught in a historical behavioural vacuum, charged with racism. The actions and agencies of the missionary women are accorded meaning by treating the missionary archive as textual representations located within the logics of metropolitan trajectories of social change and gender relations. Thus the depiction of

Indian women as other assumes an effect within the history of the pro-fessionalisation of middle-class women's occupations and employ-ments in Britain. The consequences of this, and of the activities of the missionary women, for Indian histories, are neither assumed nor denied, but given a potentiality in terms of their local context. In the process, it seems to me that the concept of 'women' as a putative cat-egory of identity and relation is not deconstructed to the point of inco-herence. Rather, it is given a complexity across time and place which surely facilitates a sound, if shifting, base for writing feminist histories able to contribute fully to contemporary feminisms.[70]

Notes

This chapter is a revised version of a paper first published as *The Past in the Present: Writing the History of the Mission of Sisterhood*, Discussion Papers in Women's Stud-ies, Centre for Women's Studies, University of Waikato, Hamilton, NZ, ed. Professor Anna Yeatman, 1992.

1 Chilla Bulbeck, 'New histories of the memsahib and missus: the case of Papua New Guinea', *Journal of Women's History*, 3:2 (1991), p. 82.
2 See especially Claudia Knapman, *White Women in Fiji 1835–1930: The Ruin of Empire?* (Sydney, Allen and Unwin, 1986); Helen Callaway, *Gender, Culture and Empire: European Women in Colonial Nigeria* (London, Macmillan, 1987); Margaret Macmillan, *Women of the Raj* (London, Thames and Hudson, 1988); C. Bulbeck, *Australian Women in Papua New Guinea: Colonial Passages 1920–1960* (Cam-bridge, Cambridge University Press, 1992), for studies which explicitly engage with the stereotype of the racist memsahib. Other works which look at the way male his-torians have portrayed white women as the inaugurators of racist relations in the colonies are: Margaret Strobel, *European Women and the Second British Empire* (Bloomington and Indianapolis, Indiana University Press, 1991); Nupur Chaudhuri and Margaret Strobel (eds), *Western Women and Imperialism: Complicity and Resistance* (Bloomington and Indianapolis, Indiana University Press, 1992); and Kumari Jayawardena, *The White Woman's Other Burden: Western Women and South Asia During British Rule* (New York and London, Routledge, 1995).
3 Janaki Nair, 'Reconstructing and reinterpreting the history of women in India', *Jour-nal of Women's History*, 3 (1991), pp. 8–34, and Jane Haggis, 'Gendering colonialism or colonising gender? Recent women's studies approaches to white women and the history of British colonialism', *Women's Studies International Forum*, 12 (1990), pp. 105–112.
4 Bulbeck, 'New histories', p. 99.
5 This debate has been wide-ranging and prolific. Some key texts are: L. Newman, 'Critical theory and the history of women: what's at stake in deconstructing women's history'; J. Williams, 'Domesticity as the dangerous supplement of liber-alism'; L. Vogel, 'Telling tales: historians of our own lives'; J. Newton, 'A feminist scholarship you can bring home to dad?'; all in *Journal of Women's History*, 2:3 (1991), pp. 58–105; E. Fox-Genovese, 'Placing women's history in history', *New Left Review*, 133 (1982), pp. 5–29; G. Bock, 'Women's history and gender history: aspects of an international debate', *Gender and History*, 1:1 (1989), pp. 7–30; D. Riley, '*Am I That Name?' Feminism and the Category of 'Women' in History* (Minneapolis, University of Minnesota, 1988); J. Scott, *Gender and the Politics of History* (New York, Columbia University Press, 1988); J. A. Bennett, 'Feminism and history', *Gender and History*, 1:3 (1989), pp. 251–272; J. L. Newton, 'History as usual? Fem-inism and the "new historicism"', in H. Aram Veeser (ed.), *The New Historicism*

(London and New York, Routledge, 1989); D. Clark Hine, 'Black women's history, white women's history: the juncture of race and class', and R. Roach Pierson, 'Colonization and Canadian women's history', both in *Journal of Women's History*, 4:2 (1992), pp. 125–156; E. Barkley Brown, '"What has happened here": the politics of difference in women's history and feminist politics', and I. Berger, 'Categories and contexts: reflections on the politics of identity in South Africa', Symposium: Intersections and collision courses: women, blacks, and workers confront gender, race, and Class, *Feminist Studies*, 18:2 (1992), pp. 284–312; R. Roach Pierson, 'Experience, difference and voice in the writing of Canadian women's history', in K. Offen, R. Roach Pierson and J. Rendall (eds), *Writing Women's History: International Perspectives* (Bloomington and Indianopolis, Indiana University Press, 1991), pp. 79–106.

6 Scott, 'Gender and the politics of history', esp. ch. 1.
7 *Ibid.*, p. 10.
8 D. Birkett and J. Wheelwright, 'How could she? Unpalatable facts and feminists' heroines', *Gender and History*, 2:1 (1990), p. 49.
9 L. Stanley, 'Moments of writing: is there a feminist auto/biography?', *Gender and History*, 2:1 (1990), p. 58.
10 Birkett and Wheelwright, 'How could she?', p. 49.
11 *Ibid.*, p. 46.
12 The tension between the roles of mother and wife in the lives of expatriate women in the colonies, and how this impacted on their view of the colonial environment, has been explored in several studies. Knapman, *White Women in Fiji*, and Callaway, *Gender, Culture and Empire*, draw on a conceptual framework similar to Bulbeck's, suggesting white women were essentially outside the masculine sphere of colonial authority. P. Grimshaw, *Paths of Duty: American Missionary Wives in Nineteenth Century Hawaii* (Honolulu, Hawaii University Press, 1989), and M. Jolly, '"To save the girls for brighter and better lives": Presbyterian missions and women in the south of Vanuatu – 1848–1870', *Journal of Pacific History*, 26:1 (1991), pp. 27–48, situate white women in a more relational context in which norms of gender ideologies dictate the specific aspects of white women's involvements in domestic and non-domestic life.
13 See Haggis, 'Gendering colonialism'.
14 M. Jolly, 'Colonising women: the maternal body and empire', undated mimeo, p. 21.
15 Barkley Brown, '"What has happened here"', p. 298.
16 *Ibid.*, p. 297.
17 *Ibid.*
18 *Ibid.*
19 *Ibid.*, p. 299.
20 See particularly G. Chakravorty Spivak, 'Three women's texts and a critique of imperialism', *Critical Inquiry*, 12:1 (1985), pp. 243–261, and E. W. Said, *Culture and Imperialism* (London, Chatto and Windus, 1993).
21 See particularly C. Talpade Mohanty, 'Under Western eyes: feminist scholarship and colonial discourses', in C. Talpade Mohanty, A. Russo and L. Torres (eds), *Third World Women and the Politics of Feminism* (Bloomington and Indianapolis, Indiana University Press, 1991), pp. 51–80, and G. Chakravorty Spivak, 'French feminism in an international frame', in *In Other Worlds: Essays in Cultural Politics* (New York and London, Methuen, 1987), pp. 134–153.
22 R. Pierce Beaver, *American Protestant Women in World Mission: History of the First Feminist Movement in North America* (Grand Rapids, Eardmans, 1980); S. S. Garrett, 'Sisters all: feminism and the American Women's Missionary Movement', in T. Christensen and W. R. Hutchinson, (eds), *Missionary Ideologies in the Imperialist Era 1880–1920* (Denmark, Aros, 1982), pp. 221–230 ; P. R. Hill, *The World Their Household: The American Women's Foreign Mission Movement and Cultural Transformation 1870–1920* (Ann Arbor, University of Michigan Press, 1985); J. Hunter, *The Gospel of Gentility: American Women Missionaries in Turn-of-the-Century China* (New Haven and London, Yale University Press, 1984); Grimshaw,

Paths of Duty; S. M. Jacobs, 'Give a thought to Africa: black women missionaries in Southern Africa', in Chaudhuri and Strobel, *Western Women and Imperialism*, pp. 207–228; M. King, 'American women's open door to Chinese women: which way does it open?', *Women's Studies International Forum*, 13:4 (1990), pp. 369–379; G. B. Paul, 'Presbyterian missionaries and the women of India during the nineteenth century', *Journal of Presbyterian History*, 62 (1982), pp. 230–236.

23 The London Missionary Society was established in 1795. Although putatively non-denominational, the Society was closely associated with the Congregational community in England. Its first missionary undertaking was to the 'South Seas' in 1796. The Society launched its mission to India by smuggling two men in via the Danish territory of Tranquebar in South India, as a consequence of the East India Company's opposition to missionary activities in territories under its jurisdiction. One of these, a Prussian named Ringeltaube, found his way to Travancore, a Hindu kingdom on the far south-west coast of India, in 1807. The South Travancore District was, by 1851, the most successful of the Society's Indian establishments with one of the largest convert communities of any missionary station in India, a position it retained for much of the nineteenth century. The South Travancore District extended to Quilon in the north and the border between Travancore and Madras Presidency in the east, at which points the Church Missionary Society, affiliated with the Church of England, assumed territorial rights to convert loyalties.

24 J. S. Dennis, *Christian Missions and Social Progress: A Sociological Study of Foreign Missions* (Edinburgh and London, Oliphant, Anderson & Ferrier, 1899), vol. 2, p. 46.

25 E. R. Pitman, *Heroines of the Mission Field: Biographical Sketches of Female Missionaries Who Have Laboured in Various Lands Among the Heathen* (London, Cassell, Petter, Galpin & Co., *c.* 1881), p. 7.

26 E. Stock, *The History of the Church Missionary Society* (London, Church Missionary Society, 1899), vol. 3, p. 369.

27 The movement of middle-class women into the labour force during the years 1870 to 1914 has been called a 'white blouse revolution': see G. Anderson (ed.), *The White Blouse Revolution: Female Office Workers Since 1870* (Manchester, Manchester University Press, 1988). There was a massive increase in the percentage of women employed in teaching, nursing, shop and clerical occupations and the civil service. One estimate puts the overall increase at 161 per cent between 1881 and 1911: see L. Holcombe, *Ladies At Work: Middle Class Working Women in England and Wales, 1850–1914* (Hamden, Connecticut, Archon Press, 1973).

28 M. Vicinus, *Independent Women: Work and Community for Single Women, 1850–1920* (London, Virago, 1985), p. 1.

29 Vicinus, *Independent Women*, p. 33.

30 L. Davidoff and C. Hall, *Family Fortunes: Men and Women of the English Middle Class 1780–1850* (London, Hutchinson, 1987), p. 117.

31 G. K. Hewat, *Vision and Achievement 1796–1956: A History of the Foreign Missions of the Churches United in the Church of Scotland* (Edinburgh, Thomas Nelson, 1960), p. 11.

32 Stock, *History of the Church Missionary Society*, vol. 1, p. 108.

33 Mrs Marshman, of the Baptist Missionary Society, is credited with having established the first girls' school at some point soon after her arrival in Bengal in 1799: M. Weitbrecht, *Women of India and Christian Work in the Zenana* (London, J. Nisbett, 1875), p. 145.

34 Commenting on the departure of the first missionary couples despatched to Ceylon in 1804, the Directors of the LMS wrote: 'Mrs Vos and Mrs Palm have also an important service to occupy their zeal, in the instruction of the female natives, and in assisting in the education of children': R. Lovett, *The History of the London Missionary Society 1795–1895*, vol. 2 (London, H. Frowde, 1899), p. 18. Fiancees and wives were vetted by the missionary societies as part of the application process for missionary candidates. In 1837, Mr Abbs applied as a missionary to the LMS. Confidential references were called regarding his fiancee's suitability to accompany him as his wife, her pastor describing her as a valuable teacher in the Sunday school,

with a 'zeal and heartiness in the cause of the Redeemer'. *Council for World Mission*, Home and General, Candidates Papers, Box 1, Envelope 1, Letter: Dryden, 1 August 1837.

35 *History of the Society for Promoting Female Education in the East* (London, E. Suter, 1847), p. 5.

36 *History of SPFEE*, p.6.

37 Although Jemima Luke, an early member of the SPFEE, wrote in her memoirs that 'opposition and sarcasm have given place to respect and sympathy', I have as yet found no evidence of any concerted or organised opposition to the establishment of the SPFEE and its operations. J. Luke, *Early Years of My Life* (London, Hodder and Stoughton, 1900), p. 155.

38 See F. Prochaska, *Women and Philanthropy in Nineteenth Century England* (Oxford, Oxford University Press, 1980), for a general history.

39 *History of SPFEE*, p. 5.

40 *Ibid.*, p. 45.

41 Mrs Corrie was the first to approach the Church Missionary Society in this regard in 1815. The Committee responded that it would be against 'Christian decorum and propriety' to send single women out to India unless they were 'sisters accompanying or joining their brothers': Stock, *History of the Church Missionary Society*, vol. 1, p. 125; see also J. S. Isherwood, 'An analysis of the role of single women in the work of the Church Missionary Society 1804–1904', University of Manchester, Theology MA (1979).

42 The SPFEE had a clause in its bylaws binding all appointed agents, should they voluntarily relinquish their post or leave to marry within five years, to repay the Committee 'the sum expended by them on her less one fifth deducted for each year she did her job', *History of SPFEE*, p. 280. In 1842, one of the ladies sent out by the Edinburgh Society married one of the male missionaries who had been amongst those most eager for 'a lady from Scotland' to be sent to his mission to start women's work there. The Society felt so strongly about this that they tried, unsuccessfully, to demand compensation from the male missionary's society: A. S. Swan, *Seed Time and Harvest: The Story of the Hundred Years Work of the Women's Foreign Mission of the Church of Scotland* (London, Thomas Nelson and Sons, 1937), pp. 47–49.

43 *History of SPFEE*, p. 31.

44 Luke, *Early Years*, p. 73.

45 CWM, Home and General, Committee Minutes, Ladies Committee, Box 1, Printed Notice, 13 July 1875.

46 CWM, Home and General, Committee Minutes, Ladies Committee, Box 1, Printed Letter, 13 July 1975.

47 LMS, Annual Report, 1891.

48 CWM, Home and General, Committee Minutes, Ladies Committee, Box 1, 9 June 1891.

49 The vetting process is particularly visible in the case of candidates who were ambiguously located in class terms. Susannah Hodge had earned her own living as a milliner, maintaining herself out of a sense of 'duty' to her widowed mother, she wrote in a letter to the Committee (CWM, Candidates Papers, Box 7, Envelope 46, Letter, 5 July 1890). Her minister wrote that 'she had received a better education than is usual with persons in her position; and I should think she has come from a home of some refinement' (CWM, Candidates Papers, Box 7, Envelope 46, Letter, 17 June 1890). However, despite attending an interview and completing the Printed Questionnaire required of all candidates, the Committee still felt they required a 'more intimate knowledge'. Only after Committee members had seen Susannah in their homes and had reported 'the favourable impression produced on them ... by her manner and personal appearance' was her application accepted, six months after her initial enquiry (CWM, Committee Minutes, Ladies Committee, Box 1, 15 July 1890 and 4 November 1890).

50 The importance of Indian Christian women in actually carrying out missionary 'work' is also noted by Geraldine Forbes in her brief study of single women mis-

sionaries who served with the Society for the Propagation of the Gospel in Bombay between 1858 and 1914. Forbes emphasises the important role of Indian Christian women in the development of female education, a point borne out in my own research. G. H. Forbes, 'In search of the "Pure Heathen": missionary women in nineteenth century India', *Economic and Political Weekly*, 21 (1986), Review of Women's Studies, WS2–WS8.

51 One missionary, serving in South Travancore in the 1880s, related in his Annual Report how a star graduate from his wife's boarding school had been sent, under mission auspices, to undertake midwifery training at a medical school for women in North Travancore, a considerable distance from her home: 'As she had a family of four young children it was not an easy matter for her to leave her home and go for two years with only occasional holidays to a place over sixty miles off. ... Her husband who is a schoolmaster ... felt it very difficult of course to spare his wife for two years and take charge himself for so long a time of three or four young children but he finally decided to do so' (CWM/Home and General/India/South India/Travancore/Reports/Box 3/1888).

52 For a more detailed consideration of the class, race and gender dimensions of the representation of the Bible women see J. Haggis, 'Good wives and mothers or dedicated workers: contradictions of domesticity in the Mission of Sisterhood, Travancore, South India', in K. Ram and M. Jolly (eds), *Maternities and Modernities: Colonial and Postcolonial Experiences in Asia and the Pacific* (Cambridge, Cambridge University Press, forthcoming, 1998).

53 *India's Women*, vol. 1 (1880), preliminary issue, p. 3

54 *India's Women*, 1:9 (1882), p. 134.

55 *India's Women*, 4:22 (1884), p. 180.

56 *India's Women*, vol. 1 (1880), preliminary issue, p. 3

57 H. White, *Tropics of Discourse: Essays in Cultural Criticism* (Baltimore, Johns Hopkins University Press, 1978), p. 43.

58 T. Asad, 'The concept of cultural translation in British social anthropology', in J. Clifford and G. E. Marcus (eds), *Writing Culture: The Poetics and Politics of Ethnography* (Berkeley, University of California Press, 1986), p. 163.

59 Asad, 'The concept of cultural translation', p. 163, emphasis in original.

60 E. W. Said, *The World, the Text and the Critic* (Cambridge, Mass., Harvard University Press, 1983), p. 4.

61 *Ibid.*, p. 12.

62 *Ibid.*, p. 13.

63 E. W. Said, *Orientalism* (Harmondsworth, Penguin, 1985); see also P. Chatterjee, *Nationalist Thought and the Colonial World: A Derivative Discourse* (London, Zed Books Ltd., 1986).

64 Weitbrecht, *Women of India*, p. 194

65 J. M. MacKenzie, *Propaganda and Empire: The Manipulation of British Public Opinion 1880–1960* (Manchester, Manchester University Press, 1984).

66 See D. Ludden, *Peasant History in South India* (Delhi, Oxford University Press, 1989), and S. Bayly, *Saints, Goddesses and Kings: Muslims and Christians in South Indian Society 1700–1900* (Cambridge, Cambridge University Press, 1990), for histories of South India which attempt to set colonialism within the context of an existing indigenous historical dynamic.

67 See Haggis, 'Good wives and mothers'.

68 See A. Burton, *Burdens of History: British Feminists, Indian Women and Imperial Culture 1865–1915* (Chapel Hill, University of North Carolina Press, 1994).

69 Barkley Brown draws a direct analogy between the description of jazz music as a 'true democracy' and history as 'everybody talking at once' (p. 297). However, she does not really address in her article the problems of power and authority as an issue for the writing of history I've tried to raise here.

70 On the issue of feminist history and its contribution to feminist theory see Antoinette Burton, '"History" is now: feminist theory and the production of historical feminism', *Women's History Review*, 1:1 (1992), pp. 25–38.

PART II

Reactions and resistances

CHAPTER THREE

Indian Christian women and indigenous feminism, *c.*1850–*c.*1920

Padma Anagol

The gender and women's history of India has expanded considerably in recent years, adding to our knowledge of various aspects of women's lives.[1] These have included the marginalisation of women in the economy and popular culture; the impact of colonial law and administrative policies on the role and status of women; the reconstitution of patriarchies via the recasting of the concept of 'womanhood';[2] the cultural politics of gender and the significance of masculinity for the imperial enterprise;[3] and more recently, the historical visibility of women.[4] While these studies represent significant contributions to the field, this chapter shifts the focus to tackle directly the twin issues of consciousness and assertion among Indian women in the colonial era.

Over the years, the position of women in Indian society has been looked at either as part of broader studies in the social and cultural history of India[5] or, more directly, in the attempt to trace the changing role of women in the colonial period.[6] Improvements in the status of women came about from the nineteenth century onwards, such scholars argue, not as the product of a process of conscious assertion on the part of Indian women, but through programmes of social reform devised and carried out by Indian men and the colonial state. In many ways the picture which emerges of Indian women as passive recipients in these processes, has been predetermined by the approaches which scholars have adopted. In the Western impact/Indian response paradigm which informs their work there is little room for women as conscious agents. Instead, women are reduced to mere beneficiaries of the 'awakening' experienced by their menfolk as a result of contact with Western influences. Similar problems arise with studies informed by post-structuralism where the focus is on colonialist and nationalist discourse rather than the female subject.[7] However, if Indian women are to be studied merely as 'representations' or as a 'site' for the play of dominant discourses we are in danger of erasing them completely from history.[8] Indeed, it is ironic that an approach which attempted to critique Orientalist essentialism has done so much to reinforce the image of the passive Indian woman.

The approach adopted here is informed by a conception of agency which is not limited to issues of 'consent' or 'coercion',[9] nor does it reduce autonomy to mere resistance – essentially reactive to the interventions of the colonial state or Indian men.[10] Rather, a much broader view of agency is configured where the focus is on uncovering the intentions and experiences of Indian women as they asserted their rights, addressed social inequalities and rejected tradition in an engagement with the world around them in what amounted to a unique indigenous feminism.[11] These issues are explored in a study of Maharashtrian women who converted from Hinduism to Christianity from the late nineteenth century onwards. Although the relationship was to become more ambiguous, Christian missions were seen by many scholars as central to the colonialist agenda leading to their exclusion from mainstream histories of South Asia.[12] By treating Indian Christian women as agents it is hoped that a serious gap in Indian historiography will be redressed. Also, in older mission histories women converts were depicted as merely following the dictates of their husbands. However, when the focus shifts to the experiences of women themselves and the process of conversion which they went through, a much more complex picture emerges. This chapter traces the inner struggles which these women went through after the conversion of their husbands, the prolonged resistance which many exhibited and the reasons which they gave for their ultimate conversion. Finally, it will attempt to trace the character of this indigenous feminism and determine whether this consciousness went beyond the question of individual empowerment to encompass a wider conception of women as a group which could be used as the basis for collective action.

The historical context of the missions in Maharashtra

As early as the 1820s, missions from the Scottish Board and the Church Missionary Society had established roots in Bombay and were highly successful in developing high schools, while the American Board prospered at Ahmednagar. Some of the first male converts were from influential Parsi and Brahmin families in Bombay and Ahmednagar. Members of indigenous elites aspiring to a professional education for their children in the 1820s and 1830s had little choice but to send their boys to mission schools. Undoubtedly, the first converts were products of schools run by missionaries. By the last decade of the nineteenth century the missions of the American Board, the Free Church of Scotland, the Church Missionary Society and the Society for the Propagation of the Gospel were firmly established in larger towns like Bombay and Poona and were slowly spreading into smaller towns and villages. Together, they boasted a 'native Christian' population of approximately 60,000.[13]

Not surprisingly, the first female converts were the wives, mothers or sisters of the first Brahmin, Muslim or Parsi converts. However, as early as the 1820s the education of women had been a key strategy of missionary activity. Their programmes rested on the belief that the 'womanhood of India' was 'the protectress and zealous adherent of traditional heathenism'.[14] As grandmothers, mothers and wives Hindu women were thought to plant the first seeds of idolatry and ritual in children. Thus, conversions were unlikely unless the influence of women was combated. These trends were reinforced by developments in Europe and America. In the later half of the nineteenth century the complexion of missionary activity changed with the beginnings of women's movements in the West. Historians have shown how European and American women in their quest for self-definition and alternative roles began to interest themselves in the cause of the 'heathen' woman.[15] More recently Geraldine Forbes, Antoinette Burton and Barbara Ramusack have examined the roles of missionary and non-missionary white women's activities in the colonies.[16] They argue that white women who went to colonies in the nineteenth century constructed and relied on the notion of 'enslaved' Indian women which served the purposes of their own programmes of emancipation. Overseas opportunities not only provided space for the surplus 'genteel' population of white women but empowered them through collaboration in the ideological work of empire.

These developments were soon to have an impact on India. In the 1860s the first women's auxiliary units of various missions such as the Society for the Propagation of the Gospel and the London Missionary Society began to arrive in India. Between 1858 and 1871, according to Richter, there were eight women's auxiliary units of Anglican and American missions in India.[17] Such was the enthusiasm among female circles in England that the Church of England Zenana Missionary Society alone sent 214 women between 1887 and 1894. They brought a new angle to the old missionary enterprise, a concern for the 'desolate plight of Indian womanhood'. Combating *sati* or widow-burning and infanticide, providing refuge homes for deserted wives and widows, educating women in *zenanas* or women's quarters – all these appeared prominently on missionary women's agendas. Missionaries regarded the Bombay Presidency, especially the Marathi-speaking region, as ideal ground for their conversion programmes. In missionary literature typical accounts note that, historically, the region appeared to have been little influenced by Muslim practices. Women having greater freedom of movement and the unveiled Maharashtrian women provided fewer obstacles for the work of Western missionary women.

However, this concern with the woman's question was not cited as a reason for conversion by prominent male converts in Maharashtra. Though individuals like Baba Padmanji expressed concern at the suffering of Hindu widows in his work, just as missionary tracts did, the treatment of women in the various religions was not a major issue for male converts.[18] This was despite the fact that this question had become a major bone of contention for many Hindus, with an increasing number of tracts dealing with the question of the salvation of Hindu women.[19] The emerging Indian intelligentsia in the early half of the nineteenth century was faced with an eclectic culture. On the one hand it was marked by missionary activity, and on the other by the reforming zeal of influential Brahmins who criticised the contemporary state of Hindu society and the practices of a corrupt Brahmin priesthood. Baba Padmanji, a prominent male convert, recorded how he benefited from this eclectic atmosphere:

> The *Dnaynodaya* [Christian newspaper] convinced me of the truth of Christianity and the futility of the claims of the Shastras [Hindu religious books] to divine inspiration; the *Prabhakar* [newspaper edited by a Hindu reformer] destroyed my religious reverence for the Brahmans; and the *Dnyan Prakash* [newspaper concerned with theological questions] had preserved me from falling into the quagmire of atheism.[20]

In a manner similar to Baba Padmanji many educated male converts arrived at an acceptance of Christianity after an intellectual engagement with the religious precepts of Hinduism and Christianity, exhibiting a formidable knowledge of the scriptures of both religions.[21] In short, for Hindu males conversion was born out of a major questioning on abstract theological issues, whether in relation to questions of 'revealed' religion or on the inconsistencies of the Hindu religious texts.

In contrast, while women converts did not simply follow the dictates of their husbands in converting to Christianity, nor was the relative validity and truth of each religion the primary issue for them. For high-caste educated women like Pandita Ramabai, Krupabai Satthianadhan and Soonderbai Powar it was the treatment of women in each religion which emerges as the main issue in their process of conversion and their adherence to Christianity.[22]

Reconstituting Indian womanhood: critiques of Hinduism by high-caste educated women

The earliest signs of the creation of feminist consciousness among Maharashtrian women are discernible in their evaluation of the position of women in various religions and their eventual acceptance or rejection of them. Given the rigours of high-caste oppression, the conversion of low castes to Christianity has been seen as unproblematic. Later, it will be argued that their conversion was a much more complex process than the above generally accepted view implies. For the moment, however, it is important to ask why high-caste educated Hindu women became attracted to Christianity. One of the most vociferous sections of Maharashtrian feminists were converts from Hinduism, not just prominent converts, who, it could be argued, were merely following the dictates of their husbands, but a host of relatively unknown high-caste women who converted of their own volition. Many of these women showed great resistance to conversion, continuing their opposition years after their husbands' initial conversion. Conversion took place after a gendered critique of Hinduism and Christianity in which the former was found wanting.

Even among those women who followed their husbands a certain prioritisation of desires is evident. Wives of male converts usually had the choice of staying with their parents or their extended family. Moreover, they had heard of the great persecution converts were subjected to by Hindus, yet they chose to follow their husbands. In fact, quite a few of them had dramatic escapes from their enraged kith and kin. For example, Ganderbai Powar told the court that she had been imprisoned in her own home and prevented from joining her husband for years.[23] Not all women were successful in resolving conflicts over religious issues and quite a few cases ended tragically. Lakshmibai, another woman, entered a period of intense introspection and remained with her parental family for seven years before deciding to rejoin her husband only to find that he had given up on her and re-married. She died a year later.[24] Anandibai Bhagat, who accompanied Pandita Ramabai on her trip to Wantage, England in 1882, committed suicide.[25] In her case the anxieties of conversion were accompanied by the tensions brought on by her interaction with missionaries.[26] In order to get a complete picture of the conflicts, ambivalences and resolutions of women's struggle to create a social space for themselves we have to look at their experiences of the processes of conversion.

As a first-generation convert, the views of Pandita Ramabai (1858–1922) are crucial and through her writings she provides us with a key to the growing feminist consciousness among women in

Maharashtra.[27] Born into a Chitpawan Brahmin family of Mangalore district, Karnataka (South India), her father, Ananta Shastri Dongre, was a priest and taught at the Peshwa's (regional ruler's) court. He taught his wife to read and write and she in turn taught Ramabai. Ramabai was a child prodigy. At the age of twelve she had committed to memory 12,000 verses of the ancient Sanskrit scriptures. Along with her brother, Srinivas, she travelled all over North India and at the age of twenty reached Calcutta. Here she was drawn to the reform circles and in an open competition with male pandits on Hindu theology and philosophy she won the title 'Pandita Saraswati'. In June 1880, she married Bipin Behari Das, a Bengali Kayasth, considered a rebellious act as Maharashtrians viewed Kayasths as low castes. At twenty-two, she was fluent in five Indian languages (she would eventually master Greek, Latin and Hebrew), and in 1882, she learned English with Ramabai Ranade (a prominent Hindu female reformer) and amalgamated the latter's Ladies' Association with other women's groups to form the Arya Mahila Samaj, a premier women's organisation of Maharashtra. Her first book in Marathi, *Stri-Dharma Niti* (Prescribed Laws and Duties on the Proper Conduct of Women), earned her funds to travel to England. In England she stayed with the Wantage Sisters and studied Christian theology, converting in 1883. For a while she held the Chair of Sanskrit at Cheltenham Ladies College. Between 1885 and 1887 she travelled in America and studied the kindergarten system of education. Meanwhile her vision for liberating Indian women had crystallised and she lectured extensively on the pitiable condition of Indian women and the need to emancipate them. Her next book in English, *The High-Caste Hindu Woman*, a powerful feminist tract, caught the imagination of the American public from Quakers to Evangelicals who formed sixty-five 'Ramabai Circles' and pledged to make her projects successful. The circles were coordinated under an elected Board called The American Ramabai Association. Pandita Ramabai was awarded the Kaisar-i-Hind medal by the Indian government in recognition of her services to Indian women.

In her earliest analysis of Hinduism's treatment of women, written for the *Cheltenham Ladies College Magazine* in 1885, she argued that Hinduism gives central importance to men while women's functions were merely to worship their husbands. It was only through her husband that a Hindu wife could secure a place in heaven. It was women's lack of 'personal responsibility' to God which created dissatisfaction within Pandita Ramabai.[28] She quoted the Code of Manu, the ancient Hindu law-giver, to show how a Hindu wife is supposed to obey and worship her husband as a god, however reprehensible he may be. By removing 'personal responsibility' to God, Ramabai argued that there was nothing to sustain a wife unlucky enough to be married to an unworthy husband. A wife in such a position was robbed of the personal dignity which a Christian woman could claim. Hindu women, she reflected, could not reach the 'true dignity of womanhood' since Hinduism did not respect women as independent human beings. This conclusion led Ramabai to investigate the manner in which the unjust treatment of the sexes evolved in the practice of Hinduism. Her sense of acute dissatisfaction with Hinduism in this respect is set out in her autobiographical work – *A Testimony*.[29] She found a common strand linking all the Sanskrit texts of the *Mahabharata*, Dharma Shastras, Vedas, Smritis and the Puranas to the modern poets and popular preachers of the day, which was that:

> women of high and low caste, as a class, were bad, very bad, worse than demons, as unholy as untruth, and that they could not get Moksha as men. The only hope of their getting this much-desired liberation from Karma and its results, viz., countless millions of births and deaths and untold suffering, was the worship of their husbands. The woman has no right to study the Vedas and Vedanta and without knowing Brahma no one can get liberation, i.e., Moksha ... My eyes were being gradually opened, and I was waking up to my own hopeless condition as a woman, and it was becoming clearer and clearer to me that I had no place anywhere as far as religious consolation was concerned. I became quite dissatisfied with myself, I wanted something more than the Shastras could give me ...[30]

Reading the Vedas (an act forbidden to women) only served to increase her discontent. However, it was only in 1883, three years after her husband's death, that she went to England and saw the work of the Wantage Sisters of Fulham (Church of England), among whom her interest in Christian doctrine was awakened.

Pandita Ramabai recognised the work of the Wantage Sisters, through whom she realised that 'fallen women' (prostitutes) could be brought back into society. She contrasted their work with the contemporary Hindu practice of shunning prostitutes as the greatest of all sinners and unworthy of compassion. She asked the Sisters why they cared for prostitutes and learned from them about 'Christ's meeting with the Samaritan woman' and his teachings on the nature of true worship which excluded 'neither male nor female'.[31] It was then that she realised that 'there was a real difference between Hinduism and Christianity', and was convinced that Christ alone, in her words, 'could transform and uplift the downtrodden womanhood of India and every land'.[32] Once again, it is the feminisation of missionary Christianity which appealed to Ramabai. The rhetoric of a religion that did not exclude women had a practical application for Ramabai. On returning to India, she translated into action some of her borrowings from mission Christianity by founding the Kripa Sadan (or Home of Mercy), probably the first home for the rehabilitation of prostitutes in India.

In 1883 Pandita Ramabai was baptised along with her daughter Manoramabai. She records that finally she felt at peace with herself, having found a 'religion which gave privileges equally to men and women; and where there was no distinction of caste, colour or sex in it'.[33] Her rebellion, then, was against Hinduism – a religion she perceived as one that preached inequality between the sexes, which counterposed good and evil respectively in men and women. She rejected the Vedantic or Hindu teachings about the 'unreality' (illusion) of life and showed a preference for a religion which conceived of human life as 'reality' because this philosophy opened a multitude of possibilities, especially the potential to live intensely and with a purpose. Mission Christianity through the practice of 'good deeds' allowed Indian women to participate in public life. In a similar manner to Pandita Ramabai, other Hindu women who had been educated in mission schools embraced Christianity through a learning process. An interesting case was that of Gunabai, who studied at a mission school in Ahmednagar where she was impressed by the 'Christian values' of compassion and mercy. Her daughter Shewatbai recollected that John Bunyan's *Pilgrim's Progress* had such an impact on her that she lost all traces of hesitancy and reserve about the wrath of her family and community and ran away to the mission house and was disowned by her parents.[34] Through missionary discourse Christianity had a profound effect on the perceptions of a certain small but influential section of such literate Maharashtrian women.

Pandita Ramabai's critiques were improved and extended by a second generation of Christian women who concentrated more on the exposition of the role and status of women in Hinduism in their efforts to empower Indian womanhood. Second-generation Christian women were much more systematic in their analysis, addressing men as the original culprits in the vilification of women through their coding and encoding of Hinduism. Soonderbai Powar (1856–1921) was the daughter of first-generation Christians, Ganderbai and Ramachandra. The first booklet she wrote was aimed at encouraging disheartened missionaries and was entitled *Is Zenana Work a Failure?* She was well known in Britain and India for her involvement in anti-opium and temperance movements. In 1883, she met Pandita Ramabai and became her 'right hand' for seven years. Once she felt confident that Ramabai's work had stabilised she left to open a Zenana Training Home in Poona. This school flourished on funds she had secured from her campaigns in England, Scotland and Ireland. Among her writings, the book *Hinduism and Womanhood* most clearly expressed her views on women's issues.

Like Pandita Ramabai, Soonderbai Powar located women's servitude in Hindu religion and social customs, but she elaborated on Pandita's critique by highlighting the role of men with much greater clarity. Soonderbai described Indian women as 'slaves' who had been forced to merge their personal freedom and individuality in the personality of man. Through an acute observation of Hindu mannerisms, the expressions used on the birth of a female child, the popular sayings about wives and widows and the offensive language used against women, she tried to show the ways in which woman is devalued by Hinduism, making it impossible for her to be an inspiring companion to her husband or a wise and responsible mother to her children.[35] Weaving a narrative through the life-histories of the students in her Zenana Training Home, she concluded that, if Hindu women were in 'bondage', it was one imposed by selfish men through the rules of a religion which made them perceive woman 'as nothing more than a soulless animal to be used for the pleasure of man'.[36] Dissecting Hindu customs like early marriage, female infanticide, the harsh treatment of widows, the dedication of girls as temple prostitutes and the dowry system, she labelled them as the 'bitter fruits of Hinduism', Soonderbai claimed that: 'in the name of their religion, Hindus do many wicked things and have many bad customs which cruelly limit or destroy the liberty of the subject, and strangle social and family happiness'.[37] According to Soonderbai, such customs derived sanction from the inviolable principles of their religion and philosophy and Hindu men would do nothing to alter them because they had themselves created them. She felt, therefore, that only the Christian religion could free women from such bondage.

Krupabai Satthianadhan (1862–93), another second-generation Christian woman, went further in her analysis, not only investigating Hindu men's resistance to granting equal rights to women but also showing how Hinduism negatively affected the attitudes and stunted the personalities of Hindu women. Krupabai's parents, Haripant and Radhabai Khisty, were among the earliest Brahmin converts in the Bombay Presidency. Krupabai turned out to be a precocious child and the American mission at Ahmednagar offered her the option of enrolling as a teacher or studying further. Krupabai had made up her mind to be a doctor so she was sent to Madras Medical College, which had opened its doors to women. While in Madras she met a Cambridge-returned Indian Christian, S. Satthianadhan, and married him. In her own time, she was widely known and held a national and international audience for her writings. Her known writings comprise about twenty essays, two novels and many poems. Her novels were compared to Jane Austen's because of her eye for details, satiric tones and for exposing domestic hypocrisies of the time. Of particular note here are her feminist critiques, exposition of white racism and her criticisms of the English-educated Indian middle classes. Due to failing health she was forced to discontinue her studies and died at the age of thirty-one.

Krupabai's critique of the nature of women's oppression in Hindu society and her arguments for the education of women helped women not only to counteract the onslaught of Hindu vilification and contempt for women but, in a larger sense, to help women break through the rigidity of the roles prescribed for them.[38] In the first place she maintained that marriage should not be the only goal of a woman's life. Second, she argued that education led women to develop some freedom of thought and action, to begin to question the social tyranny and injustice they were subjected to, and to become self-reliant. Third, she argued that this process of women's self-realisation was the only way for the Indian nation to progress.

Krupabai began her analysis with the general proposition that the independence of women was anathema to Hindu men. Because of the high status that a man commanded in Hindu society, the minute a male child was born he was treated like a king. As a result of this he grew up to be a 'petted, spoiled despot, or a selfish ease-loving lord'.[39] To his 'inflated, self-satisfied nature' the very idea of an intellectual wife, in any way superior to him, 'will be gall-wormwood'; qualities that he lacked would not be tolerated in his wife.[40] The second rationale she outlined was a psychological one. Hindus, argued Krupabai, had lost their power as rulers and had been in servitude for centuries, thus, exercising authority at home was an important compensation for the Hindu male which he would never let go willingly. The third reason she gave was the economic necessity of exploiting the labour services of women for the efficient functioning of Hindu joint families. She concluded that if Hinduism entailed inferior status and lack of rights for women, Hindu men were heavily implicated in the process.

The critiques of second-generation Christian women were closely linked to contemporary male discourse on female education. One of the commonest allegations of male progressives was that women were the greatest opponents of education: they preferred to be ignorant; their interests could never rise above petty gossip and trifles; they blocked reform work.[41] Krupabai challenged these arguments by placing responsibility for intrigues and gossip among women on the shoulders of selfish Hindu males. She pointed out:

[88]

How few of our educated men ever trouble themselves about their women – as to how they spend the whole day, whether or not they find the hours hanging on their hands, whether the leading of an idle existence is hateful to them or not! They only look upon the women as mere appendices to their great selves ... They [women] are not to be blamed; they know of no higher mode of existence: there is nothing to occupy their minds; no interest is taken in them: they are treated as toys and play-things, and are humoured and pleased with gilded trinkets or any such trifles.[42]

What we observe here is a rigorous contesting of the knowledge about women claimed by Hindu men. Second-generation women gave a cultural explanation for Hindu women's inferior status, rather than rooting it in a biological theory of the weakness of the 'gentle sex'. If Hindu women were ignorant and bigoted, the reasons were external to them. Krupabai's analysis of the attitudes of Hindu men and the atmosphere in Hindu homes eventually led her to argue that it was only by leaving Hinduism that women could redeem themselves.

Krupabai set up a model of independent/dependent women and opposed it with another binary pairing of Christianity/Hinduism. Her ideas are best expressed in the two novels written by her in the English language in the 1890s, under the titles *Kamala: A Story of Hindu Life* and *Saguna: A Story of Native Christian Life*. Kamala's life is described as 'dark' and a prolonged sadness permeates it. Kamala is a young, beautiful and sensitive girl who is brought up in isolation by her father, a Brahmin pandit who has chosen to be a recluse. Kamala is married early to an English-educated man called Ganesh. The couple's love-life is fractured by the machinations of a jealous mother-in-law and scheming sisters-in-law, a common plot of novels during this period of social reform. Ganesh comes under the influence of Sai, a profligate though accomplished woman, who is described as one 'attached to a dramatic company', probably an actress, a profession which had terrible connotations during the nineteenth century. Ganesh spends less and less time with his wife, who is ill-treated by her in-laws. Eventually, Ganesh dies of cholera and Kamala gives birth to a child which also succumbs to fever. Distraught, Kamala rejects her only choice of happiness, the proposal of her childhood betrothed, Ramachander Row, who is willing to marry her despite her being a widow. The author comments that 'Her religion, crude as it was, had its victory.'[43]

Through the narrative of the novel, we learn of the origins of Kamala's convictions. We are told that Kamala became resigned to her lot, and it was her crude religious convictions that enabled her to do so.[44] Kamala had learned from her father that whether she was good or bad, whether she enjoyed pleasure or suffered pain, she ought not to grumble but accept it meekly, 'for it was her fate'. Caught in a turmoil between her heart, which wished to follow Ramchander, and her mind, which enjoined the duty of a faithful wife, Kamala reasoned that if women like Sita and Savitri – the ideal women from the ancient Hindu past – could not get their due in this world and had to submit to fate, then how could an ordinary mortal like her protest against it? Krupabai's message was that Hindu teachings gave women very little consolation even when it taught them to be resigned to their fate through passive role-models like Sita. Hinduism made women listless, 'feeble in purpose and in will', resulting in their complete non-interest in life as 'life itself was a poor spiritless affair'.[45] No matter how much Hindu women tried to assert and control their lives, Krupabai felt that 'the book of fate would come to pass do what she could to avert it'.[46]

Saguna, the subject of Krupabai's second novel, is presented as a complete contrast to Kamala. Her life is described as 'bright' in comparison to Kamala's 'dark' one. Saguna's life is influenced by the 'new order of things', which Krupabai says is sweeping all over India.[47] The 'new order of things' refers to the introduction of Christianity as a choice for Indians dissatisfied with the old order of life. Saguna's childhood is described as a 'sweet and innocent' one nurtured in domestic peace and quiet, where learning was encouraged and her freedom of speech and action was unchecked. Her eldest sister is treated as an equal and a friend by her father and her brother. Patience and kindness suffuses the Saguna household, and comfort in suffering and contentment in poverty mark their lifestyle. It is suggested that Christian life is of a 'purer faith' and 'higher culture' than Hindu life and that it encourages open-mindedness in those who profess it. Thus, Saguna is given complete choice in pursuing a profession – a freedom unthinkable for Hindu girls of her day except in the most radical circles. Saguna's female friends are allowed to interact freely with young men and choose their own spouses – once again, contrasted with Hindu customs. In the mission school, Saguna meets Christian girls, all of whom had a 'definite work in view' and were receiving training for it.[48] Through the voice of Saguna, Krupabai tries to get across to readers that Christianity held open the possibilities of leading a more independent life.

Saguna is later enthused with the idea of serving and improving the condition of her Indian sisters. She enrols in a medical college to become a doctor. To her, Christianity was the only religion which inculcated the idea of respect for other human beings. This was a more appealing philosophy than a religion which, in her view, reduced the idea of duty solely to the husband, regardless of the latter's worthiness. Krupabai thus focused the entire narrative on the growth of Saguna through Christian influence into a confident and independent 'new woman'. Among Indian Christian women's writings, Krupabai's analysis offers the most intricate link between religion and a woman's identity and role. Although it has been suggested so far that second-generation women's critiques were sharper, a notable continuity with the first-generation converts is their common conviction that Hindu women were helpless and passive due to their adherence to Hinduism.

The 'God of widows and deserted wives': illiterate women and Christianity

A large number of semi-literate women converted to Christianity towards the end of the nineteenth century, many at Pandita Ramabai's Sharada Sadan – the largest school for Brahmin widows in India at the time. In 1892, 12 out of 49 widows and 13 non-widows at Sharada Sadan converted to Christianity. Interestingly, all of them were adult Brahmin women and faced the possibility of ill-treatment (as a result of their conversion) from their relatives and/or guardians. In 1899, only 8 out of the 108 women at Sharada Sadan remained Hindus, while Pandita Ramabai claimed in 1905 (the year she publicly dropped secular teaching) that 1,500 out of 2,000 pupils in her schools were Christians.[49] Because of the highly structured organisational and managerial aspects of her schools, it is unlikely that she had any direct influence on the girls' decisions. The Executive Committee of the American Ramabai Association had drawn up the constitution of Sharada Sadan as a 'secular' institution. It made it clear to Pandita Ramabai that if there was any cause for dissatisfaction, the funding of her school would stop, as it was being supported by an annual grant of about $10,000 drawn from an eclectic American public of all persuasions on the specific understanding that the school would be non-sectarian. Moreover, the Managing Committee, drawn up by the American Ramabai Association, largely consisted of Maharashtrian male Hindu reformers whose list of guidelines allowed the Pandita access to her students only in the lecture rooms.[50] We have to look elsewhere for an explanation of the huge numbers of conversions.

The views of the converts can be constructed from the exhaustive personal interviews with pupils carried out by Judith Andrews, Chair of the American Ramabai Association.[51] Many of the Brahmin widows who converted to Christianity revealed that on their entry into Sharada Sadan they were not compelled to fast or shave their heads, as Hindu society demanded they do. The widows were informed in the classrooms that the spirit of their dead husbands was not linked to the hair on their head, as Hindu practice would have them believe, and for the first time they read about a God who did not believe in persecuting them for so-called lapses in good behaviour.[52] In Ramabai's school they did not have to endure the concepts of pollution of touch and sight associated with widows. The widows quickly attributed their misery to Hindu religious customs and eventually accepted Christianity, as a way of escaping some of the hardships of Hindu strictures. From the interviews it is apparent that mission Christianity was helping them to cope with their everyday existence much better than Hinduism. Thus an extremely pragmatic approach governed their acceptance of Christianity. One of Sharada Sadan's more exceptional students, Nurmadabai, who was removed from the school after the first uproar over the conversion issue in 1893, confirmed the reason for the many conversions. She had attended Sunday school since the age of seven and at the age of ten she was admitted to the Sharada Sadan. It was in this school that she felt for the first time that there was 'something real about this religion'.[53] She told Judith Andrews that a large number of girls had previously experienced no happiness in their own homes but in Sharada Sadan, instead of abuse, they were given affection and kindness.

Part of the explanation for the voluntary acts of conversion can be surmised from Pandita Ramabai's method of instruction. As early as 1886, she had mused that Manu's Code of Law and the earliest Hindu scriptures ought to form part of the syllabus in girls' schools in order to make them realise their true position in Hindu religion and society.[54] Certainly the Puranas (Hindu scriptures) were taught in her schools.[55] It is possible that women were encouraged to think on these issues as a result of her teaching. To many of these illiterate widows from oppressive families, Christ was represented as a 'saviour' of 'deserted wives, prostitutes and widows'.[56] Such a notion had a tremendous appeal to harassed and tormented women. The statistics available for Pandita Ramabai's schools show that two-thirds of the pupils were widows. A significant proportion of the widows who were not bound by any kinship ties or guardians were swift to see the advantages of freeing themselves from caste restrictions such as cooking food prepared by their own hands and from a religion that seemed to offer no comfort for women, especially widows. In 1896 only a handful of women in the Sharada Sadan remained Hindus but they had indicated to Pandita Ramabai that this was only because of pressure from powerful relatives.[57] Ramabai herself was constantly surprised by the behaviour of orthodox Hindu girls, who within a few days of their arrival thought of breaking caste rules. Hindu women, compelled to fast and shave their heads and perform endless rituals in their own homes, once freed of that compulsion, were able to quickly rekindle their aspirations and needs.

A third category of women converts were the wives of the male converts drawn from low castes, such as tanners, carpenters and masons. Their conversions, it appears, were prompted by issues of personal morality. These women initially followed their husbands and agreed to live with them in the belief that a Hindu wife's duty was to serve her husband. However, they remained opposed to their husbands' conversions and expressed disapproval by keeping a separate house, serving separate meals to their husbands and continuing Hindu rituals for several years. The reasons they gave for their eventual conversion are based on the transformation they experienced in their menfolk's attitude and conduct towards them. Ganderbai, for example, narrated that when her husband was a Hindu, he was hot-tempered, petulant and harsh to her but was 'all kindness' after he became a Christian.[58] Women like Sakubai argued that Christianity must be a superior religion since her husband had not remarried in spite of her refusal to live with him for two whole years.[59] Christianity in colonial India was perceived by many women to embody customs that favoured women in contrast to what they saw as the harsh reality of Hinduism.

The category of women who turned to Christianity on the basis of the issue of 'morality' approached it from a subjective point of view. This is better understood when we contrast women's attitudes to male converts who used the 'morality' argument. A well-known male Maharashtrian Christian of the late nineteenth century, Nehemiah Goreh, argued that the monotheist god in Hinduism as described in the most important texts of Hinduism, the Vedas and Upanishads, had sublime attributes yet no sense of morality, being unable to distinguish right from wrong.[60] The Hindu god, according to Goreh, was immoral and adulterous. How can one worship God, they reasoned, if he claims to be immortal but is full of mortal failings? Issues of morality are not considered by Goreh from a subjective point of view but as an abstraction. The question of literacy did not pose a barrier to the conversion of low caste women. Semi-literate and illiterate women arrived at the same conclusions regarding the 'purer spirit of Christianity' but from a subjective viewpoint rather than through a philosophical exposition. The appeal of an alien religion was thus quite differently perceived and experienced by men and women. In the transition from disapproval to acceptance of Christianity many illiterate or semi-literate women displayed no knowledge of the theological constructs of either religions. But, after their baptism, they were given basic training in Christian doctrines. In the capacities of Bible women and catechists, they were able to relay religious precepts in a simple manner to villagers and thus proved to be some of the most enthusiastic workers in the proselytisation programmes of the missionaries.

Indian women's interaction with missions: conflicts over belief and methods

Despite the sense of liberation which conversion brought to Hindu women, their rejection of Hinduism was never absolute and their relationships with the Western agents of their new religion were not unproblematic. When Indian Christian women forged links with the West, an important mediator was the white female missionary. The missions of various denominations befriended Indian Christian women and rendered services to them through forming their beliefs, clearing their doubts and helping them in times of financial distress. Indian Christian women readily acknowledged this help.

On arrival in India, as we shall see, these women did not encounter a docile set of Indian Christians who could be manipulated at will. In terms of organisational work Indian women Christians differed in approach and methods of action. Although the various missionary creeds profoundly affected the beliefs of Christian women, this was not an uncritical adoption. The more influential among them filtered these ideas, throwing out what did not suit the interests of their enterprises. The strength of their feminist consciousness is revealed in the cases of Soonderbai and Pandita Ramabai. They were attacked by Western missionaries as well as influential male Indian Christians and were severely criticised throughout their careers for their unconventional religious beliefs. Neither belonged to any church nor did they profess any kind of attachment to a particular denomination. Various accusations were hurled against them and they were called mercenaries exploiting Christian sympathy to promote the welfare of 'high caste Hindu women'.[61] The careful mapping of boundaries by Indian Christian women between themselves and missionaries represented the formation of an indigenous variety of feminism. Although firmly rooted in an alien religion, it held women's issues at the heart of its concerns. Indian Christian women indigenised Christianity because of their woman-centred approach to religion. This stemmed from the belief that any compromises with organised Christianity, apart from their own selective borrowing, would undermine their programmes for the advancement of Indian women.

It is important to explore the reasons why Indian Christian women resisted belonging to any particular creed or sect. All of these women believed that in the spirit of Christ there was neither male nor female.

Their feminist critique of Hinduism led to their rejection of it. For them, Hinduism preached inequality between the sexes either as part of Hindu doctrines themselves or through the interpretation of Hindu priests. As Christians they were frequently pressured into accepting a particular church in order to carry on their work. However, Pandita Ramabai was very critical of divisive tendencies within the Church as a whole. Her correspondence on theological questions clearly reveals the reasons behind her opposition. In a letter to Sister Geraldine, in 1885, she wrote: 'I have just with great efforts freed myself from the yoke of the Indian priestly tribe, so I am not at present willing to place myself under another similar yoke by accepting everything which comes from the priests as authorised Command of the Most High.'[62] Obedience to the law and to the Word of God, according to her, were quite different from obedience to priests alone. Soonderbai also conducted her work on non-denominational lines in the belief that allegiance to a particular church meant subordination to mediating agencies. Neither of them wanted any intermediaries between God and themselves. Soonderbai, on her tours in Britain, was constantly asked about her denominational status, to which she wittily replied 'King's Own'.[63]

Christian women critically examined the Indian past with a view to understanding the position of Indian women and their gradual decline in status.[64] Krupabai and Pandita Ramabai attributed this to the gradual ascendancy of the priestly class among Hindus. Nothing, according to them, marked the constitution of Hindu society as much as the power and influence that the Brahmin priesthood commanded over Hindus.[65] In their opinion, it served the priest's interests to keep the Hindu woman as credulous and ignorant as possible, since learned and clever women, especially widows, would be able to manage their own affairs and estates without the aid of the family priest. Thus, the Hindu priesthood had taken every opportunity to decry women's learning, and blamed learned women for every misfortune that fell upon a family in India. With such an analysis of the role of the Hindu priesthood it was not surprising that Indian Christian women were reluctant to accept church mediation.

Many Indian Christian women, especially those who had visited Britain, discerned the ways in which Victorian values were reinforced by the Church's views on female sexuality. Giving allegiance to a particular church entailed an acceptance of Victorian values. Among these were sex segregation and the biological determinist theories which outlined separate spheres for men and women. These issues were of prime importance to Indian Christian women. For someone like Pandita Ramabai, who taught carpentry and masonry to women, the natural division theory was an unacceptable one.[66] On one occasion, as the Professor of Sanskrit at Cheltenham Ladies College, Ramabai offered to teach British officers as part of their preparation for India. However, when she sought permission to do so through the Principal, Dorothea Beale, she was told that the clergy would not allow a woman to teach men because it was a transgression of natural laws. In late-nineteenth-century India, in contrast, rapid changes had not yet crystallised into rigid rules. Women such as Cornelia Sorabji taught for a year at a male college in Ahmedabad while Pandita Ramabai frequently addressed all-male Indian audiences. Any strict conformity to church laws would mean a curtailment of their freedom of speech and action. Likewise, Soonderbai rejected modern interpretations of the Bible and taught her own versions which she felt were closer to the true spirit of the Bible. Indian Christian women had a clear notion of the balance of power between the sexes and it was their belief that in accepting a male intermediary, a necessary condition of belonging to a church, their freedom of speech and action would be curtailed.

The tensions between Indian Christian women and their Western 'sisters' increased towards the end of the nineteenth century. While bearing the brunt of missionary attacks on their belief and work, Indian Christian women were themselves active in criticising Western missionary attitudes towards Indian culture and Indians. The earliest commentaries on 'racism' among women were by Indian Christian women. Saguna, Krupabai's literary self, noted, at the age of fourteen, the insolence and arrogance of Western missionaries towards Indians. She recalled her humiliation and anger at the way her mother had tried to console her by saying: 'How can you expect them to be friends. Don't you see the difference, they are white and we are black. We ought to be thankful for the little notice that they take us.'[67] Cornelia Sorabji also called for a 'certain change in the attitude of the mind' if Westerners wanted a genuine interaction with Indians.[68] Indian Bible women also observed the differences between 'old' and 'new' missionaries. The 'new' ones they felt were 'cold, unemotional and kept barriers with supercilious airs', and they predicted that with such attitudes Western missionaries would not convert a Hindu in a thousand years![69]

Indian Christian women were among the first to criticise the 'Orientalist' notions of Western missionaries. Indian women drew attention to the missionaries' tendency to address Indians as 'benighted heathens' and their habit of constantly classifying them. They felt that the contempt and unjustified arrogance of Western missionaries arose through such classifications. Pandita Ramabai insisted that all missionaries who embarked on a voyage to India should study the history and literature of the Hindus.[70] She was convinced that Western missionaries were alienating Indians and thus harming the cause of Christianity in India. Further, she argued that St Paul himself, as an apostle, became a Jew to the Jews, and a Greek to the Greeks, and that 'God's method of work' was 'building on the old foundations, keeping that which is good, and destroying only that which is evil, decaying, ready to perish'.[71] She saw no rationale in decrying everything in the Indian scriptures, and expected missionaries to argue with Indians on an intellectual level regarding the particularities of each religion.

Indian Christian women were constantly emphasising 'Indianness' and maintained Indian dress, diet and etiquette.[72] Manoramabai went to the extent of telling missionaries eager to work at her mission at Mukti that they ought to be aware of the fact that Mukti was a 'thoroughly Indian mission' and if they were not prepared to accept this style of life they should not come at all![73] Indian Christian women continued to stress their 'Indianness', and in many books authored by them, careful foreword writers mentioned that the authors had not 'denationalised' themselves. Indian women felt the need to distinguish themselves from Western missionaries in order to be able to work ably in their welfare schemes for women without the negative connotations that Westerners were rapidly acquiring with their racist approach. The immense correspondence between Indian Christian women and missionaries points to the fact that the former considered their emancipatory programmes for women as a 'fledgling' which needed nurturing and sensitive treatment. Towards this end they adopted wholly 'Indian' methods of evangelical work. With this in mind Pandita Ramabai once delivered a *kirtan* (a religious discourse in verse) in a temple to a female audience. She defended her action on the ground that women in small towns were not only shy and timid but had no conception of Western public lectures and meetings. With this in mind she had used the *kirtan* to communicate practical lessons on social philosophy chosen from some of the Puranas and delivered them in a new style of lecture. When she was attacked by the Indian Christian community, she countered by pointing out that missionaries employed means like the 'magic-lanterns shows' and *tamashas* (Maharashtrian folk entertainment) to convey their message and so she felt justified in doing the same.[74] The 'Indianness' which Christian women stressed lay also in the method of worship which they consciously adopted from Hinduism and retained as good practice. Lakshmibai, Soonderbai and Pandita Ramabai believed in the *bhakti* form of worship, an emotional expression of love of God, practised from medieval times in India. In the 1900s a great 'revival' was reported with large numbers of girls and women embracing Christianity. When Western missionaries sharply rebuked these forms of worship as expressions of paganism, Indian Christian women defended them as legitimate forms of female worship forming a crucial part of women's lived realities.

This 'Indianness' must not be read as nascent nationalism or patriotism. In fact, a great number of Christian women were opposed to the nationalist activity carried out by the Indian National Congress. Although the fashioning of identity amongst Christian women was taking place through asserting difference from the West, the rationale for this was not nationalistic. Rather, it was associated with their emancipatory agenda for Indian women. Indian Christian women's growth in consciousness and resistance to organised Christianity was often manifested by quoting the biblical verse 'there is neither male nor female' (Galatians 3:28), stressing the equality between the two sexes. Indian Christian women carved out an indigenous feminism through Christianity within the missions in Maharashtra, which defied the norm of male-dominated missionary enterprises. Women missionaries like Pandita Ramabai were highly influential, with a powerful international standing. In the beginning, Western missionaries had attracted many Indian Christian women with the message that women were equal to men. Having experienced and exercised a greater degree of autonomy it was hardly likely that they would give it up. To this end many Christian women in their correspondences to each other expressed the desire to be self-sufficient financially, which would have enabled them to cut their dependence on Western sources of funding.

Conclusions

During the colonial era Indian Christian women developed a strong feminist consciousness on the basis of a critique of the status of women in the two opposing choices of religion – Christianity and Hinduism. By shifting the focus to the analysis of the reasons behind their conversion, it has been demonstrated that these women broke away from the inherited Hindu past and found a new sense of freedom of thought, liberty of action, an avenue for self-definition and self-expression, as well as religious consolation. However, this was not by any means an uncritical acceptance. An analysis of their views illustrates that they selectively chose from the dominant male discourses of the time and sought the independence which would enable them to fashion Christianity in the cause of Indian womanhood, in a way that set them apart from missionary, reformist and nationalist discourses. As such, the actions of these women amounted to more than individual empowerment. Because they displayed a keen awareness of women as a distinct group in society and acted upon this to improve the quality of women's lives, a strong sense of the emergence of a distinct feminist consciousness is clearly discernible. They demonstrated the indigenous roots of Indian feminism by maintaining a cultural distance from European Christianity and by separating themselves from denominational allegiance.

A dynamic women's movement had begun in Maharashtra towards the end of the nineteenth century and Christian women played an important part in this pioneering effort. Their greatest contribution was the crucial support they gave to Hindu women, not only through their institutions but as path-breakers who showed the courage to step beyond accepted boundaries. This movement was marked by the prominence of dynamic Indian Christian women who in many ways laid its foundations – through their ideology, organisation and entry into the public arena. In the first quarter of the twentieth century, Hindu female leaders like Ramabai Ranade, who had been infused with strength from their Christian counterparts, built on this legacy and continued the movement until the coming of Gandhi. In contrast to the widely accepted view that Indian women were passive and uncritical subjects for the reforming activities of others, it has been established that through their development of a feminist consciousness they were active agents in processes of change at the height of colonial rule.

Notes

I owe an enormous debt to the staff of Mukti Mission, especially Ms Johnstone, who made valuable primary source material on Indian Christian women available to me, especially the Annual Reports of the American Ramabai Association, without which this chapter could not have been written. I have also benefited from the comments of participants at the Annual Conference of the British Association of South Asian Studies, 1992, where it was presented. I would like to thank Patrick McGinn, Geraldine Forbes and Jeffrey Cox, who took the trouble of reading early versions of this chapter and whose detailed criticisms helped me greatly to revise it.

1 For a broad historiographical survey see B. Ramusack, 'From symbol to diversity: the historical literature on women in India', *South Asia Research*, 2 (1990), pp. 139–57, and A. Basu, 'Women's history in India: a historiographical survey', in K. Offen *et al.* (eds), *Writing Women's History: International Perspectives* (Basingstoke, Macmillan, 1991), pp. 181–210.

2 See for example the collection of essays in K. Sangari and S. Vaid (eds), *Recasting Women: Essays in Colonial History* (New Delhi, Kali for Women, 1989), and J. Krishnamurthy (ed.), *Women in Colonial India: Essays on Survival, Work and the State* (New Delhi, Oxford University Press, 1989).

3 M. Sinha, *Colonial Masculinity: The 'Manly Englishman' and the 'Effeminate Bengali' in the Late Nineteenth Century* (Manchester, Manchester University Press, 1996).

4 The task of recovering women's voices has begun through the translations of autobiographies and through emphasis on lesser-known women who have written

unique texts questioning gender relations. For a sample see S. Mazumdar, *Memoirs of an Indian Woman*, ed. G. Forbes (Armonk, Sharpe, 1989); T. Shinde, *For the Honour of my Sister Countrywomen: Tarabai Shinde, the Critique of Gender Relations in India*, ed. R. O'Hanlon (New Delhi, Oxford University Press, 1995); and the anthologies edited by S. Tharu and K. Lalitha, *Women Writing in India, 600 B.C. to the Present*, Vols I and II (New York, Feminist Press, 1991).

5 See for example C. Heimsath, *Indian Nationalism and Hindu Social Reform* (Princeton, Princeton University Press, 1964), and David Kopf, *British Orientalism and the Bengal Renaissance: The Dynamics of Indian Modernization* (Berkeley, University of California Press, 1969).

6 Until recently the focus has been on Bengal and representative works are: M. Borthwick, *The Changing Role of Women in Bengal, 1848–1905* (Princeton, Princeton University Press, 1984), and G. Murshid, *Reluctant Debutante: Response of Bengali Women to Modernisation* (Rajshahi, Sahitya Sansad, 1983).

7 Sample studies in a growing field are: L. Mani, 'Contentious traditions: the debate on *sati* in colonial India', in Sangari and Vaid (eds), *Recasting Women*, pp. 88–126; P. Chatterjee, 'Colonialism, nationalism and colonialised women: the contest in India', *American Ethnologist*, 17:1 (1989), pp. 622–33.

8 One of the more extreme positions is that of Gayatri Spivak, who has argued that the subaltern woman cannot speak and cannot be heard: 'Can the subaltern speak?', in C. Nelson and L. Grossberg (eds), *Marxism and the Interpretation of Culture* (Urbana and Chicago, University of Illinois Press, 1988), pp. 271–313; and 'The Rani of Sirmur: an essay in reading the archive', *History and Theory*, 24 (1985), pp. 247–72.

9 The historiography on the subject of *sati* provides a good example of the process by which female agency has been reduced to simplistic notions of volition. For a recent critique on the literature see A. Loomba, 'Dead women tell no tales: issues of female subjectivity, subaltern agency and tradition in colonial and post-colonial writings on widow immolation in India', *History Workshop Journal*, 36 (1993), pp. 209–27.

10 For a conception of agency as resistance see the essays in the collection by D. Haynes and G. Prakash (eds), *Contesting Power: Resistance and Everyday Social Relations in South Asia* (Berkeley, University of California Press, 1991).

11 The complexities of an emergent feminist consciousness of Maharashtrian women between 1850 and 1920 is studied in greater detail in my forthcoming monograph, *Beyond the Courtyard: Gender, Social Reform and Politics in Colonial India*.

12 J. Cox has pointed out that South Asian Christians are victims of the critiques of imperialism/colonialism, wherein missionaries are portrayed as imperialists, reducing Indian Christians to 'collaborators' and Pakistani Christians to 'heretics': 'Audience and exclusion at the margins of Imperial History', *Women's History Review*, 3:4 (1994).

13 S. Satthianadhan, *Sketches of Indian Christians Collected from Different Sources* (London, Christian Literature Society for India, 1896), pp. 188–9.

14 J. Richter, *A History of Missions in India* (Edinburgh, 1908), p. 329.

15 N. Cott, *The Bonds of Womanhood: 'Woman's Sphere' in New England, 1780–1835* (New Haven, 1977), especially chapter 4.

16 G. Forbes, 'In search of the "Pure Heathen": missionary women in nineteenth century India', *Economic and Political Weekly*, 21:17 (1986), pp. 2–9; A. Burton, '"The White Woman's Burden": British feminists and Indian women, 1865–1915', *Women Studies International Forum*, 13:4 (1990), pp. 295–308; and B. Ramusack, 'Cultural missionaries, maternal imperialists, feminist allies: British women activists in India, 1865–1945', *ibid.*, pp. 309–21.

17 Richter, *A History of Missions*, p. 342.

18 It was only after his conversion that Baba Padmanji wrote a novel, *Yamuna Paryatan* (Yamuna's Rambles) (Marathi) (Bombay, 1937), in which he highlighted the problems of Hindu widows through the trials of the heroine Yamuna.

19 For a sample of this literature see B. H. Khare, *How is Woman Treated by Man and Religion?* (Bombay, 1895); B. R. Row, *Women's Right to Salvation* (Madras, 1887).

20 B. Padmanji, *Once Hindu, Now Christian: The Early Life of Baba Padmanji, an Autobiography*, trans. J. Murray Mitchell (London, 1890), p. 71.

21 Nilakantha Goreh for example was a Brahmin priest who had begun by refuting Christian doctrines and ended as a staunch Christian. See his *A Rational Refutation of the Hindu Philosophical Systems*, trans. Fitz-Edward Hall (Calcutta, 1862).

22 Keeping in mind that nineteenth-century Christianity in colonies embodied certain aspects of cultural imperialism, I use the term 'Christianity' in a qualified sense, i.e., representations of Christianity.

23 H. S. Dyer's Preface in S. Powar, *Hinduism and Womanhood* (London, n.d.), p. 6.

24 Padmanji, *Once Hindu*, p. 136.

25 Anandibai's letter to the Head of the Mission School in Bombay reveals the turmoil caused by the major changes in her life and her unhappiness and fear of having displeased her patron, Mrs Mitchell, a prominent missionary. See her undated letter in A. B. Shah (ed.), *The Letters and Correspondence of Pandita Ramabai* (Bombay, 1977), pp. 11–14.

26 Anandibai's case is similar to the traumatic experiences of Lily Moya recounted in S. Marks (ed.), *'Not Either an Experimental Doll': The Separate Worlds of Three South African Women* (London, The Women's Press, 1987).

27 Scholarship on Pandita Ramabai has expanded considerably in recent years. However, many scholars still consider her coming to consciousness within a religious framework. For example, A. B. Shah labels her a 'rebel in religion' in 'Pandita Ramabai: a rebel in religion', in A. B. Shah (ed.), *Religion and Society in India* (Bombay, Somaiya, 1981), pp. 196–224; Ram Bapat calls her a 'religious revolutionary' but 'certainly not a feminist': see 'Pandita Ramabai: faith and reason in the shadow of the East and West', in V. Dalmia and H. V. Stietencron (eds), *Representing Hinduism: The Construction of Religious Traditions and National Identity* (New Delhi, Sage, 1995), pp. 224–52; and Leslie Flemming argues that both Pandita Ramabai and Krupabai 'found their primary identities in religious communities': see her article, 'Between two worlds: self-construction and self-identity in the writings of three nineteenth century Indian Christian women', in N. Kumar (ed.), *Women as Subjects: South Asian Histories* (New Delhi, Stree, 1994), pp. 108–24. The variety and richness of her writings are accessible in the English language, see S. M. Adhav, *Pandita Ramabai* (Madras, Christian Literature Society, 1979), and A. B. Shah (ed.), *The Letters and Correspondence of Pandita Ramabai* (Bombay, Maharashtra State Board Publications, 1977).

28 P. Ramabai, 'Account of the life of a Hindoo woman', *Cheltenham Ladies College Magazine*, 12 (Autumn 1885), p. 143, Institutional Collection of Mukti Mission (hereafter ICMM).

29 In a personal communication Saraswathi Bhat informed me that this book is given as a gift to female children in South Karnatak Christian families to this day on their attaining the skills to read and write. I would like to thank Meena Siddharth for introducing me to the Christian community of S. Karnatak.

30 P. Ramabai, *A Testimony* ([1907] Kedgaon, 6th edn, 1964), p. 8.

31 P. Ramabai, *A Short History of the Kripa Sadan, or Home of Mercy* ([1908] Kedgaon, 1964), p. 2.

32 *Ibid.*, pp. 2–3.

33 Ramabai, *A Testimony*, p. 13.

34 Recollections of Shewatbai, Mistress of Epiphany School, Poona, on her mother's conversion, *Magazine of Panch Howd*, St Mary Convent (Poona, 1892), n.p. (ICMM).

35 Powar, *Hinduism and Womanhood*. An earlier version of this book was published by her, probably in the 1890s, under the title *The Bitter Fruits of Hinduism* (details unknown).

36 *Ibid.*, p. 31.

37 *Ibid.*, p. 18.

38 Krupabai develops these themes in four consecutive essays: 'Women's influence at home', 'Home training of children', 'Female education' and 'Hindu social customs', in *Miscellaneous Writings of Krupabai Satthianadhan* (Madras, Srinivas

Varadachari and Co., 1896), pp. 1–33.

39 Krupabai, 'Female education', p. 18.

40 *Ibid.*, p. 19.

41 This view is echoed by a great number of Hindus whether revivalists or reformers. Vernacular literature and contemporary press writings are replete with this viewpoint.

42 Krupabai, *Miscellaneous Writings*, p. 21.

43 K. Satthianadhan, *Kamala: A Story of a Hindu Life* (Madras, 1895), p. 207.

44 *Ibid.*, p. 57.

45 *Ibid.*, p. 57.

46 *Ibid.*, p. 58.

47 This is a semi-autobiographical novel and Krupabai can be seen clearly in the role of Saguna here: K. Satthianadhan, *Saguna: A Story of Native Christian Life* (Madras, 1895).

48 *Ibid.*, p. 166.

49 A huge controversy broke out in Maharashtra among Hindus over the issue of conversions in Pandita's school. Most of the turmoil took the form of rumours and allegations regarding her supposedly pernicious influence over students. The vernacular press active in denouncing her was chiefly led by B. G. Tilak, a prominent Hindu conservative who turned the Age of Consent debate from a feminist to a nationalist one. Pandita was accused of dishonesty and even received death-threats from orthodox Hindus.

50 It is therefore hardly possible to see any direct coercion by her of her students. Disturbed by the furore caused over the conversions, the American Ramabai Association sent their President Mrs Andrews to investigate the matter in 1893. After a fact-finding tour lasting six months, she submitted an extensive report describing the allegations against Ramabai as 'baseless fabrications'. Ramabai, however, conceded to Mrs Andrews that she may have had indirect influence over her students through her lifestyle. *Annual Report of the American Ramabai Association*, 11 March 1894, pp. 16–19 (ICMM).

51 The guardians of students were also requested to send their opinions. D. K. Karve, an important Hindu male social reformer who married Ramabai's first pupil, reported that in her four-year training at the school his wife had never been coaxed or cajoled into embracing Christianity and had remained a Hindu. See his letter to Mrs Andrews dated 2 Feb. 1894, *Annual Report*, 1894, pp. 27–9.

52 Explanations offered in popular Hinduism in order to comfort and provide a rationale for regarding the austere life ahead of them.

53 In 1893 when Nurmadabai was removed from Sharada Sadan she refused to go to any other school and after two years, seeing her conviction and obstinacy, her parents allowed her to go back to Ramabai's school. From Nurmadabai's Address at the Annual Meeting of the American Ramabai Association, *Annual Report*, 1903, pp. 40–2.

54 Ramabai, 'Account of the life of a Hindoo woman', p. 146.

55 *Mukti Prayer Bell* (Magazine of Mukti Mission), Dec. 1904 and Oct. 1905 (ICMM).

56 'The story of Jivi and others', typed manuscript, n.p. (ICMM).

57 P. Ramabai to Dr Donald, President of American Ramabai Association, 13 Sept. 1902 (ICMM).

58 K. Storrie, *Soonderbai Powar: A Noble Worker for Indian Womanhood* (London, n.d.), pp. 6–7.

59 A. Hastings, in his work on the ambiguities of the impact of missions on African women, notes a similar trend: 'Were women a special case?', in F. Bowie, S. Ardener and D. Kirkwood (eds), *Women and Missions: Past and Present* (Oxford, Berg, 1993), pp. 109–24.

60 N. Goreh, *Four Lectures Delivered in Substance to the Brahmos in Bombay and Poona* (Bombay, 1875), pp. 1–11.

61 S. M. Adhav, 'Pandita Ramabai', paper read at Church History Association of India, Western India Branch, 12 March 1978, p. 1 (ICMM).

62 P. Ramabai to Sister Geraldine, 12 May 1885, in Shah (ed.), *Letters and Correspondence of Pandita Ramabai*, p. 59.
63 Storrie, *Soonderbai Powar*, p. 45.
64 For further elaboration of Christian women's critiques of the Indian past, see my forthcoming book, *Beyond the Courtyard*.
65 K. Satthianadhan, 'Female education', *Miscellaneous Writings*, pp. 16–17; P. Ramabai, *Stri-Dharma Niti: Prescribed Laws and Duties on the Proper Conduct of Women* ([1882] Kedgaon, 33rd edn, 1967), pp. 40–5.
66 P. Ramabai to Rev. Dr Pentecost, 6 Dec. 1892, in *Pandita Ramabaicha Chikat Pustak* (Notebook of Pandita Ramabai) (Marathi, Rajas Dongre Collection).
67 Satthianadhan, *Saguna*, p. 108.
68 C. Sorabji, 'Social relations', *Pan-Anglican Papers*, pp. 1–4 (ICMM).
69 Satthianadhan, *Saguna*, pp. 132–40.
70 P. Ramabai, 'Indian religion', *Cheltenham Ladies College Magazine*, 13 (Spring 1886), pp. 106–18 (ICMM).
71 *Ibid.*, p. 107.
72 Lakshmibai notes how in dress, Indian Christian women rejected the trailing gowns and skirts of Western women and instead wore a modified version of the Indian sari and a blouse. It differed from Maharashtrian Hindu women's dress in that the sari was not divided and drawn between the legs and tucked at the back but fell loosely like the pleats of a skirt and the blouse was modified to the extent of having wrist-length sleeves. They also wore no ornaments except two bangles on each wrist. L. Tillak, *I Follow After: An Autobiography*, trans. J. Inkster (London, Oxford University Press, 1950), p. 168.
73 'Notes to a would-be worker abroad', Manoramabai's Papers (ICMM).
74 P. Ramabai's letter, 25 July 1889, *Dnyanodaya* (Marathi).

CHAPTER FOUR

National liberation movements and the question of women's liberation: the Irish experience

Margaret Ward

Women in the Irish nationalist tradition have played many different roles: at times acquiescent and passive, at times highly radical and deeply critical of restrictions based upon gender. In the exploration of the gendered nature of that tradition, women's own words are vital witnesses. No critique can be truly convincing if the testimony of those who participated is not considered. Personal experiences, with their attendant hazards of romanticism and idealisation, are obviously not the only source of evidence: consideration of the extent to which women's liberation was facilitated or impeded by movements for national liberation needs also to include the conditions in which those struggles took place. As a historian, I believe that the material context defining those varied experiences must remain the crucial starting point for all critiques.

Analysis of the gendered nature of Irish nationalism has become an expanding area of study, one increasingly informed by the disciplines of cultural and literary studies and possessing a sophistication unknown a mere decade ago. Discourse analysis has done much to foreground power relations between the sexes as an essential factor in future considerations of Irish nationalist discourses. Dazzling insights and complex theories can present a welcome challenge to conventional wisdoms but I have considerable doubts about the political direction of much of this work. My disquiet stems from an awareness that the shift away from the empirical to the discursive has enabled theorists unsympathetic to nationalism to depict a masculinist tradition in which women remain 'the other' without any requirement to examine opposing evidence. One critic recently coined the phrase 'the great patrilineage of Irish liberation' in her analysis of the unequal relationship between women and the male-dominated movement for Irish national independence.[1] A highly potent phrase, but concentration upon the deconstruction of texts which are easily available to the non-specialist (and which are seldom those written by women) allows for serious misrepresentation, as women's efforts to become agents of change in their own right remain peripheral. Unintentionally perhaps, women are seen as victims of circumstance instead of actors consciously attempting to influence policies and events. For those who want to emphasise the 'patrilineage' to the exclusion of other evidence, this poses no problems but, equally, it can be argued that this is to distort historical fact.

Two recent works, by Mary Condren and Sarah Benton, both conclude that the military struggle engaged in by Irish nationalists in the 1916 period of military uprising reaffirmed a masculinist discourse which ultimately disempowered women and ensured their eventual relegation to the domestic sphere.[2] In such a reading women, if not actually colluding in this process, offered little resistance. Conclusions based upon essentialist claims that nationalism is automatically hostile to women's interests need to be interrogated and placed in historical perspective. While Mary Condren has, rightly, described the 1914–16 era as one when the discourse on 'manhood' reached 'almost pathological proportions', it needs to be remembered that this was also an era in which women were highly visible in labour, suffrage and nationalist organisations. Singleminded focus upon one particular aspect of the struggle against British rule ignores other significant chapters in the Irish nationalist narrative, all of which are of importance. Is it the case that women's subordinate status in the post-independence Irish state was an inevitable result of the campaign of military resistance to British rule? If so, must we conclude that women should never take part in wars of national liberation?

Methods of resistance to British colonial rule have, over several centuries, taken many forms – political, cultural, military. What has not varied has been the gendered nature of this resistance. In symbolic form, in nationalist-inspired literature, the ideological imperatives of the struggle created a gendered discourse in which the category of female was deemed passive, defenceless, in need of rescue by a maledom which was in the process of recovering its virility through the taking up of arms. Iconographic images of Ireland have ranged from the romanticism of Roisin Dubh (Dark Rosaleen), to the sorrowing Shan Van Vocht (Poor Old Woman), to the triumphant Cathleen ni Houlihan – the old woman transformed into a radiant young queen because men who had regained their gallantry were fighting for her honour. So potent was the mix of literature and politics that on the eve of the 1916 Rising young men were lectured that there was no such person as Cathleen ni Houlihan calling upon them to serve her.[3]

Literary evidence would appear to substantiate the contention that nationalism is overwhelmingly gendered in ways that deny agency to women. However, in contradiction of the assumption that there is only one reading of literary symbolism, some nationalist women interpreted mythology and history in woman-centred terms, thereby constructing an alternative version where female power was equally essential to the evolution of the Irish nation. Some of the power of legend is suggested by Lorna Reynolds in a survey of Gaelic legend and literature that concludes, 'the women of Ireland, whether we look for them in legend, literature or life, do not correspond to the stereotypes that have, so mysteriously, developed in the fertile imaginations of men'.[4] In the early decades of the twentieth century, political activists like Ella Young and Crissie Doyle used their literary skills to promote women's entry into the political arena. As Loftus has remarked, 'Cathleen ni Houlihan and the female figures associated with her represented individual as well as national freedom.'[5] In other words, unlike their male comrades, the women were not undertaking some chivalric rescue but were fighting on their own behalf – they *were* Cathleen ni Houlihan just as much as Cathleen was the personification of the ideal. When Maud Gonne, founder of the nationalist–feminist organisation Inghinidhe na hEireann (Daughters of Ireland), played the title role in W. B. Yeats's play *Cathleen ni Houlihan*, she symbolised nationalist women's determination to break with the tradition which relegated them to a purely supportive role. One of the leading members of Inghinidhe na hEireann, Constance Markievicz, was very clear on women's ultimate goal. In 1909 she urged members not to forget that their own emancipation was part of the struggle for freedom: 'Fix your minds on the ideal of Ireland free, with her women enjoying the full rights of citizenship in their own nation.'[6] Six years later, on the eve of the 1916 Rising, she was urging nationalist women to 'dress suitably in short skirts and strong boots … and buy a revolver'.[7]

Anne McClintock, in a study of women's relations to competing national narratives and struggles in South Africa, starts from the premiss that 'nationalisms are from the outset constituted in gender power'.[8] Despite the full participation of women in the South African national liberation movement, it was only in the last years of the struggle against the apartheid regime that women's empowerment was 'recognised in its own right, distinct from the national, democratic, and socialist revolution'. McClintock's survey of women's contributions to nationalist and socialist revolutions leads to the conclusion that 'nowhere has feminism in its own right been allowed to be more than a maidservant to nationalism'. There is no evidence from the Irish experience to contradict this assertion. It is nevertheless important to consider moments from that history when women did attempt the development of alternative discourses of empowerment, rejecting their reduction to the status of totemic symbols of nationhood. In this exploration of women's relationship with Irish nationalist movements, the focus is upon their active participation within the various organisations inspired by nationalist ideals and their continuing efforts to overcome opposition to that participation.

Nancy Curtin has provided a short account of women's contribution to the United Irishmen, the organisation responsible for the failed uprising of 1798. While acknowledging the gender-based division of labour characteristic of Irish nationalist organisations, Curtin also provides evidence to suggest that 'real republican women chafed under the constraints imposed on their participation in the cause'. Mary Ann McCracken, for example, urged her imprisoned brother Henry Joy to undertake serious consideration of the necessity for women's emancipation: 'There can be no argument produced in favour of the slavery of women that has not been used in favour of general slavery ... I therefore hope that it is reserved for the Irish nation to strike out something new and to shew an example of candour, generosity, and justice superior to any that have gone before them.'[9] The defeat of the United Irish movement was a serious blow to radical hopes. It is highly significant that less attention has been paid to the outspoken Mary Ann McCracken than to Anne Devlin, a woman who better fits the dominant image of republican heroine. Anne Devlin, who performed an invaluable service in carrying messages between the defeated insurgents after the 1803 rising, was dedicated and self-sacrificing, asking nothing for herself.[10]

The revolutionary movement to succeed the defeated United Irishmen emerged fifty years later, during the cataclysm of the Great Famine of 1845–52. 'Young Ireland' was a loose collection of intellectuals, cultural nationalists and revolutionaries. Although taking their name out of solidarity with similar revolutionary nationalist groups throughout Europe, it could also be argued that the lack of any gender-specific reference in their title (unlike the United Irishmen and the Republican Brotherhood) was some indication of greater openness as far as women were concerned. At least, it did not foreclose the possibility of women's participation. One of the most striking features of the Young Ireland movement was the number of women writers who contributed to its journal, the *Nation*.[11] Most of the writing of the female Young Irelanders concerned Ireland's colonial domination by Britain and the necessity for physical resistance to bring an end to that situation. What was not discussed explicitly was the role of women in such a movement. Such an omission needs to be placed in context: the 1848 revolutionaries in Europe did not support female suffrage, despite the presence of some outspoken women within their ranks.[12] However, within the pages of the *Nation* there were some signs that women envisaged an active role for their sex. Elizabeth Willoughby Treacy, an upper-class Protestant from Ballymena, writing under the Gaelic pseudonym 'Finola', challenged the conventional stereotypes of cultural nationalism. Instead of a 'Dark Rosaleen' waiting to be rescued, Finola's woman stood her ground and challenged her oppressors, claiming her right to fight for her country.[13]

The women of Young Ireland were able to occupy a position within the movement which, while not equal to that of the men, offered the possibility that greater egalitarianism would become acceptable to succeeding generations. But this did not happen. One of the reasons for the failure of succeeding generations of revolutionary women to build upon the tentative legacy offered by the women of the 1840s period lies in the vast material and ideological changes that occurred in the Ireland of the post-famine era – changes which had a detrimental impact upon gender relations.

Over one million people starved to death during the famine, and another million and a half fled to other lands. The famine caused the physical elimination of the poorest classes in rural society, while the 'strong farmer' class grew in significance.[14] Their determination to consolidate and improve land holdings gave rise to important demographic and cultural changes: restricted opportunities for marriage and changes in inheritance patterns were underpinned by a new puritanism in matters of sexual morality. Native Irish-speakers had either perished or left the country and Irish Catholicism lost the remnants of an easy-going Gaelicism which had not attempted to regulate personal relationships. Rome was finally able to assert its authority upon the Irish church and the impact of this upon women's position within the family and within the wider society was profound. The Catholic Church preached submission while the demise of the old village clusters, due to land consolidation, led to women being isolated on family farms, obedient to male authority. On the material level, women's economic worth was minimised as farming practices changed from labour-intensive tillage to cattle rearing. Census returns relabelled rural women as 'unproductive' and dowries became necessary as compensation for their lack of wage-earning potential.[15]

As Irish society became oppressively male (causing single Irish women to become the largest category of emigrants from any European country, signalling that Irish women were not passively accepting the imposition of this new patriarchy), so too did republicanism. While investigation has begun into the impact for women of the post-famine restructuring of society, the impact upon gender relations

within the revolutionary nationalist tradition has had little attention.[16] Once the contrast between Young Ireland and the revolutionary
movement that succeeded it, the Fenians, is made in terms of the
transformation which took place in mid-nineteenth-century Ireland,
the charge that female marginalisation is an *inevitable* outcome of
Irish nationalism's gender bias is more difficult to sustain. Material
circumstances can be the catalyst for changes that set back hopes for
a linear progression on the advancement of women's rights within
society in general, with obvious repercussions within organisations
that were themselves products of that society.

Revolutionary nationalists of the 1860s (known as Fenians after the
Fianna, warriors of ancient Ireland) formed themselves into the Irish
Republican Brotherhood – a conspiratorial, terrorist organisation, with
membership confined to men. There was, significantly, a Fenian Sisterhood in America, that land of opportunity where so many of the dis-
affected were making new lives for themselves, but in Ireland the
women who formed the Ladies' Committee, the female auxiliary of
the IRB, concentrated their activities upon support of the prisoners.
Those who did help in preparations for the abortive Fenian Rising of
1867 did so as individual confidantes of the men, taking no oath
because they were not sworn members of the organisation.[17] Lacking
the privileges of membership they were unable, even if they had
wanted, to make any demands on behalf of their sex – a smaller-scale
reproduction of the unequal power relations of the wider society.
There is no evidence from that time that women had any specific
gender-based demands. Certainly none were expressed publicly. But
was this wholly attributable to an anti-woman bias within Irish
nationalism, or was this secretive brotherhood one manifestation of a
post-famine society suffering continued trauma and where the possibilities of a democratic conclusion to Ireland's colonial subordination
were remote? The shift away from the possibility of the more egalitarian gender relations evident in the immediate pre-famine era of
Young Ireland, to the 'separate spheres' philosophy of military-style
Fenianism needs to be understood in that context.

The outstanding exception to women's marginalised position in
nineteenth-century Ireland took place during the Land War of
1881–82. A Land League had been formed in 1879, through an alliance
of parliamentarians and Fenians, in order to mobilise tenant farmers
against the landlord class in a fight for rent reductions. Fear of renewed
famine was the spur. Women who controlled their own farms (usually
widows of farmers) had an independent economic status and therefore
were permitted to join the Land League.[18] There is substantial evidence that women were fierce fighters in their resistance to eviction.

They were after all fighting to retain a roof over their families' heads. But women as a whole were not members of the Land League and the male leadership, dominated by the concerns of Members of Parliament, ignored the disfranchised sex as possible allies. Despite this, in 1881 they were forced to agree to the formation of a woman-only organisation – the Ladies' Land League – once it became clear that the British government was determined to suppress the Land League and, if necessary, to imprison all its members. It was a landmark in the history of women's contribution to political movements. Confounding all predictions, the women proved themselves to be militant and effective opponents of landlord power. Anna Parnell, sister of Charles Stewart Parnell, leader of the Irish Parliamentary Party, and the woman most responsible for directing the work of the Ladies' Land League, has left a written account of her involvement which is suffused with indignation for the disadvantages suffered by women. Although a member of the Anglo-Irish elite she did not share the social or political views of her class. Her antagonism towards men was based upon personal experience of unwelcome economic dependency: 'if the Irish landlords had not deserved extinction for anything else, they would have deserved it for the treatment of their own women'.[19]

Gender awareness and solidarity with the dispossessed peasantry were symbiotically linked in a formidable alliance. At a public meeting where women had gained sufficient confidence to come forward to the front of the platform instead of hovering at the back, Parnell commented: 'I observe that we have succeeded today in getting rid of the men nearly entirely – and I am sure that we all feel much more comfortable in consequence.'[20] The male sex, however, possessed political and economic power. The direction taken by the Ladies' Land League suited neither the British government nor the Irish parliamentarians and an explicitly gendered alliance ensured that the Ladies' Land League was disbanded and militant agitation discontinued. The Irish National League, the moderate organisation based upon the parliamentary party, which was formed in its wake, described itself as 'an open organisation in which the ladies will not take part'.[21] For eighteen months some of the sisters and daughters of the emerging Irish middle class (in addition to the Protestant Parnell) had been able to break away from their gender-defined roles and through their experience of organising resistance to landlord power had begun to question other power relations.

The strategic and political differences that emerged between the male and female organisations during the Land War had unhappy consequences for a whole generation of women. They now found themselves barred from membership of all political and cultural organisations. In 1890 the upper-class English woman Maud Gonne, attempting to gain membership of various nationalist organisations, asked for some explanation for her ineligibility. A former Land League member stated bluntly that the Ladies' Land League women had done 'too good work and some of us found they could not be controlled'.[22] Irish society had many visibly gendered divisions: national schools had separate entrances for boys and girls; men and women sat on opposite sides in church; the pub, focus for much of rural social life, was not an accepted place for women.

The process of breaking down some of those barriers between the sexes could be said to begin in 1893, with the formation of the Gaelic League as an organisation to revive the native culture and language. The League was considered revolutionary in its admittance of women to membership and in many rural areas nationalists encountered great hostility from the local parish priest for permitting the sexes to study together. Male League members, many of whom later participated in the military struggle against British rule, found that this experience was invaluable in developing a recognition that women could take part in the national liberation struggle. Nevertheless, the small group of feminists that emerged in the early years of the twentieth century warned against reading too much into this partial acceptance of women. Recognition of women as transmitters of cultural narratives was not the same as accepting their right to equal participation in national movements; 'it is primarily in her capacity as mother and housekeeper, not as individual citizen, that these movements have of necessity recognised her importance', warned Hanna Sheehy-Skeffington, founder of the Irish Women's Franchise League.[23]

Only in 1900, almost twenty years after the dissolution of the Ladies' Land League, was there another political organisation to which women could belong. This was Inghinidhe na hEireann, a woman-only group, formed by women who 'resented their exclusion' from all other groups.[24] Included within their ranks was the charismatic Maud Gonne. The moral support Inghinidhe members gave to each other as they redefined their own identities (including the adoption of noms de plume derived from the strong women of Ireland's Celtic past) helped to create a spirit of sisterhood which enabled Irish women to feel a pride in their sex. By the time of the publication of their journal Bean na h-Eireann (Woman of Ireland) in 1908 they had succeeded in extending women's political boundaries. Members were elected to executive positions in Sinn Fein, which they had helped to found in 1905. For the first time ever in Irish political life, women and men were equal participants in an organisation. From the pages of the Bean, they argued for a range of policies to be pursued by the nationalist movement. They often advocated physical force as a weapon of resistance to British rule, urging the importance of making the 'final sacrifice' long before Padraig Pearse and the future leaders of the 1916 Rising were doing so.

Inghinidhe women refused to ally themselves with the growing suffrage movement, but not because they did not agree with the principal of women's right to vote. Their objection centred around the unacceptability of Irish nationalists making any demand for legal change to the British parliament, whose jurisdiction they repudiated. Their battle cry was 'freedom to the nation and the complete removal of all disabilities to our sex'. National freedom and women's emancipation were complementary goals, to be worked for simultaneously. The rift between nationalist women and feminists who put the fight for suffrage first continued until 1918, when the granting by the British government of the vote to British and Irish women over thirty finally removed the issue from the political arena. It was a long-standing difference in emphasis, yet another consequence of the distortions of colonial rule, one which seriously undermined the ability of women in Ireland to put forward a united programme of demands. Those who have been engaged in researching Inghinidhe's contribution would agree with the conclusions of historian Maryann Valiulis:

> The Daughters of Eireann delineated a wider definition of what was appropriate for women – more than that, what it was women's obligation to do – for the nationalist movement. Their gender ideology expanded women's role into the public sphere where women would work as partners with men in the broader political scene. Woman as citizen was their ideal.[25]

Some male nationalists were prepared to consider women as valuable allies, but many continued to insist that 'there was no room for the ladies'.[26] These opposing views came into starkest relief in the years 1913–21, beginning with the establishment of military-style organisations by both unionists and nationalists and followed by the outbreak of the First World War, the Easter Rising of 1916 and the gradual escalation of military resistance to British rule in Ireland.

The nationalist Irish Volunteers did not allow women as members. A woman's organisation, Cumann na mBan (Irishwomen's Council), was formed in 1914, a compromise between those who wanted equality of status for women and those who did not believe a physical force movement required the presence of women in any capacity. It was an auxiliary organisation, its role intended as support for the 'fighting men'.[27] While some questioned this, the need to maintain a united nationalist front meant that areas of possible controversy were avoided. Suffragists from the Irish Women's Franchise League demanded that nationalist women be given representation on the Irish Volunteer executive, on the grounds that those who were raising funds had the right to determine how those funds were spent. This argument was dismissed by members of the Irish Volunteers and greeted with a mixture of embarrassment and anger by members of the Cumann na mBan, who refused to admit that their separate organisation was a set-back to women's hopes of parity of status. However, Constance Markievicz, although a Cumann na mBan member, admitted that 'These Ladies' Auxiliaries demoralise women, set them up in separate camps, and deprive them of all initiative and independence.'[28]

**Cumann na mBan members in the Civil War, 1922–23
(courtesy of Beyond the Pale Publications)**

Of the remaining members of Inghinidhe na hEireann, almost all transferred their loyalties to the more egalitarian Irish Citizen Army, formed to defend Dublin trade unionists in the Lock-Out of 1913. Under the leadership of the socialist James Connolly, a strong supporter of the militant suffrage movement, the Citizen Army women were not excluded from attaining officer status or from decision-making. During the Easter Rising those few who wanted to take up arms were able to do so. All had participated in the same rigorous training. Although a minority tendency within the overall nationalist movement, the example they set imbued those who flocked to join Cumann na mBan in the years following the Rising with a determination to ensure that their participation in the struggle would be on less restrictive gender lines.

Once militarism dominated the nationalist discourse it would appear as if the struggle to incorporate women's emancipation within the final goal of the movement for national liberation had been lost. Frank Sheehy-Skeffington, a pacifist and a militant supporter of the suffrage cause, had stated his unease in an open letter to Thomas MacDonagh, an Irish Volunteer friend: 'Why are [women] left out? Consider carefully why; and when you have found and clearly expressed the reason why women cannot be asked to enrol in this movement, you will be close to the reactionary element in the movement itself.'[29]

However, the situation contained more potential for transformative change than the immediate rhetoric would suggest. Different discourses – cultural, military and economic – all played a role in establishing the conditions which made an armed uprising an inevitability in the circumstances of the First World War. Not all were reactionary. The women's movement – incorporating suffrage, nationalist and labour organisations – with its discourse of gender equality, succeeded in staking its claim. The principles of equal citizenship and equality of opportunity that were written into the Proclamation of the Republic gave recognition to these different claims. The publication of the Proclamation signalled the start of the uprising and '[legitimated] women's role in the new state and gave formal recognition to their place in the nationalist movement'.[30]

Those events came to symbolise the birth of the Irish nation-state; however, the radical hopes of that generation were not to be realised. The eventual establishment of a conservative state, in which Catholic social and religious values were constitutionally enshrined, has enabled those hostile to nationalist aims to condemn the 1916 revolutionaries for initiating the process which resulted in the creation of that anti-woman environment. Revisionist historians have blatantly incorporated that political stance into their rewriting of the past (although not out of concern for women's oppressed status) and it now appears as though feminist critics, informed by an anti-nationalist perspective, are engaging in a similar exercise. Condren and Benton argue that the pursuit of war, in heightening the cult of 'manliness', reinforces gender divisions to the extent that women's right to full citizenship in the future nation-state becomes a contested issue.

Mary Condren concentrates upon the 1916 period, using the Easter Rising as a 'festival paradigm' in order to explore the 'sacrificial discourse' within the Irish republican tradition. For her, the lessons of history are clear. Women's interests are never served by war: 'the release of the death drives (regardless of any spurious female inclusion in war/sacrifice) can only work to reinscribe gender boundaries, at women's expense'.[31] Women are therefore urged to 'refuse the sacrificial social contract with its easy options of sacrifice or self-sacrifice, in favour of a genuine self-awareness and service to humanity'.[32] There are thought-provoking insights in her discussion, but she does not make explicit what alternative path women should have taken. It is difficult, for example, to know what type of alternative 'service to humanity' women in Ireland could have engaged in, in the context of the First World War, unionist opposition to Home Rule and the determination of revolutionary nationalists to stage an armed uprising in order to stake Ireland's claim to be considered as a 'small nation' in the final peace settlement following the conclusion of the war. The suffragist Hanna Sheehy-Skeffington implicitly endorsed the Rising by carrying supplies to the insurgents' headquarters and conveying messages between outposts. She had been informed that she would be a member of a civil provisional government planned to come into existence if the Rising was prolonged.[33] Sheehy-Skeffington's objections as a feminist centred less upon the notion of military uprising than on women's subordinate status in Cumann na mBan. She did not join Cumann na mBan but she did become a prominent member of the post-Rising Sinn Fein.

In Condren's reading of history, there is no possibility of movements for national liberation containing a transformative potential not only to liberate the nation from its colonial past but also to empower the individual as citizen of a new state-in-the-making. In her festival paradigm, defined by reference to anthropology, linguistics and psychoanalysis, 'womanhood' has collapsed while 'manhood' reaches exacerbated levels. What remains unexplored by the paradigm, but succinctly articulated by McClintock, is the contention that refusal to participate in a nationalist revolution contributes to powerlessness in the post-revolutionary era: 'as the lessons of international history portend, women who are not empowered to organize during the struggle will not be empowered to organize after the struggle'.[34]

Women's own testimony concerning the years immediately following the Rising reveals there to have been considerable numbers of women working hard to gain some commitment to a radical social programme. The confidence engendered by their participation in the military conflict and the recognition of women's right to equality asserted by the Proclamation transformed women's consciousness of the importance of gender-based issues. They were to the fore in arguing for a democratic programme that would enlist the energies of a wide spectrum of society and they formed a woman-only organisation in order to maximise their impact upon the wider political organisation. Widows of some of the executed leaders were amongst the activists who, in 1917, formed the League of Women Delegates (later renamed Cumann na dTeachtai). They succeeded in having four of their members co-opted onto the ad-hoc executive of Sinn Fein, making the point that their claim was based

> on the risks women took, equally with the men, to have the Irish Republic established, on the necessity of having their organised cooperation in the future struggle to free Ireland and the advantage of having their ideas on many social problems likely to arise in the near future.[35]

At the all-important Sinn Fein Convention of 1917 Cumann na dTeachtai had a resolution passed binding the organisation to promoting the equality of women in all its proceedings.[36] They also began tentative approaches to the non-nationalist suffrage organisations for joint campaigns on such issues as government regulations regarding venereal disease that were particularly discriminatory towards women.[37]

Women made other gains, particularly in the area of local government, where a substantial number were elected. By the time the Treaty was agreed upon in 1921, more women had been elected to public office and women made strong representations against acceptance of the Treaty, partly on the grounds that the state that would come into existence as a result – modelled on British standards of liberal democracy – would not be the type of egalitarian society they had been fighting for. The fact that the pro-Treaty majority in the Dail refused to wait until the electoral registers had been revised in order to allow women between the ages of twenty-one and thirty to vote on the issue symbolised women's alienation from the state.

Six years after the Easter Rising a partial independence had been achieved by all except six counties in Ulster. Women's involvement in those years of war had incorporated a variety of roles: support for the flying columns of guerillas; propagandists; elected political representatives; prison campaigners; bereaved relatives. Sarah Benton includes the War of Independence and the Civil War in her discussion, but not all women activists abandoned their interests '[as] the price women had to pay for the right to belong', and neither did the Irish struggle simply place women 'firmly in the roles of auxiliaries, grievers, and those who kept the home fires burning', as Benton concludes her assessment of the Irish national struggle.[38]

This focus upon masculinity in discursive analysis distorts reality through neglect of women's agency. Other writers have come to different conclusions. There clearly *were* differences between the conception of national freedom held by many of the male leaders and the aspirations of their female colleagues, but women continued to argue their case. Carol Coulter usefully places this in a political context by contrasting those who were 'mainly preoccupied with constitutional issues, with state-formation and international legitimacy' (a tendency which dominated the first Irish government) to those of the original revolutionary leadership, who were 'concerned with the social and cultural content of the new society they hoped to create'.[39] There was enormous tension within the movement as to the appropriate role for women in the post-1916 era. Some of the male leadership attempted to ensure that women's relation to the national struggle was either focused upon their role as biological mothers of the people or, if transmitters of cultural narratives, only by virtue of their maternal role rather than through independent economic activity, such as writing or teaching. Eamon de Valera, the most senior surviving figure, had notoriously refused to allow women into his command during the Rising, exhorting them to return home. Post-1916 determination to ensure that women were removed from the public arena had echoes of the male refusal to allow female participation to continue in the aftermath of the Land War. The nadir of the new cult of domesticity was reached in the 1930s when de Valera, by now leader of the Irish government, eulogised at the funeral of Margaret Pearse: 'But for the fame of her sons the noble woman at whose grave we are gathered would perhaps never have been heard of outside the narrow circle of her personal friends.'[40]

De Valera's insistence upon the primacy of woman's role as homemaker was enshrined in the 1937 Constitution, clauses of which have become the site of intense gender-based conflict since the 1970s. But was there a dreadful inevitability to this process? Was it a product of the military struggle against British rule in Ireland in which women's support of guerrilla warfare, supposedly in deadly replication of male and female gender roles, paved the way for women's future subordination, or was it partly at least an effect of the defeat of radical forces during the civil war that followed the signing of the Treaty between Britain and Ireland?

I have in the past argued that women's political representation during the brief years comprising the War of Independence was largely due to the fact that circumstances had made it too difficult for men to undertake that role. There was no guarantee that women would retain such positions once military conflict came to an end.[41] While true, this is only half the picture because it ignores the considerable efforts made by women to ensure that they would not be sidelined in such a manner. Failure to nominate more than two women in the parliamentary elections of 1918, and a suspicion that Sinn Fein was not wholehearted enough in campaigning for the female candidates, were causes of internal dissension only partly ameliorated by the victory of Constance Markievicz as the first woman Member of Parliament. A further five women were elected to the second Dail (the alternative assembly established in defiance of the British parliament) in 1921. The existence of an organised caucus of women would seem to suggest that participation in a war of liberation had engendered sufficient confidence to ensure that women would not be easily deflected from their purpose in promoting issues of gender.

Cumann na dTeachtai members, in private and in discussion with male nationalists, were surprisingly outspoken on their insistence that women be treated as complete equals in all respects. These were women who had previously been critical of feminists for putting women's interests first. At the same time, women who had refused to join nationalist organisations prior to the Rising, on the grounds that feminists could not participate in groups that refused to recognise women's rights to citizenship, joined Sinn Fein afterwards with the specific intention of ensuring that gender issues would be well represented in the future. The bitter divisions between nationalist and feminist that had hampered the development of a strong women's movement lessened considerably once the dilemma of prioritising the campaign for the vote or the fight for national freedom had disappeared as an issue. There were certainly enormous difficulties barring the way towards women's liberation, but the possible outcome, for a time at least, was not unfavourable to women.

The assertion that 'Imperialist wars are openly aggressive while colonized societies often develop political identities by rigidly asserting their moral purity over against the foreign "invader"'[42] would appear to offer an explanation for the deeply conservative and Catholic state that emerged, but only at the expense of ignoring a complexity of causal factors. The Irish Free State did not simply develop its identity as a reverse image of the secular British nation-state. Its formation was distorted by the effects of a civil war which had reduced radical opponents of the regime to a powerless faction. In that context, the defeat of women's struggle for an equality of rights was a defeat for socialists, a defeat for liberals and ultimately a defeat for all those who believed in the separation of Church and state and the development of a secular democracy. The fragility of women's entrance into the public arena enabled the conservative backlash to begin with attacks on women's rights, in the guise of creating a stable society free from the upheavals of war.

It has been stated that women's participation in that war, and in particular their support for those who took the anti-government side during the Civil War, created the conditions for curtailing women's right to participate in public life in the post-colonial era.[43] But no one has attempted to argue that women would have been granted rights of citizenship if they had remained outside of the anti-colonial movement. In critiquing the Irish nation-state, Condren fails to consider what type of society might have emerged if women had refused 'the sacrificial social contract'. She provides an original and challenging attempt to understand the nature of the highly gendered, sexually repressive social order which emerged in Ireland in the aftermath of the anti-imperialist struggle. What it lacks is historical perspective.

It often appears, particularly in the context of a war that has been fought, in its most recent manifestation, for twenty-five years in the north of Ireland, that political attitudes towards contemporary issues have determined (and justified) the conclusions put forward in academic contexts.[44] The approach of historians is not value-free, but empiricism has merit at least in that it can allow for a greater consideration of evidence. Maryann Valiulis, for example, in an analysis of the construction of gender in the Free State, has insisted that this process be placed in context. Her focus upon ecclesiastical discourse in the legitimation of political restrictions against women leads to the conclusion that this was not a process unique to post-colonial Ireland. There was a general increase in conservative movements throughout Europe in the inter-war years, culminating in the rise of fascism and renewed discourses of militarism and motherhood.[45] Irish women suffered severely from the imposition of gendered legislation which removed their rights to serve on juries, limited their employment rights and eventually restricted them to the domestic sphere, but the explanation for this needs to be centred around Roman Catholicism, the dominant discourse in many European countries, rather than in the aftermath of the Irish national liberation struggle. Irish radicals, male and female, were defeated over the Treaty, but they remained in existence. The defeat of radical hopes epitomised by the Spanish Civil War (a cause for which many Irish republicans fought) left progressive forces internationally isolated and unable to make alliances while conservative leaders triumphed.

Nationalism is undoubtedly a heavily gendered concept and wars of national liberation have not necessarily included women's emancipation within their frame of reference. Nevertheless, it can be argued that even if 'nationalism' is too problematic to be considered without reference to a specific context, feminist historians who have applied themselves to the task of uncovering women's roles within past movements of national liberation are providing emancipatory tools for a new generation. Such tools can only be of use if they are the best available – and that requires a willingness to look at the evidence from the writings and actions of women themselves and to interpret male nationalist discourse within its shifting historical context.

Notes

1 M. Condren, 'Work-in-progress: sacrifice and political legitimation: the production of a gendered social order', *Journal of Women's History*, 6:4/7:1 (1995), 160–189.

2 S. Benton, 'Women disarmed: the militarization of politics in Ireland 1913–23', *Feminist Review*, 50 (1995), 148–172. For other recent works see also: C. L. Innes, *Woman and Nation in Irish Literature and Society 1880–1935* (Hemel Hempstead, Harvester, 1993); C. Nash, 'Remapping and renaming: new cartographies of identity, gender and landscape in Ireland', *Feminist Review*, 44 (1993), 39–57; T. O'Brien Johnson and D. Cairns (eds), *Gender in Irish Writing* (Buckingham, Open University Press, 1991); S. Sharkey, 'Frontier issues: Irish women's texts and contexts', *Women: A Cultural Review*, 4:2 (1993), 125–135. I am not suggesting that these, other than the overtly political stance taken by Benton, are informed by anti-nationalism. Sharkey is explicitly anti-imperialist in her comments.

3 D. McCartney, 'Gaelic ideological origins of 1916', in O. Dudley Edwards and F. Pyle (eds), *1916: The Easter Rising* (London, Macgibbon and Kee, 1968), pp. 41–49.

4 L. Reynolds, 'Irish women in legend, literature and life', in S. F. Gallagher (ed.), *Women in Irish Legend, Life and Literature* (Buckinghamshire, Colin Smythe Ltd, 1983), p. 25.

5 B. Loftus, *Mirrors: William III and Mother Ireland* (Dundrum, Picture Press, 1990), p. 62.

6 C. Markievicz, 'Women, ideals and the nation', in M. Ward (ed.), *In Their Own Voice: Women and Irish Nationalism* (Dublin, Attic Press, 1995), pp. 30–32.

7 C. Markievicz, *Irish Citizen*, 23 October 1915, reprinted in Ward, *In Their Own Voice*, pp. 46–47.

8 A. McClintock, '"No longer in a future heaven": women and nationalism in South Africa', *Transition*, 51 (1991), 104–123.

9 N. Curtin, 'Women and eighteenth-century Irish republicanism', in M. MacCurtain and M. O'Dowd (eds), *Women in Early Modern Ireland* (Dublin, Wolfhound, 1991), pp. 133–144.

10 C. Coulter, *The Hidden Tradition: Feminism, Women and Nationalism* (Cork, Cork University Press, 1993), p. 12.

11 L. Curtis, *The Cause of Ireland: From the United Irishmen to Partition* (Belfast, Beyond the Pale, 1994), p. 56.

12 B. Anderson and J. Zinsser, *A History of Their Own: Women in Europe from Prehistory to the Present*, Vol. II (London, Penguin, 1988), p. 284.

13 B. Anton, 'Northern voices: Ulsterwomen in the Young Ireland Movement', in J. Holmes and D. Urquhart (eds), *Coming into the Light: The Work, Politics and Reli-*

gion of Women in Ulster 1840–1940 (Belfast, Institute of Irish Studies, 1994), pp. 60–92.

14 Christine Kinealy, This Great Calamity: The Irish Famine 1845–52 (Dublin, Gill and Macmillan, 1994).

15 J. Bourke, Husbandry to Housewifery: Women, Economic Change and Housework in Ireland 1890–1914 (Oxford, Clarendon Press, 1993); M. Luddy and C. Murphy (eds), Women Surviving: Studies in Irish Women's History in the 19th and 20th Centuries (Dublin, Poolbeg, 1990).

16 R. Rhodes, Women and the Family in Post-Famine Ireland: Status and Opportunity in a Patriarchal Society (New York, Garland, 1992); J. Nolan, Ourselves Alone: Women's Emigration from Ireland, 1885–1920 (Lexington, Kentucky University Press, 1989). A comprehensive bibliography on the subject of Irish women and emigration is contained in A. Rossiter, 'Bringing the margins to the centre: a review of aspects of Irish women's emigration', in A. Smyth (ed.), Irish Women's Studies Reader (Dublin, Attic Press, 1993), pp. 177–202.

17 Curtis, The Cause of Ireland, p. 69.

18 J. TeBrake, 'Irish peasant women in revolt: the Land League years', Irish Historical Studies, 28:109 (1992), 63–80.

19 A. Parnell, The Tale of a Great Sham, ed. D. Hearne (Dublin, Arlen House, 1986), p. 86.

20 M. Ward, Unmanageable Revolutionaries: Women and Irish Nationalism (London, Pluto, 1983), p. 16. See also J. Côté, Fanny and Anna Parnell: Ireland's Patriot Sisters (Dublin, Gill and Macmillan, 1991).

21 Ward, Unmanageable Revolutionaries, p. 36.

22 Maud Gonne MacBride, A Servant of the Queen (London, Victor Gollancz, 1974 [1938]), p. 96.

23 H. Sheehy-Skeffington, 'Nationalism and feminism', Bean na h-Eireann, November 1909, in Ward, In Their Own Voice, pp. 32–34. Her discussion of the varying forms that women's relationship to nationalism can take resembles that suggested by N. Yuval Davis and F. Anthias (eds), Women-Nation-State (London, Macmillan, 1989).

24 Ward, Unmanageable Revolutionaries, pp. 40–87; Innes, Woman and Nation, pp. 128–143.

25 M. Valiulis, 'Free women in a free nation', in B. Farrell (ed.), The Creation of the Dail (Dublin, Blackwater Press, 1994), pp. 75–90.

26 Ward, Unmanageable Revolutionaries, p. 92.

27 For the history of Cumann na mBan, see L. Conlon, Cumann na mBan and the Women of Ireland, 1913–1925 (Kilkenny, Kilkenny People, 1969); D. Hearn, 'The Irish Citizen 1914–1916', Canadian Journal of Irish Studies, 18:1 (1992), 1–14; B. McKillen, 'Irish feminism and national separatism, 1914–1923', Eire/Ireland, 17:3 (1981), 52–67 and 17:4 (1982), 72–90; Ward, Unmanageable Revolutionaries, pp. 88–247.

28 Markievicz, Irish Citizen, 23 October 1915, reprinted in Ward, In Their Own Voice, pp. 46–47.

29 Francis Sheehy-Skeffington, 'Open letter to Thomas MacDonagh', Irish Citizen, 22 May 1915, in Edwards and Pyle, 1916, pp. 149–152.

30 Valiulis, 'Free women', p. 82.

31 Condren, 'Work-in-progress', p. 175.

32 Ibid., p. 182.

33 L. Levenson and J. Natterstad, Hanna Sheehy-Skeffington: Irish Feminist (Syracuse University Press, 1986), p. 78; R. M. Fox, Rebel Irishwomen (Dublin, Progress House, 1967 [1935]), p. 76.

34 McClintock, '"No longer in a future heaven"', p. 122.

35 M. Ward, 'The League of Women Delegates and Sinn Fein 1917', History Ireland, 4:3 (1996), 37–41.

36 Sinn Fein Convention (1917), in Ward, In Their Own Voice, pp. 75–76.

37 R. Cullen Owens, Smashing Times: A History of the Irish Women's Suffrage

Movement 1889–1922 (Dublin, Attic Press, 1984), pp. 122–125; L. Ryan, 'Women without votes: the political strategies of the Irish suffrage movement', *Irish Political Studies*, 9 (1994), 136.

38 Benton, 'Women disarmed', pp. 169–170.

39 Coulter, *The Hidden Tradition*, p. 22.

40 M. Valiulis, 'Neither feminist nor flapper: the ecclesiastical construction of the ideal Irish woman', in M. O'Dowd and S. Wichert (eds), *Chattel, Servant or Citizen: Women's Status in Church, State and Society* (Belfast, Institute of Irish Studies, 1995), p. 169.

41 Ward, *Unmanageable Revolutionaries*, pp. 2–3.

42 Condren, 'Work-in-progress', p. 180.

43 L. O'Dowd, 'Church, state and women: the aftermath of Partition', in C. Curtin, P. Jackson and B. O'Connor (eds), *Gender in Irish Society* (Galway University Press, 1987), pp. 10–11; Valiulis, 'Free women', pp. 85–86.

44 See, for example, C. Murphy, 'Suffragists and nationalism in early twentieth-century Ireland', *History of European Ideas*, 16:4–6 (1993), 1009–1015. Murphy, unsympathetic to nationalism, begins her article: 'Diverse loyalties place great stress on activists in every country and many find that at some stage in their movement a decision has to be made and an allegiance must be decided.'

45 Valiulis, 'Neither feminist nor flapper', pp. 177–178; see also O'Dowd, 'Church, state and women', p. 4.

CHAPTER FIVE

Australian frontier feminism and the marauding white man

Marilyn Lake

'Here in Australia,' Louisa Lawson, editor of the feminist journal *Dawn*, observed with characteristic matter-of-factness, 'it is considered more a crime to steal a horse than ruin a girl.'[1] On the Darling Downs, at the turn of the century, another pioneering wife explained, 'Women in the farming districts don't occupy a very high place in the masculine community – being classed usually according to their degree of usefulness with the other animals.'[2] (And thanks to Anne Maree Collins's work on bestiality the extent of the usefulness of the other animals is only now beginning to be fully appreciated.)[3] Yet a third female pioneer, some twenty years later, had reason to return to the comparison of women with the 'other animals'. Millicent Preston Stanley, the first woman to enter the New South Wales parliament, when campaigning for the establishment of a chair in obstetrics at the University of Sydney, observed that several new positions had recently been granted in veterinary science: 'if the university is able to grant the means in the case of the horse, it should be equally able to grant "horse-rights" for women'.[4]

Frontier societies, women have long observed, enshrined masculine values and interests. In frontier societies white men roamed free, but men's mobility seemed to spell women's misfortune. In 1926, the British Commonwealth League, a London-based feminist organisation formed to promote women's citizenship rights, resolved that 'it was felt necessary to stress responsibility to the wandering member of the British race, who may be without ties in a new country. For such members may work great damage to their own and to other races if they have not means of recreation or of fellowship, but live in dangerous loneliness.'[5] In feminist discourse, mobile men were dangerous men and the wandering members of the British race – the nomad tribe, the swagmen, the men on the track – became a bunch of marauding white men. The mobility of men, that condition said to characterise the frontier and to be definitive of freedom, was assumed, by men and women alike, to be inherently threatening to women. The discursive emphasis on the freedom of men in frontier societies resulted in turn in a heightened perception of women's situation as one of 'isolation', 'vulnerability' and 'defencelessness': women were in need of 'protection'.

In this chapter I want to explore the ways in which the outlook of feminism in Australia, from the 1880s to the 1940s, was crucially shaped by the historical context of the frontier and to suggest that the frontier, as a conceptual and geographical space, acquired its meaning within an imperial as well as national context. I shall be arguing the importance of gender relations and the family to the imperial project in Australia and conversely the centrality of colonialism to gender politics and feminism in the settler colonies. In 1888, the same year in which Louisa Lawson chose to relinquish the editorship of the *Republican* newspaper in order to establish the *Dawn* (a 'journal for Australian women'), colonists in New South Wales celebrated a centenary of British settlement. Aboriginal Australians meanwhile mourned the loss of their lands, their culture and their people consequent upon this British invasion. It has been estimated that more than 20,000 Aboriginal people died in frontier warfare during the nineteenth century and many thousands more were lost as a result of disease and deprivation.[6] When the six British colonies federated in 1901 to form the new nation-state – the Commonwealth of Australia – the indigenous people were officially excluded from membership. Most were denied the franchise and associated citizen benefits. The same federal legislation that gave white women the vote denied it to the majority of Aborigines, following parliamentary debates that routinely invoked distinctions between 'women' and 'lubras' (the derogatory term for Aboriginal women).[7] Officially segregated on reserves and missions, far removed from the sight of the vast majority of white Australians, who lived in towns and cities clustered along the eastern seaboard, Aboriginal people were conveniently deemed to be a 'dying race'.[8]

Nationalist writers and many historians of Australia have tended to represent the frontier experience as emblematic of the national experience. On these 'outskirts of civilisation' the essential meaning of what it was to be Australian was somehow distilled or laid bare – the truth of Australian life exposed. For Russel Ward it was the birthplace and forcing ground of the legendary Australian – the practical man, rough and ready, independent and anti-authoritarian, a man given to few words, but resourceful and supportive of his mates.[9] For historians of Aboriginal dispossession, such as Henry Reynolds, it was on the frontier that the criminality, brutality and violence that characterised the settlement of Australia were most fully exposed.[10] Feminists, too, have shared this tendency to represent the frontier experience as paradigmatic. In the early twentieth century, feminist writers often portrayed strong women as the backbone of rural pioneering communities, offering models for Australian women to come. From the 1920s, however, the marauding frontiersman began to figure in many feminist representations as the true representative of the Australian frontier, the white man's systematic abuse of Aboriginal women suggestive of the inherent degradation that characterised free sexual relations. These otherwise divergent depictions of the frontier – the nationalist, the post-colonial and the feminist – shared this assumption: that 'on the border' white men could 'do as they liked', as residents of the Port Philip district informed Aboriginal Protector George Augustus Robinson.[11] For white men, the frontier was a fantasy of freedom; for white feminists it became a focus of fear and anxiety, a place beyond their ken, where undomesticated men roamed wild.

Writing of the genesis of modern feminism, Maggie Humm reminds us that although distinctive as a movement, feminism has been variously shaped by the 'cultural, legal and economic policies of particular societies' in which it was formed. 'Feminist campaigns are inevitably shaped by national priorities and national politics.'[12] I wish to suggest that the outlook of Australian feminism in the late nineteenth and early twentieth centuries was shaped by the context of an imperial frontier in four main ways. First, in the context of a British colonial settlement white women assumed a special authority as the agents of civilisation and custodians of the race. Second, a pioneering society was a masculine society. In these male-dominated colonies, there was a particular feminist emphasis on the need to reform characteristically masculine behaviours (drinking, gambling and a predatory sexuality) which seemed to flourish on the frontier, but which increasingly came to be seen as antithetical to civilisation and women and children's welfare. Third, in response to perceptions of women's special vulnerability in a masculinist society, there was a heavy emphasis in Australian feminist campaigns on the need to provide 'protection', rather than, say, 'emancipation', for women and girls. Writing about leading New South Wales feminist Rose Scott, Judith Allen has suggested that 'although overseas suffragists also pursued the vote as a principal means to the end of challenging men's sexual behaviour and power', Scott articulated this connection fully, clearly 'influenced by late nineteenth century conditions in Australia'.[13] Following on from this, I would suggest, further, that it was the spectacle of white men's systematic sexual abuse of Aboriginal women and 'unprotected' white women and girls in a male-dominated and homosocial society that confirmed twentieth-century Australian feminists in their view of sexuality as inherently degrading for women. Unlike some of their peers in the United Kingdom and the United States, it was not until the 1960s (at precisely the moment when, coincidentally, Aboriginal women tended to disappear from feminist view) that Australian feminists began to claim rights as sexual subjects.

In characterising the distinctiveness of the Australian version of frontier feminism, I want to suggest that the crucial conceptual dynamic underpinning the Australian feminist project in the early twentieth century was what I have called elsewhere feminists' sense of 'double difference' – their construction of a New World identity and politics marked by difference from, and temporal advancement beyond, both the feudal oppressions of the European Old World and the 'primitivism' of the Stone Age culture of Aboriginal Australians.[14] Australian feminists saw themselves as nation builders, consciously engaged in the project of fashioning a new order of protectionist state. As white women in the outposts of the British Empire, they were authorised to pursue their work of reform, all the while understanding their identity in relation to, but distant from, Chinese and black women.

Nineteenth-century colonial discourses which drew distinctions between primitive/barbarous societies and civilised/Christian ones allocated a special place to white women as the bearers of culture, morality and order. As Adele Perry, the Canadian historian of the backwoods of British Columbia has observed, in such a world quite ordinary white women were assigned an awesome responsibility as the most civilised representatives of the civilised race.[15] They were also agents of the 'governing race', as delegates to the British Commonwealth League noted.[16] This positioning was the source of their authority as activist reformers and feminists, authorised and enjoined to take their mission of purity out into the world. The imposition of 'purity' could be seen as especially important in the Australian colonies, given the possibilities of contamination from the convict legacy and the existence, and in some parts of Australia, the close proximity, of indigenous societies.

This meant that white women had a special responsibility as exemplars of civilised standards: drinking and sexual promiscuity were regarded as especially heinous offences in women. Thus it was decreed that 'sexual lapses of women must ever be held more deplorable than those of a man simply because the offence in the woman's case causes more harm within her environment and more rapid and permanent injury to her own more delicate moral and intellectual fibre'.[17] This tyrannical double standard was enshrined in law and became a major focus of feminist reform – not in the direction of claiming increased

[126]

sexual liberties for women, as would be the case in the 1960s, but in demanding that men, too, discipline and control themselves – that they literally live up to the 'civilised' standards that they invoked to justify their political power.

In this colonial nation-building context, as Perry observed of British Columbia, women were allocated and assumed a particular responsibility to reform men's behaviours to bring them into line with more 'civilised' standards. As New South Wales feminist Rose Scott explained, 'licensed or unlicensed vice can only mean evil, and ... a really great nation can only be built by inculcating the virtues of self-control and purity'.[18] This was an urgent task in frontier societies, where the predominance of single, mobile men fostered a strong homosocial national culture, sustained by bonds of mateship between men, casual sex with animals, other men, indigenous and other 'unprotected' women and girls, as well as the dissolute practices of gambling and drinking. As I noted in the mid-1980s, in a masculinist context which in Australia saw the elevation of these practices to the status of a national culture, women's mission of respectability could acquire a particularly subversive, threatening dimension.[19] It was one thing for women to attempt to work changes on men in private, wooing them from public house to private home, with their own good housekeeping as envisaged by the *Queenslander*, for instance:

> Bright, educated, companionable, capable women will make cheerful, economical homes, keep the men from gambling and other bad habits, render embezzlement and speculation unnecessary and generally purify life. That is provided they are thoroughly good. This crowns all.[20]

The exercise of private influence was woman's prerogative. It was quite another matter for women to attempt to lay down the law, but feminists embarked on public campaigns to do just that, seeking to outlaw drinking and to restrict men's sexual access to women and girls. Temperance reform assumed a particularly important place in the politics of frontier feminism. The preoccupation with men's behaviour also led to a particular concern to protect Australian boys from the models of manhood around them. Whereas the difficult position of daughters attracted the attention of British feminists, as Barbara Caine has noted, Australian feminists worried about the vulnerability of their sons.[21] 'Is it not a painful fact to contemplate', asked Louisa Lawson, 'that according to present conditions it can be looked upon as a miracle should a boy reach man's estate and escape the contaminations of vice which daily example makes him familiar with from boyhood. To be able to smoke, swear, drink and gamble like a man is the Alpha and Omega of his infantile dreams.'[22] Rose

Scott also deplored the fact that 'boys are taught by public opinion that it is manly to know life! To drink, to gamble and to be immoral.'[23] Australian boys had 'as great a right to be safeguarded for purity and self-control' as did girls, declared 'Irven' in *Labor Call* over twenty years later.[24]

Immorality was thought to accompany the nomadic lifestyle of frontiersmen. Unsettled men posed a particular sexual threat to the women and girls who shared their terrain. Cases such as the following were widely reported in colonial newspapers. In 1871 twelve-year-old Ammelie Weise was sent to the head station at Hirst Vale near Dalby, to collect food supplies. When she returned some hours later, her dress was torn and she was crying. The girl explained to her mother that a shearer temporarily in the area had followed her from the station and demanded a kiss. She refused; the man told her that he would 'see about that' and forced her to the ground and assaulted her.[25] Feminist campaigns aimed at curbing this freedom of men to do as they pleased, that condition which was seen as definitive of life on the frontier.

In this scenario, the key to the consolidation of colonies into nations was the settlement and domestication of a mobile and dangerous manhood. Feminists were emboldened to attempt a transformation of the free-wheeling, independent Lone Hand into a responsible, caring, temperate, chaste, self-controlled, considerate, selfless Domestic Man. Needless to say, their intentions met with considerable resistance. 'Am I likely to get married?', wrote George Underwood, a young selector in southwest Queensland, to his family. 'Yes, just as I am to produce a pair of wings and fly. I am a real bachelor just now … I cook for myself, wash my own clothes, in short am my own housekeeper.'[26] Or in the words of Randolph Bedford's father, who encouraged him to 'go bush':

> You're me all over again, lad. There's only one thing that will tie you down, and that's responsibility. A wife and children will put the hobbles on you. You'll look over the fence at the horses who are going somewhere; but you'll have to stay in the paddock.[27]

(Again the colonial tendency to identify with the horses).

In the metropolis, in Britain, in the nineteenth century, surplus women – also called redundant women – were deemed to constitute a major social problem. The difficulty of their existence – their lack of opportunity – became a major preoccupation of British feminists, who put much time and energy into reforms such as promoting access to education, which would enable single women to live independent lives. As Barbara Caine has written, for Victorian feminists in Britain, 'the plight of single women was of the utmost importance'.[28] In frontier societies such as Australia there was a surplus of men, but they were not, of course, conceived of as redundant or superfluous. They were for feminists, however, a problem. The situation in Queensland, deemed by commentators to be 'the most Australian' of all the colonies, was especially marked: at the turn of the century there were 171 males for every 100 females. The preponderance of men had important social consequences, notably a very high marriage rate for women. In all the Australian colonies marriage was the common condition of women over a certain age, and the nature of marriage and the condition of married women became major concerns of Australian feminists. Frontier feminism tended to be more concerned with the condition of mothers and wives than the tribulations of spinsters. For several decades feminists in Australia focused on attempts to elevate the marriage relationship – lifting it from being a species of prostitution to a 'sweet companionship' and, by the twentieth century, attempting to end the 'sex slavery' of the wife through the introduction of motherhood endowment.[29]

As a result of the perceived vulnerability of women and girls in a masculinist society, feminist campaigns concentrated on providing 'protection'. Colonial settlements were, in effect, extensive white men's protectorates, purporting to provide protection to those groups most vulnerable to white men's own depredations – Aborigines, Chinese, women and girls. But who would protect these groups from their protectors? Men were allegedly women's natural protectors – thus one Queensland politician was moved to remark of his colony in the 1860s: 'women are in a more defenceless position than at home, from our limited population and scattered habitations, and consequently they are very liable to violence in the absence of their natural protectors'.[30] In such a construction of the problem, the subjects actually perpetrating the violence were rendered anonymous, but as the American feminist Charlotte Perkins Gilman was moved to comment: 'As a matter of fact, the thing a woman is most afraid to meet on a dark street is her natural protector.'[31]

Nineteenth-century feminist activism in Australia was animated by the conviction that men had failed in their ordained role as protectors – women themselves would henceforth take responsibility for this task, authorised by their status as mothers. As Louisa Lawson argued, 'If we are responsible for our children, give us the power and sacredness of the ballot and we will lift ourselves and our brothers to a higher civilization.'[32] This political mobilisation of the identity of mother to promote a form of maternal government was a crucial dimension of the concomitant decline in the importance in the role of the helpmeet/wife, who was increasingly conceptualised as an exploited creature of sex. In frontier societies, feminists found their voice as

[129]

mothers: motherhood was conceptualised as women's common condition and the source of their political authority. It also provided, as Susan Sheridan has noted, a potential affinity between women of different classes and races.[33] As the feminist journal *Woman Voter* argued in opposition to the racially discriminatory clause of the Maternity Allowance of 1912, 'it is the White Australia policy gone mad. Maternity is maternity whatever the race'.[34]

The protection of women and girls gave priority to particular reforms: temperance, raising the age of consent, opposition to contagious diseases legislation, custody rights for mothers, the appointment of women to a range of public offices – as gaol warders, doctors, factory inspectors, police officers – so that women need never fall into men's hands. By the 1920s and 1930s, feminist activists attempting to reform the conditions of indigenous women and children in Western Australia and the Northern Territory demanded the appointment of women protectors to Aboriginal administration, because they would better defend their 'less favoured sisters' from the marauding white man.[35] Returning from a trip to northern Australia in the early 1930s, Mary Bennett reported: 'the worst thing I have seen is the attitude of the average white man to native women – the attitude not of the mean whites but of the overwhelming majority of white men'. 'Wherever there is a white man's camp there is a need for protection for these girls', said Bennett. 'It is the average ordinary white man who is to blame for this trouble.'[36] In feminist discourse, the heroic pioneer was exposed as the average, ordinary white man.

The consequences of white men's uncontrolled behaviour on the frontier were seen to be most destructive in the area of sexual relations – for both Aboriginal and non-Aboriginal women. Louisa Lawson wrote about the degrading position of white women forced to endure their husbands' sexual relations with Aboriginal women. In a preface to her poem 'The Squatter's Wife', Lawson referred to the actual case of a 'beautiful and gifted girl' who had married a squatter only to find on her arrival at his property that there were two bark huts – one for herself and the other for 'her husband's black mistress and family'. For the white woman, men's lusts rendered the frontier a place of loneliness and debasement. Lawson addressed the squatter's wife in these terms:

> Lonely hut on barren creek,
> Where the rotting sheep-yards reek,
> Far away from kith and kin,
> None save thee and native gin
> Many a weary mile within –
>
> Alice Gertler

The legendary freedom of the frontiersman was reconceptualised by Lawson, in racist terms, as an especially base form of licentiousness:

> Bound to one who loves thee not,
> Drunken off-spring of a sot;
> Even now at wayside inn
> Riots he in drink and sin,
> Mating with a half-caste gin –

Alice Gertler[37]

Whereas Lawson's depiction of the white man's sexual relations with Aboriginal women focused on the degradation visited on the white woman, twentieth-century feminists increasingly expressed outrage at the abuse of Aboriginal women themselves.

As white colonists, feminists assumed their racial superiority, but as women they identified a common condition of sexual exploitation. 'The plight of native women is pitiful', wrote Ada Bromham, member of the Woman's Christian Temperance Union and independent 'women's candidate' for the 1921 West Australian election; 'if we can do nothing for them how can we hope to protect our own women[?]'[38] There was a general principle involved: 'If a woman whether white or black has not the control of her body she is a slave', declared Edith Jones, one time president of the Victorian Women's Citizen's Movement.[39]

By the 1920s a number of feminists in organisations such as the Women's Service Guild, the Woman's Christian Temperance Union, the Australian Federation of Women Voters and the Women's Non-Party Association of South Australia came to see white men's sexual abuse of indigenous women as paradigmatic of uncontrolled masculinity. The appalling condition of Aboriginal people was a direct consequence of white colonisation and thus a national responsibility. 'We must never forget', an Australian speaker informed the British Commonwealth League (BCL) conference in 1931, 'that the whole continent of Australia having been seized by the British Government as Crown lands the Aborigines became British nationals and subjects of the British Empire.'[40] 'The terrible plight of the civilised Aborigines', wrote Mary Bennett, 'is the logical conclusion of our own dealings with them.'[41]

To these feminists the large increase in the mixed-descent population between the wars – the 'half-caste problem' – provided dramatic evidence of the extent of white men's depredations. Feminists such as Bennett, Edith Jones, Bessie Rischbieth, Ruby Rich and Constance Cooke organised national and international campaigns to draw attention to the trafficking in Aboriginal women and girls.[42] They also argued that men's uncontrollable lusts were undermining the moral authority of White Australia, of the new nation in the Pacific. 'I cannot

[131]

see how white supremacy can last out this decade even', despaired Bennett in the 1930s. 'We, I mean, white supremacy, is in the most imminent danger, and everybody is blind. In my view, our only chance of survival is to put our "spiritual" house in order and to do it mighty quick.'[43] In losing sexual control, the white man forfeited moral authority and would lose political control.

What was to be done? Mary Bennett was clear and insistent in language that echoed Rose Scott's claims of some forty years before. She spoke of 'the loving protection needed by these girls and women, native and half-caste, in the state of transition from native culture to white civilisation and the shielding from the terrible crop of evils that have sprung up in this borderland of transition'.[44] This space – the border-lands – emblematic of Australia at large – was an anarchic and unstable space of transition where the freedom of the white man had led to the systematic degradation of women and girls. In one of the few documents recording the response of Aboriginal women themselves to these 'protectionist' initiatives, a petition from the 'Half-Castes of Broome' echoed the demand that sympathetic 'lady protectors' be appointed to Aboriginal administration in place of police, but it diverged from the feminist emphasis on economic independence in voicing the plea that they be allowed to marry whom they liked. 'Sometimes we have the chance to marry a man of our choice ... Therefore we ask for our freedom, so that when the chance comes along, we can rule our lives and make ourselves true and good citizens.'[45]

Feminism on the frontier was authorised by colonial discourses that positioned white women as the moral guardians of civilisation. But I would emphasise that feminism was not contained by colonial discourses: feminism was complicit in the paternalism of the imperial project, but it also challenged some of its most fundamental assumptions, notably that women should occupy a familial dependent status in the colonies and new nation and that 'unprotected' women were fair game. By the 1920s and 1930s, major feminist organisations were demanding a place in the new nation for both black and white women as independent citizens. The 'half-caste problem', according to Bennett, resulted from the women's economic dependence – 'Economic dependence [was] the root of all evil.'[46] Because they had been deprived of their land, Bennett told a BCL meeting in 1933, Aboriginal women endured all the suffering of serfdom. They were, furthermore, deprived of education, medical services, wages and 'a political standing by which they might obtain other rights due to them'.[47] Feminist reformers campaigned for a variety of reforms in the condition of Aboriginal women and girls, such as land rights, custody rights, economic independence and citizenship rights.[48]

From the 1920s 'progressive' government officials moved to abandon the older segregationist policies in favour of a programme of assimilation, that is the 'absorption of the blacks by the whites' through the removal of children of mixed descent from Aboriginal mothers and the intermarriage of half-caste women and white men. In place of this 'controlled interbreeding' envisaged by government officials, the feminist reformer and educationalist Mary Bennett embarked on schemes to render Aboriginal women independent and self-supporting in their own communities. She personally taught them weaving and craft skills with this aim. Bennett described her work to Bessie Rischbieth, President of the Australian Federation of Women Voters, in these terms:

> The money thus earned goes back to the workers. It is enough that the women and the girls can be self-supporting and are self-supporting. Economic dependence is the root of all evil. ... The evils of the patriarchal system have become commercialised, the unfortunate women having acquired value as merchandise from white settlement. ... And so, though all the hunting grounds have been taken up as sheep stations, and the native culture has been completely destroyed, there has been an extraordinary recrudescence of polygamy for prostitution. ... But the women intrinsically are fine and ready for a position of respect and independence. This is why I have asked that they shall be permitted to invoke and obtain the protection of the law of the land.[49]

Bennett's appeal to 'the protection of the law of the land' is important here. It speaks to a historic convergence of forces that came to shape and define the Australian feminist investment in a protectionist nation-state. The stress on the necessity of women's protection in a frontier masculinist society coincided with a nationalist commitment to building a new order of nation-state, which would produce, in the words of Bessie Rischbieth, 'the sort of civilisation women of all countries dream about'.[50] The defining elements of this new order were nicely captured in Lilian Locke-Burns's celebration of the Labour government's introduction of the maternity allowance in 1912, to be paid directly by the state:

> In no other part of the civilised world as far as one can ascertain, is so much being done by the State in the way of providing for mothers and children as in the Australian Commonwealth. And yet how far we are still from a proper realisation of the value of a child as an asset of the State, and how little we realise the true position ... the mothers of the community would occupy in a properly organised social system, where the economic independence of women was fully recognised and assured. In Great Britain and some other countries which lay claim to some share in democratic reforms, the mothers are only protected (if protection it

may be called) under some form of social insurance. In the American states also very little has been done so far in this direction beyond some attention to delinquent children and the usual institutional efforts that we find in most countries which have evolved beyond the barbaric stage. Neither in England nor America do we hear of any such humanitarian provision as the Australian maternity allowance.[51]

This tribute is interesting both in its identification of the New World civilised nation's mission as the protection of women and its definition of that mission as the responsibility of the state. For Australian women citizens, the state was envisaged as a powerful beneficial force, enabling them to resolve the seeming contradiction posed by their twin ideals of 'protection' and 'independence'. Feminists enlisted the state as a crucial ally, able to provide the protection that would make possible women's independence from men. Arguing that their sex was more nurturing, loving and peace-loving than men, feminists endorsed the idea of a separate maternal citizenship for women, who were excused and excluded from the work of national self-defence abroad and enjoined to seek the protection of the state at home. Paradoxically, then, feminists contributed to the processes whereby women in the new nation were locked into the status of the protected sex and arguably into a psychology of helplessness and defencelessness that continues to pose a major dilemma for feminists today. The protected ones could not know real freedom. Moreover, as the inheritors of frontier feminism, Australian women still confront the contradictions posed by living in a strongly masculinist culture (which has just proclaimed Anzac Day to be the national day of remembrance), which has nevertheless institutionalised the power of a protectionist femocracy.

The particular emphases and orientations of feminism as a movement in Australia between 1890 and 1940 were crucially shaped by the historical context of British imperialism and relatedly its geographical location – 12,000 miles away from Europe. The masculinist character of colonial settlements led feminists to define their mission as one of protection, which encouraged them in turn to position themselves as mothers to all the vulnerable ones. In the condition of Aboriginal women and girls, feminists saw the condition of all women writ large. As colonists and nation builders – proud that their equality as citizens was granted within one year of the new nation-state's formation – Australian feminists placed much faith in the state as the guarantor of women's freedom. The state, they expected, would provide women with protection and independence from men. As colonists active in fashioning a new order of protectionist nation-state, Australian feminists were thus, like feminists elsewhere, complicit in, but also critical of, the imperial project of which they were part.[52]

[134]

Notes

1 Louisa Lawson, 'First public speech', 13 June 1891. Lawson family papers, Mitchell Library, Sydney, MS A1898.
2 Quoted in Katie Spearitt, 'The poverty of protection: women and marriage in colonial Queensland 1870–1900' (unpublished Honours thesis, History Department, University of Queensland, 1988), p. 58.
3 Anne Maree Collins, 'Woman or beast? Bestiality in Queensland, 1870–1949', *Hecate*, 17:1 (1991), pp. 36–50. Men charged with bestiality said they had made 'use of the [animal] as if it were a woman' (p. 38).
4 Quoted in Gail Griffith, 'The feminist club of New South Wales 1914–1970: a history of feminist politics in decline', *Hecate*, 14:1 (1988), pp. 56–67.
5 'Women and overseas settlement and some problems of government', British Commonwealth League Conference, 22–23 June 1926, Report. Fawcett Library, London.
6 Henry Reynolds, *Frontier Aborigines, Settlers and Land* (Sydney, Allen and Unwin, 1987), pp. 180, 189.
7 Abigail Belfrage, 'Citizenship and the vote at the time of Australian Federation, or How the white man shared his burden' (unpublished BA Hons, La Trobe University, 1993).
8 Susan Sheridan, *Along the Faultlines: Sex, Race and Nation in Australian Women's Writing 1880s–1930s* (Sydney, Allen and Unwin, 1995), chs 9 and 10.
9 Russell Ward, *The Australian Legend* (Melbourne, Oxford University Press, 1966).
10 Reynolds, *Frontier Aborigines*.
11 *Ibid.*, p. 52.
12 Maggie Humm (ed.), *Modern Feminisms: Political, Literary, Cultural* (New York, Columbia University Press, 1992), pp. 2, 7.
13 Judith Allen, *Rose Scott* (Melbourne, Oxford University Press, 1994), p. 96.
14 Marilyn Lake, 'Between Old World "Barbarism" and Stone Age "Primitivism": the double difference of the white Australian feminist' in Lake (ed.), *Australian Women: Contemporary Feminist Thought* (Melbourne, Oxford University Press, 1994).
15 Adele Perry, '"How influential a few men and a few families become": white women, sexuality, family and colonialism in nineteenth-century British Columbia', paper presented to the 18th International Congress of Historical Sciences, Montreal, August 1995. On white women's assumed authority as civilisers, see also Vron Ware, *Beyond the Pale: White Women, Racism and History* (London, Verso, 1992), and Napur Chaudhuri and Margaret Strobel (eds), *Western Women and Imperialism: Complicity and Resistance* (Bloomington, Indiana University Press, 1992).
16 British Commonwealth League Report, 22–23 June 1926. Fawcett Library, London.
17 Quoted in Spearitt, 'The poverty of protection', p. 26.
18 Quoted in Allen, *Rose Scott*, p. 134.
19 Marilyn Lake, 'The politics of respectability: identifying the masculinist context', *Historical Studies*, 86 (1986), pp. 116–31. Reprinted in Susan Magarey, Sue Rowley and Susan Sheridan (eds), *Debutante Nation: Feminism Contests the 1890s* (Sydney, Allen and Unwin, 1993).
20 Quoted in Spearitt, 'The poverty of protection', p. 39.
21 Barbara Caine, *Victorian Feminists* (Oxford, Oxford University Press, 1993), p. 36.
22 Louisa Lawson, 'First public speech'.
23 Rose Scott, 'Womanhood suffrage', speech notes, March 1898. Rose Scott Papers, Mitchell Library, Sydney, MS 38/38.
24 Irven, 'Sex hygiene', *Labor Call*, 19 June 1919, pp. 14–15.
25 Quoted in Spearitt, 'The poverty of protection', p. 31.
26 *Ibid.*, p. 25.
27 Lake, 'The politics of respectability', p. 118.
28 Caine, *Victorian Feminists*, p. 36.
29 On the reform of marriage see, for example, Patricia Grimshaw, 'Bessie Harrison Lee' in Marilyn Lake and Farley Kelly (eds), *Double Time: Women in Victoria, 150 Years* (Melbourne, Penguin, 1985), pp. 139–47; and on motherhood endowment,

Marilyn Lake, 'A revolution in the family: the challenge and contradictions of maternal citizenship' in Seth Koven and Sonya Michel (eds), *Mothers of a New World: Maternalist Politics and the Origin of Welfare States* (New York, Routledge, 1993), pp. 378–95.

30 Spearitt, 'The poverty of protection', p. 30.

31 Quoted in Judith Hicks Stiehm, 'The protected, the protector, the defender', *Women's Studies International Forum*, 5:3/4 (1982), p. 373.

32 Lawson, 'First public speech'.

33 Sheridan, *Along the Faultlines*, pp. 124–5.

34 Quoted in Marilyn Lake and Katie Holmes (eds), *Freedom Bound 2: Documents on Women in Modern Australia* (Sydney, Allen and Unwin, 1995), p. 7.

35 Fiona Paisley, 'Ideas have wings: white women challenge aboriginal policy 1920–1937' (unpublished PhD in Women's Studies, La Trobe University, 1995), ch. 4.

36 Mary Bennett reported in *West Australian* and *Daily Mail*, Rischbieth papers, National Library of Australia, Canberra, MS 2004/12/351.

37 Louisa Lawson, 'Scrapbook', Vol. I, Lawson papers, Mitchell Library, Sydney, MS A 1895.

38 Newspaper report of conference of Australian Federation of Women Voters, Rischbieth papers, National Library of Australia, Canberra, MS 2004/12/327. See also Marilyn Lake, 'Between Old World and New: feminist citizenship, nation and race – the destabilisation of identity' in Melanie Nolan and Caroline Daley (eds), *Suffrage and Beyond: International Feminist Perspectives* (Auckland, Auckland University Press, 1994), pp. 277–94.

39 Conference of Representatives of Missions, Societies and Associations interested in Welfare of Aborigines with Minister of Home Affairs following submission of Bleakley report, 12 April 1929. Rischbieth papers, National Library of Australia, Canberra, 2004/12/506.

40 'The Australian Aborigine woman: is she a slave?', Rischbieth papers, National Library of Australia, Canberra, MS 2004/12/314.

41 Mary Bennett, 'The Aboriginal mother in Western Australia in 1933', Rischbieth papers, National Library of Australia, Canberra, MS 2004/12/218.

42 Fiona Paisley, '"Don't tell England!" Women of empire campaign to change Aboriginal policy in Australia between the wars', *Lilith*, 8 (Summer 1993), pp. 139–52.

43 Mary Bennett to Bessie Rischbieth, 6 November 1934, Rischbieth papers, National Library of Australia, Canberra, MS 2004/12/64.

44 Mary Bennett to Bessie Rischbieth, April 1932, Rischbieth papers, National Library of Australia, Canberra, MS 2004/12/23.

45 Quoted in Lake and Holmes (eds), *Freedom Bound 2*, pp. 63–7.

46 Mary Bennett to Bessie Rischbieth, April 1932, Rischbieth papers, National Library of Australia, Canberra, MS 2004/7/62.

47 Bennett, 'The Aboriginal mother in Western Australia'.

48 Paisley, 'Ideas have wings', ch. 3.

49 Mary Bennett to Bessie Rischbieth, April 1932, Rischbieth papers, National Library of Australia, Canberra, MS 2004/7/62.

50 Bessie Rischbieth to Carrie Chapman Catt, 24 November 1924, Rischbieth papers, National Library of Australia, Canberra, MS 2004/7/62.

51 Lilian Locke-Burns, 'State provision for mother and child', *Labor Call*, 26 June 1919, p. 1.

52 Chaudhuri and Strobel, 'Introduction' in *Western Women and Imperialism*.

CHAPTER SIX

Taking liberties: enslaved women and anti-slavery in the Caribbean

Hilary McD. Beckles

'My honoured master, I hope you will pardon the liberty your slave has taken in addressing you on a subject which I hope may not give you the least displeasure or offense': thus began a letter dated Barbados 1804 from Jenny Lane, an enslaved creole black woman, addressed to Thomas Lane, her owner. The text of Jenny's letter contains a detailed proposal for the negotiation of her freedom. From Newton Plantation in the southern parish of the island colony, this correspondence, constructed in a language of submission, but bearing the ideology of self-liberation, reached its destination in the City of London through much the same channels as monthly reports from the estate manager concerning the governance of slaves. It was ironical, Thomas Lane thought, that Jenny's letter arrived at the same time as a routine correspondence from Mr Wood, his estate manager, indicating that ill-discipline and turbulence among the slaves necessitated the strict application of laws designed for their suppression.[1]

While such letters are rare, the abundance of evidence that documents women's efforts at negotiating terms of personal freedom stands in contrast to the paucity that details their direct engagement in the bloody warfare that typified the relations between enslaved blacks and whites in the Caribbean. The archives yield this much about sex, race and anti-slavery politics. Reflecting notions derived from this reading of the evidence, Morrissey asserts: 'women seldom exercised active leadership in Caribbean slave revolts. We have tended lately, therefore, to focus on their participation in indirect forms of protest.'[2] In developing this argument, she concluded:

> Women slaves did not generally fulfill prominent leadership roles in traditionally understood vehicles for revolt, that is, Maroon Communities and rebel movements. They did, however, fill subsidiary positions and give many kinds of support to male rebels. Female insurgency may have sometimes been expressed in malingering and in the refusal to conceive

and bear children. But evidence of these practices is limited, and their incidence is at odds with other more fully documented tendencies, including physiologically based female subfecundity and high levels of work productivity.[3]

The questions that follow from this statement are many. What is the political significance of an argument which says that physical combat in war should be privileged above broad-based ideological preparation? Why should the male warriors be centred and the non-violent protests of women that harnessed and directed anti-slavery politics be peripheralised? What is the influence of gender representation on anti-slavery historiography?

The search for answers to these questions should begin by recognising that during slavery the right to life and social liberty was denied blacks, not on the basis of gender, but by the race inequities of colonial culture. Differences in life experiences among males and females, however, served to demonstrate how gender constructions assisted in the promotion and maintenance of social and material inequalities. White males, who considered the project of colonialism their conquistadorial creation, believed that the system of slavery devised by them was in part the legitimate outcome of their military conquest of black males in Africa. While the initial labour preference at the frontier was for males, small numbers of black women entered the colonies in the formative stage. It was immediately recognised, however, that under favourable conditions the natural reproduction of slavery was an alternative to slave trading; also, that by securing females on a systematic basis, slave managers could meet social demands of favoured male slaves.

At two levels, then, black women were targeted by the socio-economic logic of the plantation enterprise. Their integration into this patriarchal agrarian world – of white and black males – was an entry into a gender-order that represented them as social objects of competing masculinities. On encountering the shared design of hegemonic (white) and marginalised (black) masculinities to secure their subordination within the gender-order, enslaved black women sought to develop autonomous identities by resisting oppressive ideological and institutional sources of power. But as the slave system expanded and matured, the black woman occupied positions at its centre that were of critical social and economic importance. Its survival depended upon her enslavement; as a result her survival struggle assumed more complex dimensions than that of her male counterpart whose gender ideologies she also contested.

Gender, slavery and the battle over babies

The gender conception of the enslaved black woman as the seed of unfreedom resided at the core of the meaning and social reality of slavery. Her position was ideologically constructed and socially enforced by the power of a white, male slave-owning patriarchy that understood a great deal about ideological representation, social authority and economic accumulation. Slavery was designed as a system of social relations and economic accumulation that could be self-sustained through inheritance. In order to offer the white community full immunity from the process of enslavement, patriarchy alienated the white female from the capability of producing offspring who could inherit the status of slavery. The white women were not, and indeed could not be, constructed in this way. The first generations of white women (mostly indentured servants) were imported to the colonies to perform manual labour. There was an agreement on both sides to the contract that servitude was temporary and certainly not hereditary. Slavery meant enforced labour for life and control over the physical self of the slave during non-labouring periods; it was as much about the slave's total accountability for 'self' as it was about the slave owner's legal right to demand labour. This, in part, is why Mary Prince, the West Indian ex-slave, wrote that her resistance to slavery had much to do with the denial of a right to time for 'herself'.[4]

For many blacks the unacceptability of slavery as a violently enforced pattern of relations was most acutely felt when 'free' time was rejected and their total time subjected to the authority and interest of enslavers. This is why the role of gender in an understanding of individuals' relationship to their 'body' is critical in the study of slavery. With the enslaved woman the matter of 'the body' created a special set of circumstances that centred her sex within the slave owner's gender constructions of slavery. The notion of slavery as the 'using up' of the body – day and night – had clearly differentiated sex and gender implications. The exploration of this issue should speak directly to an analysis of female slavery. It draws attention to the specific ways in which the experiences of enslaved women differed from those of men, how gender was constructed and reproduced, and how it ultimately determined the peculiar patterns and forms of anti-slavery responses.

Chattel slavery, the dominant social institution, was thoroughly gendered in its designs and functions. Throughout the Americas, European enslavers decreed that the status of an infant be derived from that of the mother. Black children were born into a social relation that was predetermined by the status of their mothers. It had absolutely nothing to do with the status of the father. Children fathered by free black men or white men were born into slavery once their mothers were slaves. Since white women, by virtue of their race, were not enslaved, their children under all paternal circumstances were born into freedom. Throughout the West Indies white women produced free-born children with enslaved men, as well as free black and free coloured men. Slavery, therefore, as a socio-legal status, depended to a considerable extent for its reproduction upon the fertility of the enslaved black woman. She was the seed, in a true sense, of the fruit of slavery, while the white woman was constitutionally alienated from slavery and represented the embodiment and conveyor of social freedom.

The entire enterprise of slavery, therefore, was organised upon the basis of race and sex, with considerable importance for the (re)production of gender ideologies and social representations. It follows that the integration of the enslaved woman into the systems of socio-economic and ideological production was rather different from that of the enslaved man – and with important far-reaching implications. Enslaved men certainly possessed the distinct privilege of being able to father free-born children. No attempt should be made to minimise the importance of this issue. Rather, it should be recognised that within the context of slave societies the issue of freedom loomed large as the most aggressively pursued, and protected, social commodity. But more importantly, the woman was perceived as a flexible and versatile investment with several streams of social, economic and psychological returns.[5]

It follows, furthermore, that enslaved women were structurally positioned and ideologically gendered to have unique experiences. A common survival response from them was to develop and maintain a network of attitudes and actions that countered efforts at the moral and political legitimation of their relationship to the system. The millions of black women who were bought and, despite resistance in Africa and the middle passage, brought to the colonies, as well as those delivered on plantations by 'enchained wombs', had set their minds against slavery. What was left to be done was to identify and determine terms of endurance consistent with survival. There were many ways to negotiate these terms, which accounted for the diverse personality types within slave villages and the overall chronic and endemic instability of the system. For this reason there was nothing peculiar about Jenny's letter or phenomenal about the two slave women in the British Virgin Islands who, in 1793, took a cutlass and severed a hand in protest against enslavement. That this case became famous in Britain speaks more to the consciousness of the imperial community than it does about the nature of women's anti-slavery attitudes.[6]

The severing of the hand that was expected to work and feed the young suggests, therefore, a complex set of relations between resistance to the labour regime and labour reproduction. It makes no sense to negate the anti-slavery importance of refusal in the area of fecundity, fertility and reproduction. Throughout the slavery period evidence indicates that enslaved women had extended their resistance network into bio-social zones associated with maternity. Child-bearing became politicised in ways that tore and tortured enslaved women to a degree that historians may never comprehend. An examination of the changing background to slave owners' natal policy, and the diverse responses of enslaved women, is therefore necessary in order to understand the battle over babies that informed women's anti-slavery.

From the mid eighteenth century, when slave prices in the British West Indies started a steady upward climb, the matter of slave 'treatment' assumed enlarged proportions among slave owners. Reacting partly to increasingly effective anti-slave-trade politics, managerial emphasis shifted slowly from 'buying' to 'breeding' as a labour supply strategy. West Indian societies entered, after the 1770s, a phase of social reform that has been described as the 'age of amelioration'. In economic terms, amelioration was no more than a policy which suggested that marginal benefits could be derived from investing the money that would have been spent on buying new slaves in a maintenance programme for existing slaves. An objective of amelioration was to create for women a pro-natalist environment in order to stimulate procreation. It entailed less work and better nutrition for pregnant and lactating women, as well as the availability of child care facilities. In addition, money was offered to women for delivering healthy children; slave midwives were offered more money than mothers, an indication of slave owners' perception of their prime responsibility for high infant mortality rates on estates.[7]

Natural reproduction, rather than importation, suggested the targeting of slave women's fertility. The systematic offering of natal incentive to women meant that slave owners considered it possible to influence the socio-sexual behaviour of enslaved women. Throughout the seventeenth century and early eighteenth century, plantation managers reported their inability to explain satisfactorily low birth rates and high infant mortality rates. Most were suspicious that slave women were applying 'unnatural' brakes upon the reproductive process. They did not know how it was done, and they speculated. The widespread belief, however, was that it was part of an anti-slavery strategy that had become endemic. By declaring gynaecological warfare upon slavery, enslaved women were accused of engaging in a most effective form of resistance.

The tragic demographic performance of slave populations up to the end of the eighteenth century in Jamaica, Barbados and the Leeward Islands cannot be explained without some understanding of these matters. By the 1780s, Barbadian slave owners, taking the lead in an effort to break this resistance, and win the baby war, had put in place the most comprehensive and far-reaching package for the encouragement of pregnant and lactating mothers. In addition to offering financial and material incentives to slave women to produce healthy children, they invested in the promotion of institutional contexts, such as access to family life, Christian marriage and labour reduction. By 1800, Barbados, unlike its neighbours, was experiencing sustained natural growth among slaves. Slave owners got their babies, and boasted in 1807 when slave trading was illegalised, that they feared having too many. Slave women also got, finally, part of what they wanted: a social and material environment which seemed less hostile to child-bearing, parenting, family and domesticity.[8]

Specific patterns of anti-slavery politics emanated from these changing forms of engagement with the slave system. Undoubtedly, some women appeared broken psychologically by the overwhelming power of slave owners.[9] Such women expressed patterns of behaviour that have been described as psychotic on account of an overt display of seemingly mindless subservience. Referred to as 'Quasheba', the female version of 'Quashee' (or Sambo), this gendered personality type could be transformed suddenly into an agent bearing unexpected social rage. Such cases can be found in abundance throughout plantation documents. In many instances slave owners would make reference to the general kindness shown the female and her positive response, before describing their shock and dismay at the violent action taken.[10] A common conclusion drawn by slave owners in these circumstances was that the loyalty and subservience projected by gender representations of slave women did not conform to social reality, which made for considerable insecurity in everyday life.[11]

Quasheba, then, who wet-nursed and raised her owner's children, was never fully trusted. She was unpredictable, however, not only in relations with her owners, but also with the black community. We see evidence of this in the judicial records when slaves appear before the criminal (in)justice system. The records of the 1736 Antigua slave plot speak to this issue. Philida, the sister of Tomboy, the alleged leader of the conspiracy, was arrested and charged with being a leading *provocateur*. She was accused of publicly making 'some virulent expressions ... upon her brother's account', an action which ran counter to her owner's perception of her character. It was also Philida, however, who allegedly provided the intelligence to her master that led to the disclosure of the rebel leadership. Her testimony indicates that she was present at the meeting when plans were designed and discussed, and that other women, most notably Obbah and 'Old Queen', also participated in leadership activity. Obbah, it was intimated, performed traditional Akan ritual functions designed to enhance secrecy and solidarity among the rebels. But it was Philida, the rebel, who was accused of divulging the information leading to the discovery of leaders.[12]

From 'rebel women' to 'natural rebels': interpreting women's resistance

Much has been said about the supportive roles that were assigned to women in the mobilisation of culture as a force in resistance politics. Bush maintains that 'women were in the vanguard of the cultural resistance to slavery which helped individuals survive the slave experience'. For her, it 'was this cultural strength, however, which helped women resist the system in their more "public" lives as workers'. In the case of the 1736 Antigua plot, the evidence indicates that 'Old Queen' may have assumed the role of a traditional Akan queen mother who held tremendous political influence in the slave yard. Certainly, this was the case with the Jamaica conspiracy of 1760 in which rebels declared their intention to appoint Abena, the Akan slave, as 'Queen of Kingston'. The relation between the ritual politics of queen mothers and the more precise roles of magico-religious leaders, the voodoo priestess in particular, is not always clear. But the quest for loyalty, as an enhancer of discipline and secrecy, was often said to be a role assigned to 'spirit mothers' whose claim to direct access to ancestral worlds was recognised and respected within slave communities. Gautier has shown, for example, that their knowledge and practice of 'le Vaudou' fortified slave troops in the successful Saint Dominique revolution.[13]

The economic culture retained by Africans in the Caribbean was also used for resistance strategies in which women gained considerable social visibility and provided consistent leadership. In West African societies women were dominant in the small-scale internal marketing of foodstuffs. Despite enslavement in the New World, this culture persisted. Huckstering of foodstuffs on street corners, in markets, and from house to house, engaged the energies of slave women in spite of hostile legislative opposition. Slave hucksters grew crops, bought and sold foodstuffs, appropriated goods from plantation stores for resale, bartered their food allowances for other goods and services, in the promotion of commercial activities. The attempted abolition of the slave huckster's market in Antigua in 1831 sparked riotous behaviour by women slaves. Earlier, the Barbadian slave owners, recognising the folly of police and legislative action in the face of such determination, had resorted to the issuing of licences as the principal method of control and regulation.[14]

Often, this rebellious commercial culture was linked to a complex network of social relationships on the estates. A case illustration of women slaves' determination to reject and restructure the pattern of distribution of estate wealth can be extracted from events on the Newton Plantation in Barbados between 1795 and 1797.[15] During this time the manager, Mr Wood, made several references to slaves' claim to a more equitable share of plantation produce. Like his predecessor, Mr Yard, Wood documents the aggressive and rebellious attitudes of slave women who appropriated 'rum, sugar, corn, and everything else which lay at their mercy'. Betsy, her sister Dolly, and their mother, Old Doll, considered the seizure of goods as just reward for the family's performance of special social services to estate management. Dolly had been Yard's mistress for many years before he was dismissed by the estate attorney. So successful were these women in their appropriations that Betsy's husband, a free black huckster, 'through these connections', was 'supplied plentifully with everything', and Old Doll's home, according to Wood, was a 'perfect out-shop for dry goods, rum, sugar, and other commodities'.[16]

Such issues raise the question of women's invisibility within historical records, a matter that has been considerably overstated. Describing the enslaved woman as essentially a 'submerged mother', Brathwaite locates her 'invisibility' within the 'archival material' and suggests that it is but an 'aspect of that general invisibility which haunts [black history]'.[17] For him, the slave woman, being black and female, suffered a 'double invisibility' which in turn promoted a historiography of neglect. There is, however, a significant conceptual and empirical problem to be tackled with respect to the 'invisibility thesis'. It has to do with the fact that the evidence historians have (over!)used as base lines for social history narratives – deeds, wills, manumission lists, diaries, plantation accounts, managers' reports, etc. – says considerably more about enslaved women than it does about enslaved men.

This characteristic of the evidence has to do with the female-centred nature of the slave system, particularly its concern with their maternity and fertility, the management of white households, and the socio-sexual expression of patriarchal power and ideology. More is recorded about slave mothers than slave fathers; more was said about female slave lovers of white males than about male slave lovers of white women. Certainly, in this last regard, enslaved men have been rendered fully invisible, though partly, it should be said, for their own safety. The general intimacy of slave women with the empowered agents of the colonial world – white male and female – placed them at the top of the documentary queue. In these records women appear in diverse social actions other than those related to labour and crime. On the whole the records yield a relatively greater visibility for enslaved women.

During the 1970s, Lucille Mair, working with Jamaican records, initiated a research project that asked some of these questions about the condition and nature of West Indian historiography and archives. On reflection, it now seems clear that the manner in which she asked these questions was an indication of the issues facing professional historians at that time in the West Indies. The anti-colonial movement had called upon historians to document and interpret the traditions of struggle against colonial domination, particularly with respect to the relatively longer and more determining period of slavery. Male historians had played prominent leadership roles in the anti-colonial labour movement, and as politicians they presented interpretations of their own actions that were rooted conceptually within the traditions of anti-slavery struggles. Newly recreated heroes of anti-colonialism were those who had led slave revolts and organised anti-slavery maroon communities.

A principal task of Lucille Mair's was to add women to the historical narrative, and to locate their anti-slavery contributions firmly within the vanguard of the political project of nation-building. Another was to challenge academics to question disciplinary and gender biases, and to approach archives with greater ideological sensitivity. The first aspect of Mair's concerns produced a body of literature on women's anti-slavery actions that resulted in a political promotion of the notion of the 'rebel woman'.[18] This figure was the quintessential anti-slavery matriarch who organised slave communities and directed their political postures with respect to survival options. Nanny, leader of an early-eighteenth-century Jamaican maroon band, took pride of place in this discourse, and now enjoys the constitutional status in Jamaica of a national heroine.

In Barbados, Nanny Grigg, a principal conceptualiser and ideologue of the 1816 slave rebellion, gained historiographical prominence. The records never hid the fact that Grigg was a central figure in the rebellion. They presented her as the person who conveyed news of developments in the Haitian revolution to other slaves, and successfully propagandised a cadre of enslaved males around its ideas and actions. Both Nanny of the Maroons and Nanny Grigg constituted matriarchal leadership within the revolutionary tradition of anti-slavery. They organised men and minds for violent anti-slavery warfare. Nanny of the Maroons led an army of enslaved men and women against British imperial soldiers and planter militia forces. Robert, a slave giving evidence before the committee established by the Barbados government to investigate the causes and nature of the rebellion, stated that Nanny Grigg told slaves on the estate that 'they were all damned fools to work, for that she would not, as freedom they were sure to get', and that the way to get it was 'to set fire, as that was the way they did it in St. Domingo'.[19] After four days of widespread arson and bloody rebellion the slaves were defeated. Nanny Grigg and 'near a thousand' slaves lost their lives in the military contest and subsequent executions carried out by imperial soldiers and planter militias.

During the 1980s the concept of the 'rebel woman' was placed within a wider context that recognised rebelliousness in different forms and shapes, ranging from collective non-violent protest to individual negotiation and compromise. In an assessment of the 'organs of discontent' on West Indian slave plantations, Dirks argued that 'when discontent arose, it was usually the female gang members who complained the loudest because everyone knew that they were less likely to be flogged than men. It earned women the reputation for being the instruments of instability and the "more unmanageable element of the work force".' While the evidence does not come down in favour of women's inequality under the whip, it does indicate a prominence for women in the creation of turmoil and the articulation of protest on plantations. Jacob Belgrave, for example, the mulatto owner of a large Barbados sugar plantation, told the authorities that shortly before the April 1816 slave revolt, he was verbally abused by a gang of slave women who alleged that he was opposed to the British parliament taking steps towards the abolition of slavery. During the revolt his estate was singled out for special treatment. He claimed property destruction of £6,720, the third highest in the island, from a total of 184 damaged estates.[20]

In this regard, Bush's work has done much to extend the parameters of the historiographic framework. In a series of essays, the themes of which occupy the empirical core of a subsequent monograph on enslaved women in the Caribbean, she demonstrated the fluidity in forms of women's struggles, and the diversity of actions and attitudes that constituted anti-slavery. Enslaved women, Bush showed, promoted a culture of intransigence in relation to work, ran away from owners, terrorised white households with chemical concoctions, refused to procreate at levels expected, insisted upon participation in the market economy as hucksters, slept with white men in order to better their material and social condition, and did whatever else was necessary in order to minimise the degree of their unfreedom. Through such 'channels', Bush states, 'women helped to generate and sustain the general spirit of resistance'.[21]

A common reaction to Bush's notion that the diversity of women's reactions to enslavement constitutes 'channels' through which a 'spirit of resistance' was fostered, is that her definition of resistance is weakened by excessive elasticity, and has lost sight of what constitutes 'political' action. Much can be said about the question of elasticity in the conception of women's anti-slavery action, especially in reaction to a feminist and post-modern context in which the 'personal' is considered the core of the 'political'. Slaves' daily negotiation for betterment, which often involved both sexual submission and refusal, as well as verbal protest, has had to struggle to find a place within the pantheon of anti-slavery activity traditionally occupied by acts of violent rebellion and marronage. The implications of this process of redefinition for an interpretation of women's social history are obviously important. In a seminal essay published in 1973 on day-to-day resistance, Monica Schuler effectively destabilised traditional definitions and perceptions of resistance. Her intentions were not guided by considerations of writing feminist or gender history, but were narrowly empirical in that she sought to list and legitimise non-violent protest actions, and a wide range of personal refusals, as acts that undermined and weakened the slave system.[22]

Schuler provided a methodological opening for a more sophisticated assessment of the range and specificity of women's reaction to enslavement. It became possible, as a result, for Bush to argue that the slave family was the crucible for resistance. Bush was keen to demonstrate that the slave family was more than a locus of conspiracy, but by virtue of its overwhelming matrifocal nature, constituted a social agency that was propelled and directed by a distinct female consciousness. Families, then, and by extension, communities, expected women to lead as ideologues – whether in the forms of 'spirit mothers', through whom ancestors speak, or queen mothers, as organisers of more secular action. The suppression of fertility by the use of abortifacients and infanticide, and the search for freedom by manumission through social and sexual intimacy with whites, all speak to the same point that actions designed to prevent the perpetuation of slavery should be considered as anti-slavery.

The concern remains that such a redefinition is tantamount to an unnecessary kicking open of the barn door. It is assumed that the specifics of women's resistance can be identified without stretching the understanding of anti-slavery to include social behaviours that were not overtly 'political' in terms of direct challenges to power and authority. Morrissey, for example, has called for a 'more critical

perspective', but accepts as common sense that slave women's commitment to kith and kin 'in specific ways contributed to tensions and
contradictions in slavery' that oftentimes drove women to kill, burn
and plunder.[23] The other side of this commitment and contradiction,
she acknowledges, drove many women to use sexuality in the pursuit
of freedom by manumission.

Among enslaved women, brown-skinned black women and mixed-
race (or coloured) women were more successful in extracting socio-
economic benefits – and legal freedom – from propertied white males
and females. Some slave women gained legal freedom through the
route of the overlapping roles of prostitution and concubinage. In these
ways, they earned the necessary money to effect their manumission,
or came in contact with clients who were prepared to assist them in
doing so. Legal freedom, however, did not always result in a distancing
from these roles. It was, therefore, very common to find freed women
continuing as prostitutes and mistresses. In 1811, the Rector of the St
Michael Parish Church in Barbados, commenting on the 'very rapid'
increase in the number of slaves freed by whites since 1802, suggested
that 'out of every four at least three' were 'females who obtained that
privilege by becoming favorites of white men'. He was supported by
Joseph Husbands, an abolitionist campaigner, who claimed that in
1831: 'By far the greater number of free colored persons in Barbados
have either obtained their freedom by their own prostitution, or
claimed it under some of their female ancestors who in like manner
obtained it and have transmitted it to the descendants.'[24]

Since the mid eighteenth century, West Indian legislators seemed
determined to restrain white males from manumitting their black and
coloured 'favorites'. In 1739, the manumission fee in Barbados had
been legally set at £50 plus an annuity of £4 local currency; the annuity was insisted upon by poor law officials as one way to prevent slave
owners from freeing old and infirm persons who could not reasonably
be expected to earn their subsistence. In 1774, a bill was introduced
into the Assembly aimed at curtailing the number of females being
manumitted. It was designed to raise the manumission fee to £100,
but was rejected on the grounds that slave owners should not be
deprived of the right to assist the 'most deserving part' of their slaves
– 'the females who have generally recommended themselves to our
"kindest notice"'.[25] The bill was defeated by a vote of eleven to five;
opposition was led by Sir John Gay Alleyne, who argued that female
slaves who gave their loyalty, love and service to masters should not
be denied the opportunity to gain freedom. Barbadians debated the
subject again in 1801, following Governor Seaforth's proposed bill to
limit female slave manumission, and to ensure that proper provisions

[148]

were made by slave owners for their manumitted slaves. The bill became law and raised the manumission fee to £300 for females and £200 for males. Slave women continued to be freed in significantly larger numbers than men for the rest of the slavery period.

The socio-economic integration of slave women into the plantation system, therefore, allowed for their use at various points along the circuit of capital accumulation. Their contribution to the overall wealth creation process of slave owners involved not only their roles as labourers, and reproducers of labour, but also as suppliers of socio-sexual services. The sex industry was an important part of the urban economy, and the relations of slavery, protected by slave codes, created societal conditions under which the maximum benefits offered by property ownership in humans accrued to slave owners. The use of slave women as prostitutes, therefore, was another way in which slave owners extracted surplus value and emphasised their status as colonial masters.

The notion of a 'rebel woman', then, seems to narrow the conceptual possibilities with respect to the understanding of women's anti-slavery activities. It speaks directly to categories of formal political struggles, rather than seeking to disclose insights into the processes through which individual women made social space in order to enjoy and endure the results of the liberties they took. Analytically, it is static and conceals the importance of diverse social experience and personal reactions in the shaping of heterogeneous anti-slavery mentalities. Brathwaite took the first step towards a critique of the concept of the 'rebel woman' as an organising category in anti-slavery discourse when he stated with respect to the multi-layered interface of slave women with the slave system: 'The whole fact of slavery affected the woman in such ways that she began to conceive of the notion of liberation naturally (liberation for the slave first of all, and secondly, at the same time, liberation of herself).'[26] Brathwaite's argument, furthermore, is that since slavery penetrated, and integrated into production, the 'inner worlds' of the woman – commodifying her maternity and sexuality – she resisted enslavement instinctively or 'naturally'.

Recognising the one-dimensionality and framed image derived from the 'rebel woman' concept, this author proceeded to confer on his book on female slavery in Barbados the title *Natural Rebels*.[27] In this text it is argued that the heterogeneity of women's actions was probably the most outstanding characteristic of their anti-slavery resistance. This position emerged from the general observation that women's vision of survival and protection of a sense of self-worth defined and shaped their resistance to everyday life which was problematised by the demands of slavery upon all spheres of existence – work, sexual relations, leisure activity and family life. The 'natural rebel' may not have been a public heroine or martyr in the way that the 'rebel woman' gained recognition. Like Jenny, who wrote letters pleading for freedom, she could have been protecting her sexuality from a rapist overseer; she could have been Quashebah, the slave at Codrington estate in Barbados, who ran away in August, September and December 1775, August 1776, January 1777 and September 1784, before she was finally confined to the stocks.[28] She could also have been Nanny of the Maroons, whose preference for death over slavery impressed followers and foes alike.

The difficulty, however, with the concept of the 'natural rebel' is that perceptions of human behaviour as 'natural' are problematic in so far as they negate the potency of cultural and environmental forces. Women's behaviour is particularly vulnerable to the ideological charge that actions emanate from some place other than the cerebral – an assertion identified with a well-known representation of women by a hostile patriarchy. The term is used in this context, however, not with any specific reference to biological determination, but in relation to a cultural proclivity by enslaved women to consciously reject and resist enforced access by slave owners to their sexuality.

Neglected aspects of slave women's resistance: relations with black men and white women

It follows, then, that an important but grossly neglected aspect of women's resistance had to do with their unequal and often unjust relation to slave men within their own communities. This point should be understood and given weight within women's anti-slavery experiences. The white male bought, sold and degraded the black woman. In the process he placed her in a social position to be further degraded and exploited by the black male, who frequently targeted her as an object with which to act out a strategy for the restoration of his crippled and dysfunctional masculinity. The 'natural rebel', on occasions, had to resist the tyranny of enslaved black men with the same degree of tenacity and may have experienced the struggle against slavery as an expedition against tyrannical male power. Such struggles were not confined to issues of sexuality, but concerned access to material resources, career opportunities and domestic arrangements.

Male slaves who were assigned privileged occupations within the production system, such as drivers, overseers and artisans, were likely to use their authority against slave women. Stedman gave an example from eighteenth-century Surinam in which a young slave girl was severely punished by a black overseer for resisting his sexual advances. Thomas Thistlewood's eighteenth-century Jamaican Diary contains references to spousal abuse by slave men and other acts of male aggression against women. 'Courrir les filles' (girl-hunting) was a pastime among male slaves in Saint Dominique, which sometimes resulted in the rape and kidnapping of women on neighbouring and distant estates. In addition, the kidnapping of women by maroon men in order to find wives and labourers figured prominently in the social history of all colonies that harboured maroon communities.[29]

Little is known of the life-experiences of slave women who were integrated into the polygynous households of elite male slaves. In maroon communities especially, women, particularly those kidnapped from the estates, performed the arduous agricultural duties. The internal relations of maroon communities have not been adequately studied for the slavery period, and it remains difficult to speak of the perceptions of these women about their social conditions. It is entirely possible, however, that some maroon women experienced at the hands of black men a continuation of the kinds of occupational and resource discrimination that typified enslavement on the plantations.

It should be emphasised, argues Moitt, 'that the structure of plantation society was sexist and that sexism was reflected in the organisation of labour'. The slave women's plight, he suggests, 'resulted largely from patriarchy and the sexist orientation of Caribbean slave plantation society which put them into structural slots that had no bearing on their abilities. This meant', he concludes, 'that women were not permitted to move into roles traditionally ascribed to [black] males.' Slave owners consistently discriminated against slave women in the allocation of access to skilled professions, and they were never allowed to hold the principal offices of head driver and overseer.[30] Victor Schoelcher, the French anti-slavery campaigner of the early nineteenth century, explained the entrapment of most women slaves in the field gangs of Martinique as follows:

> It is often the case in the field gangs that there are more women than men. This is how it can be explained. A plantation is, in itself, a small village. As it is usually established a considerable distance from major centres, it must provide of all its needs ... masons and blacksmiths as well as animal watchmen. All the apprentices who are destined to replace them are now in the field gangs (the slave driver included), and this diminishes the male population available for field work.[31]

In the sugar factories women were not trained as boilers and distillers – prestigious, high technology tasks. Slave women, then, experienced the male slave labour aristocracy as representing another level of male authority which was not necessarily supportive of their own sense of freedom and betterment.

Another neglected area has been the anti-slavery culture of black women as it relates specifically to slave-owning white females. White women, we now know, may have owned and managed as many as 25 per cent of Caribbean slaves, with a greater concentration of owner-ship in towns. We know from the slave registration records for the British colonies that during the last decades of slavery white women owned more female than male slaves. The extensive female ownership of slaves in towns was reflected in the unusually high proportion of females in the urban slave population. These records show that in Bridgetown in 1817 the sex ratio (males per 100 females) of slaves belonging to males was more than double that for female slave owners. The sex ratio of slaves belonging to males was 111, and for slaves belonging to females 49. For Berbice, in the Guianas, the slaves owned by males had a sex ratio of 132, while those owned by females had a ratio of only 81.[32]

From these data the image that emerges of the white female slave owner is that she was generally urban, in possession of less than ten slaves, the majority of whom were female. It is reasonable, then, to argue that any conceptualisation of female slavery, particularly as it relates to black women's anti-slavery activities, should proceed with a discussion of white women as principal slave owners. The perception of black women resisting their enslavement by white women poses a number of interesting questions for the discourse on the relations between race, sex, class and gender. It also highlights another set of special and unique aspects to women's resistance that has eluded scholars of anti-slavery.

Brathwaite suggests that we should begin by recognising how and why the attitudes and activities of propertied white women appeared to be mainly in the service of the establishment. How else to begin an explanation of their inability or unwillingness to offer a public politi-cal critique of slavery? Mair tells us that the white woman was socialised as the 'second sex', with the whole thrust of her upbringing designed to make her 'pretty polly, pretty parrot'. Unlike her British counterpart, she launched no missiles on behalf of anti-slavery as she was conditioned 'to rock the cradle, not the boat'.[33] Slave women, therefore, had no reason to see in their white mistress a source of ame-lioration or freedom. The available manumission records for colonies show that white males were by far the most frequent liberators of slaves. Male visitors to the colonies were consistent in reporting what Frederick Bayley did in 1833: 'female owners are more cruel than male; their revenge is more durable and their methods of punishment more refined, particularly towards slaves of their own sex'.[34] Turnbull's account of the ideas of a Cuban creole slave mistress supports this stereotyped opinion. With respect to her attitudes to domestic slaves he states:

> The mistress of many a great family in Havana will not scruple to tell you that such is the proneness of her people [domestics] to vice and idleness, she finds it necessary to send one or more of them once a month to the whipping post, not so much on account of any positive delinquency, as because without these periodical advertisements the whole family would become unmanageable, and the master and mistress would lose their authority.[35]

The daily resistance of Elizabeth Fenwick's female slaves to her authority may be indicative of the contest of race, sex, class and gender. Her letters from Barbados to Mary Hays in Britain between 1814 and 1822 detail this resistance. As a recently arrived British immigrant, she recognised the need to own slaves in order to achieve accumulation objectives, but her principal problem with respect to comfortable adjustment to colonial society sprang from the anti-slavery attitude of her domestics. They refused to work, lied, stole, ignored instructions and showed contempt for her authority. While she did not report being in fear for her life, her letters indicate the extent to which her female slaves sought to destroy whatever ambition she may have had about being an effective slave manager. They caused her 'endless trouble and vexation', refused to respond to any 'gentle and kindly impulses', and undermined any notion she cherished about Barbados as a 'paradise'. Her solution was to sell the females and purchase male slaves.[36]

Gender and anti-slavery

Jenny's letter, then, when placed within the dominant historiographic tradition, symbolised a rather complex pattern of representations. Some of these were constructed before and during her own lifetime and persist beyond the parameters of the slavery epoch. Concepts of gender are buried but skin-deep within her words, which were arranged in patterns of meaning indicative of a particular representation of the feminine experience, though concerning matters that had nothing whatsoever to do with sex or gender. It may seem altogether female, for example, within the dominant system of gender representation, for a slave to enquire about the health and well-being of a master and mistress – and their 'good' children – just to complete the enquiry with a request for freedom from their benevolence. There was no cutlass, musket or bloodshed; only determination in the sound of gentle words that managed, in this case, to throw Mr Lane, her owner, into a rage which he knew, ultimately, was of no value in the stern face of a well-reasoned claim to freedom.

Jenny's history is offered as a window through which to view the diverse experiences of different types of enslaved black women, and it is presented in order to illustrate how gender operated through the specific institutional forms of West Indian slave society. The objective of this approach is to demonstrate that while women's and gender history were divergent methodologically, they share and embrace a common end – how to document and offer historical explanation for the dynamic interactivity between lived experiences and ideological representations at specified moments. How gender worked to construct black and white masculinities, and the experiences of males in slavery are necessary prerequisites for an understanding of the experiences of enslaved women. One does not have to travel very far into the literature to encounter signposts which indicate, with respect to anti-slavery, activity, that different vehicles were often used by enslaved men and women. If female slaves expressed a more complex and contradictory set of responses to their enslavement than men, it had to do with the more diverse and dynamic patterns of female gender representations, and the multi-layered challenges of black women in their private and public lives. If many women acquiesce in the face of slave-owner power, producing the smiling, subservient but unstable, Quasheba personality type, and her male counterparts have been historiographically indicted for the capitulation that produced the stereotyped Quashee, only a merging of gender and women's history can give us the insights needed to write the social history of slavery.

Methodological connectivity can be discerned, it seems, when the slaves are allowed to speak for themselves. Chains apart, the voices of slaves – and ex-slaves – were often made vague by the very writers who committed their thoughts to print. It is necessary, however, even in such difficult circumstances, to 'feel' the texture, and hear the tone, of their indirect or engineered voices. Much can be made, for example, of the autobiographical record of Mary Prince as an instrument of literary representation. She 'cared' for the children of a mistress and valued her own 'womanness' in the process. The force of her self-understanding as a woman ran contrary to that of her mistress, who had her 'horsewhipped' for marrying without permission.

Mary Prince did much to be a loyal and 'good' slave while at the same time confronting her mistress with the idea that 'to be free is very sweet'. White people, she wrote, all had their 'liberty', and 'that's just what we want'. 'Freedom' and 'liberty' are words that appear like monuments on the pages of her text.[37] It is necessary, then, to excavate the foundations of these 'structures' for the full context of social attitudes and behaviour. In the case of enslaved women it is critical to begin the dig at the centre and work outwards. The centre of which I speak deals with the commodification of their 'inner world' and natural resistance to it, a dynamic that is only now coming in clear focus for historians of anti-slavery ideology and action.

Notes

1 Jenny Lane to Thomas Lane, 9 August, 1804, Newton Papers M.523/579, Senate House Library, London University. Jenny obtained her freedom, and in 1813 petitioned Thomas Lane for the emancipation of her sons, Robert, 26, a joiner, and Henry, 24, a tailor; Jenny Lane to Thomas Lane, 4 March, 1813, M.523/690.

2 Marrietta Morrissey, *Slave Women in the New World: Gender Stratification in the Caribbean* (Lawrence, University Press of Kansas, 1989), p. 153.

3 *Ibid.*, p. 156.

4 Moira Ferguson (ed.), *The History of Mary Prince, a West Indian Slave, Related by Herself, 1831* (London, Pandora Press, 1987), p. 84.

5 See for a discussion of these themes, Hilary Beckles, 'Sex and gender in the historiography of Caribbean slavery' , in Verene Shepherd *et al.* (eds), *Engendering History: Caribbean Women in Historical Perspective* (Kingston, Ian Randle Publishers, 1995), pp. 125–40. Also in this volume, Bernard Moitt, 'Women, work and resistance in the French Caribbean during slavery, 1700–1848', pp. 155–76.

6 Isaac Dookhan, *A History of the British Virgin Islands, 1672–1970* (Epping, Caribbean Universities Press, 1975), p. 83; also cited in Morrissey, *Slave Women*, pp. 155–6.

7 For a detailed discussion of ameliorative reforms to the British West Indian slave system at the end of the eighteenth century, see J. R. Ward, *British West Indian Slavery, 1750–1834: The Process of Amelioration* (Oxford, Clarendon Press, 1988); J. H. Bennett, *Bondsmen and Bishops: Slavery and Apprenticeship on the Codrington Plantations of Barbados, 1710–1838* (Berkeley, University of California Press, 1958); Michael Craton, 'Hobbesian or Panglossian? The two extremes of slave conditions in the British Caribbean, 1783–1834', *William and Mary Quarterly*, 3rd Series, 35 (1978), pp. 324–56; K. F. Kiple, 'Deficiency diseases in the Caribbean', *Journal of Interdisciplinary History*, 11:2 (1980), pp. 197–205; Richard Sheridan, 'The crisis of slave subsistence in the British West Indies during and after the American Revolution', *William and Mary Quarterly*, 3rd Series, 33 (1976), pp. 615–41.

8 Barry Higman, 'Growth in Afro-Caribbean slave populations', *American Journal of Physical Anthropology*, 2nd Series, 1 (1979), pp. 373–85; 'Slave populations of the British Caribbean: some nineteenth-century variations', in S. Proctor (ed.), *Eighteenth-century Florida and the Caribbean* (Gainesville, Universities Press of Florida, 1976), pp. 60–70; Stanley Engerman and Herbert Klein, 'Fertility differentials between slaves in the United States and the British West Indies: a note on lactation practices and their possible implications', *Willliam and Mary Quarterly*, 3rd Series, 35 (1978), pp. 357–74; Richard Sheridan, 'Slave demography in the British West Indies and the abolition of the slave trade', in D. Eltis and J. Walvin (eds), *The Abolition of the Atlantic Slave Trade* (Madison, University of Wisconsin Press, 1981), pp. 295–319.

9 See Hilary Beckles, 'Property rights in pleasure: the prostitution of enslaved black women in the West Indies', in Roderick McDonald (ed.), *West Indian Accounts: Essays on the History of the British Caribbean and the Atlantic Economy in Honour of Richard Sheridan* (Kingston, The Press: University of the West Indies, 1996).

10 See Kamau Brathwaite, 'Caribbean women during the period of slavery', *Caribbean Contact*, May–June, 1984.

11 See for a description of the 'Quashee' personality type, Orlando Patterson, *The*

Sociology of Slavery: An Analysis of the Origins, Development and Structure of Negro Slave Society in Jamaica (London, MacGibbon and Kee, 1967), pp. 174–81.

12 David Gaspar, '"Deep in the minds of many": slave women and resistance in Antigua, 1632–1763: a preliminary inquiry', Paper presented at the 19th Annual Conference of the Association of Caribbean Historians, Martinique, 1987. See pp. 22–5.

13 Barbara Bush, 'Towards emancipation: slave women and resistance to coercive labour regimes in the British West Indian colonies, 1790–1838', in David Richardson (ed.), *Abolition and its Aftermath: The Historical Context, 1790–1916* (London, Frank Cass, 1985), pp. 27–54.

14 See Mary Turner, 'Slave workers, subsistence and labour bargaining: Amity Hall, Jamaica, 1805–1838', and Hilary Beckles, 'An economic life of their own: slaves as commodity producers and distributors in Barbados', in Ira Berlin and Philip Morgan (eds), *The Slaves' Economy: Independent Production by Slaves in the Americas* (London, Frank Cass, 1991), pp. 92–107 and 31–48 respectively; see also Sidney Mintz, 'Caribbean market places and Caribbean history', *Nova Americana*, 1 (1980–81), pp. 333–44; Hilary Beckles and Karl Watson, 'Social protest and labour bargaining: the changing nature of slaves' responses to plantation life in 18th century Barbados', *Slavery and Abolition*, 8 (1987), pp. 272–93.

15 Sampson Wood to Thomas Lane, 1796, Newton Papers, M.523/288.

16 *Ibid.*

17 Brathwaite, 'Caribbean women', pp. 16–17.

18 Lucille Mathurin-Mair, *The Rebel Woman in the British West Indies During Slavery* (Kingston, Department of History, UWI, 1975); 'The arrival of black woman', *Jamaica Journal*, 9:2–3 (1975), pp. 1–10. See also Brathwaite, 'Caribbean women'.

19 Hilary Beckles, *Black Rebellion in Barbados: The Struggle Against Slavery, 1627–1838* (Bridgetown, Carib Research and Publications, 1987), pp. 86–106; 'The slave drivers' war: Bussa and the 1816 Barbados Slave Uprising', *Boletin de Estudios Latinoamericanos y del Caribe*, 39 (1986), pp. 85–111.

20 Robert Dirks, *The Black Saturnalia: Conflict and its Ritual Expression on British West Indian Slave Plantations* (Gainseville, University Presses of Florida, 1987), pp. 160–1. Beckles, *Black Rebellion*, p. 111.

21 Bush, 'Towards emancipation', p. 239; 'White "ladies", coloured "favourites" and black "wenches": some considerations on sex, race and class factors in social relations in white creole society in the British Caribbean', *Slavery and Abolition*, 2 (1981), pp. 253–4; '"The family tree is not cut": women and cultural resistance in slave family life in the British Caribbean', in G. Y. Okihoro (ed.), *In Resistance: Studies in African, Caribbean and Afro-American History* (Amherst, University of Massachusetts Press, 1986); *Slave Women in Caribbean Society 1650–1838* (Bloomington, Indiana University Press, 1990).

22 Monica Schuler, 'Day to day resistance to slavery in the Caribbean in the 18th century', *Association for the Study of Africa and the West Indies, Bulletin*, 6 (1973).

23 Morrissey, *Slave Women*, p. 98.

24 Parliamentary Paper, Garnette to Beckwith, December, 1811, Vol. 7 (1814–15), p. 3; Joseph Husbands, *An Answer to the Charge of Immorality Against Inhabitants of Barbados* (New York, n.p., 1831), p. 19.

25 Minutes of the Assembly of Barbados, 15 March, 1774, Barbados Department of Archives, Black Rock, Barbados.

26 Brathwaite, 'Caribbean women'.

27 Hilary Beckles, *Natural Rebels: A Social History of Enslaved Black Women in Barbados* (London, Zed Books, 1989); see Graham Hodges, 'Reconstructing black women's history in the Caribbean: Review Essay', *Journal of American Ethnic History*, Fall 1992, pp. 101–7.

28 See Beckles, *Black Rebellion*, p. 76.

29 J. G. Stedman, *Narrative of a Five Years' Expedition against the Revolted Negroes of Surinam*, 1806 (Amherst, University of Mass. Press, 1971), pp. 177–8; the Jamaica Diaries of Thomas Thistlewood, 1751–1768, Lincolnshire Records Office, England;

Leslie Manigat, 'The relationship between marronage and slave revolts and revolution in St. Dominique – Haiti', *Annals of the New York Academy of Sciences*, 292 (1977), pp. 420–38.

30 Moitt, 'Women, work and resistance', p. 162.

31 Victor Schoelcher, *Des colonies françaises: abolition immédiate de l'esclavage* (Société d'Histoire de la Guadeloupe, Basse-Terre, 1976), pp. 23–4.

32 Hilary Beckles, 'White women and slavery in the Caribbean', *History Workshop Journal*, 36 (1993), pp. 66–82.

33 Brathwaite, 'Caribbean women', p. 17.

34 See Beckles, 'White women and slavery', p. 76.

35 *Ibid.*, pp. 76–7.

36 See A. F. Fenwick (ed.), *The Fate of the Fenwicks: Letters to Mary Hays, 1798–1828* (London, Methuen, 1927), pp. 163–75.

37 Ferguson, *The History of Mary Prince*, p. 84.

PART III

The Empire at home

CHAPTER SEVEN

Anti-slavery and the roots of 'imperial feminism'

Clare Midgley

Standard histories of British feminism have had little to say about imperialism, while standard histories of imperialism have ignored feminism. Recent attempts to connect the two histories, however, have been stimulated by contemporary feminist debates concerning the problem of racism in Western feminism. In 1984 Valerie Amos and Pratibha Parmar published an article entitled 'Challenging imperial feminism' in which they set out 'to begin to identify the ways in which a particular tradition, white Eurocentric and Western, has sought to establish itself as the only legitimate feminism in current political practice'. They suggested that 'some of the unquestioned assumptions inherent in contemporary feminist demands have remained the same as those of the nineteenth and early-twentieth-century feminists who in the main were pro-imperial'.[1] In the same year Chandra Talpade Mohanty's article 'Under Western eyes: feminist scholarship and colonial discourses' critiqued the production of 'third world' women as a homogeneous powerless group of victims in Western feminist discourse, robbing them of agency and history and sustaining the idea of the superiority of the West.[2]

Since the mid-1980s historical scholarship has started to engage with such critiques of Western feminism, and to excavate 'colonial skeletons in the family cupboard' of British feminists.[3] Vron Ware's wide-ranging study of white women, racism and history offers a valuable starting point, providing interesting insights into the connections between movements for white female and black slave emancipation, into the development of feminism as a political movement in racist and imperialist society, and into how ideas about white femininity contributed to the subordination of all women.[4] Moira Ferguson has studied the analogies between the position of women and that of slaves present in early British feminist writings, and identified the emergence of an 'Anglo-Africanist' form of colonial discourse in white

British women's writing about colonial slavery between Aphra Behn's *Oroonoko* (1688) and the implementation of the Emancipation Act in 1834.[5] My own work on British women anti-slavery campaigners has explored links between white women's attitudes to enslaved black women and their views of their own position in British society in the 1790–1868 period.[6] Moving on to the period of the organised women's movement, Antoinette Burton's study of the relationship between liberal middle-class British feminists, Indian women and imperial culture in the 1865–1915 period has as it chief objective 'relocating British feminist ideologies in their imperial context and problematizing Western feminists' historical relationships to imperial culture at home'.[7] Paralleling my arguments about the input of women into anti-slavery ideology, Burton argues that women did not simply draw on existing imperial ideologies but were active in gendering these ideologies. Her conclusions concerning the emergence of 'imperial feminism' are complemented by Lucy Bland's discussions of the ways in which Darwinian evolutionary theory and eugenics, while often deployed to buttress anti-feminist arguments, were also taken up by British feminists, who argued that the further development of civilisation and regeneration of race and nation was dependent on middle-class Anglo-Saxon women's moral leadership.[8]

From such studies a picture has begun to emerge of the development of British feminist discourse in an imperial context, and the impact of late-nineteenth-century 'imperial feminism' on middle-class British women who developed the discourse, on working-class women within Britain and on colonised women overseas. Nevertheless the links between imperialism and feminism in Britain, particularly in the period prior to the emergence of an organised women's movement, remain under-researched. It is on this early period that I focus in this chapter, exploring both feminist discourse and female campaigning in the period between the 1790s and the 1860s. Jane Rendall has identified this period as marking the origins of modern feminism in Britain.[9] I wish to draw attention to the significance of the term 'modern' in this context, to bring back into view the erased term 'Western', and to think about the way in which a 'modern Western feminism' developed in Britain in the context of imperialism. I hope to draw attention both to the ways in which early feminists and campaigners for women drew on current Western discourses about non-Western societies and colonised 'others', and to the ways in which they actively contributed to the shaping of these discourses.

I approach these issues in two ways. First, I sketch the relationship between female anti-slavery campaigning, colonial reform and the emergence of organised feminist campaigning, comparing the perspectives of female anti-slavery campaigners of the 1820s and 1830s with those of the 'imperial feminists' of the 1865–1915 period discussed by Burton. Second, I explore what I have identified as a 'triple discourse' of anti-slavery in early British feminist writing of the 1790–1869 period, investigating the comparisons which feminists made between their own social position and that of enslaved Africans and women in 'Oriental' and 'savage' societies, and highlighting the centrality of such comparisons to the structuring of British feminist tracts.

Female anti-slavery campaigners, imperialism and feminism

Any attempt to place female anti-slavery in relation to the histories of imperialism and feminism entails the adoption of a critical perspective on existing historiography in both fields. Much of the history of British anti-slavery, stressing the movement's emancipatory goal, obscures the limits of the freedom it promoted. The successful slave revolt led by Toussaint L'Ouverture in the French colony of Saint Dominique involved both the emancipation of former slaves and independence from French colonial control: in contrast, white British anti-slavery campaigners aimed for Britain's Caribbean colonies to have a peaceful transition from slave to waged labour and saw close control from the imperial metropolis as an essential civilising force on West Indian society. While the transatlantic slave trade and the plantation slave system were products of early European colonial expansion, the eradication of slavery became a major justification of Britain's continuing imperial expansion in the Victorian era.[10] British women's anti-slavery activities need to be understood within this imperial framework.

Female anti-slavery also needs to be placed within the history of the development of feminism. Despite its focus on ending the sufferings of women under slavery, it is not generally viewed by historians as a feminist campaign, and, despite its co-ordinated national organisation, is not identified as marking the beginnings of the women's movement. There is some justification for this. Women were participating in a wider campaign for the emancipation of all slaves, regardless of gender, and they were part of a movement which involved men and was largely under male leadership. In addition, the links between women campaigning on behalf of slaves and campaigning for their own emancipation were less direct than in the United States, where the close links had led historians to use the term 'abolitionist-feminists'.[11] The main reason, however, lies in the tendency among contemporary white Western scholars to identify as feminist only those movements which have an exclusive focus on gender-based oppression.[12]

[163]

I would argue that female anti-slavery was a form of Western proto-feminism, which provided one of the main roots out of which full-blown 'imperial feminism' emerged. The links between the two were close both in the practical and organisational arena and in ideological terms. In my earlier work I have traced how leading anti-slavery activists moved into leadership roles in the women's movement in the 1860s and 1870s, shown how feminist organisations drew on aboli-tionist networks, and highlighted the explicit links which women made between the two campaigns.[13] Interestingly, the key feminist campaign against the Contagious Diseases Acts, which Josephine Butler labelled the 'new abolitionism', shifted from campaigning against the implementation of the Acts within Britain to campaigning against their implementation in India. Burton describes the later cam-paign as 'one example of British imperial feminism in action'.[14] What, then, were the similarities – and differences – between the ideological perspectives of the female anti-slavery campaigners whom I have stud-ied and the liberal feminists who are the subject of Burton's study?[15]

These two groups of women shared a concern for 'other' women: for non-white women in countries under British imperial control. In the anti-slavery case, this was for women of African descent in Britain's West Indian colonies; in the feminist case it was for Indian women under the British Raj. This shift in geographical focus coincided with the general shift in Britain's imperial preoccupations from the Caribbean to the Indian subcontinent. Both groups of women described colonised women in the two regions as their sisters and expressed empathy with them, stressing the common bond of moth-erhood. They were also both concerned to highlight forms of oppres-sion which were specific to women. Abolitionists attacked white planters' treatment of black women under slavery – mothers' separa-tion from children, and the flogging and sexual abuse of women; fem-inists attacked the victimisation of women caused both by British impositions such as the Contagious Diseases Act and by indigenous Indian customs such as female seclusion, child-marriage, *sati* and the prohibition of widow remarriage. Both groups accepted the validity of British imperial intervention and both sought to remould colonial societies along metropolitan lines, but there was a shift from a focus on the problems caused by colonisers to critiques of the culture of colonised peoples.

In highlighting the victimisation of black and Asian women, both anti-slavery campaigners and later feminists drew a web of compar-isons between their own positions as British women and the position of colonised women. Despite assertions of international and cross-race sisterhood, these comparisons tended to work against any notion of full equality. In both cases British social and cultural superiority is stressed, but there was a shift to a more racialised – a more racist – conception of the basis of this superiority. Anti-slavery assertions of the common humanity of African and European peoples, and the common degradation by the slave system of both white planters and black slaves, were intended to combat the language of biologically-based racial difference and hierarchy deployed by supporters of slavery. In contrast, later feminists tended to present white Anglo-Saxon women as superior by virtue of their race as much as their nationality. Thus women abolitionists contrasted the 'hapless and forlorn' lot of enslaved women with their own 'high privileges' as British females,[16] while women's suffrage campaigners represented women of the Anglo-Saxon race as the most advanced group of women in the world. This shift can be related to the wider shift in Britain in the second half of the nineteenth century towards acceptance of biologically-based racial hierarchy.

Both abolitionists and feminists represented colonised women as passive victims who were unable to defend themselves. They saw themselves as having responsibility for speaking for these silenced and helpless women and for protecting them: this, however, shifted from being the duty of privileged British women – the language of nation – to being also the 'white woman's burden' – the language of race. The language in which colonised women were described also became more negative. Thus women abolitionists stated that it was up to them 'to plead for those of their own sex, who have less power to plead than ourselves, who cannot speak their misery and their shame', while feminist campaigners similarly described the Indian woman as 'helpless, voiceless, hopeless' but also compared her with 'a dumb animal', adding an element of stupidity and dehumanisation.[17]

Their interventionist stance led women to promote a reformed and reforming imperialism on the grounds that protective, 'maternalistic' British female intervention could only benefit colonised women. From being tied to a critique of supposedly civilised men, however, this shifted to negative views of non-white men, who were seen as having an almost innate propensity to treat women badly. Thus British women abolitionists stated: 'It has wounded us to read of women's suffering and women's humiliation in countries which acknowledge British laws, which are governed, not by some half-wild, benighted Race, but by those who are connected with us by the closest ties'; while feminists stated: 'on every Oriental woman's head is set a price, she is regarded merely as a chattel', and determined 'never to rest until they have raised their Eastern sisters to their own level'.[18]

British women abolitionists and feminists both based their own claims to fuller participation in the public life of the British nation on their feminine roles as moral reformers of empire. Thus female anti-slavery petitioners claimed that they felt impelled to step outside their usual sphere by their concern for enslaved women, while feminists stressed white women's moral power to regenerate and purify the Empire as a basis for claims to suffrage and full imperial citizenship. However, here too there was a shift. Female anti-slavery petitioners expressed gratitude for 'the just and honourable level in society which they maintain',[19] whereas suffragists argued that the position of British women needed to be improved as the first step towards improving the position of women worldwide. Abolitionists presented public activism as a duty and an exceptional move outside their proper sphere in response to unique circumstances, while feminists presented it as a right and an essential and integral part of women's role in society.

Developments can thus be discerned which marked the development out of anti-slavery 'proto-feminism' into full 'imperial feminism' as the primary objective of British women's organised campaigning shifted from dutiful support for others – enslaved black women – to assertion of British women's own right to emancipation. While female anti-slavery radicalism – manifested in early support for Elizabeth Heyrick's call for immediate rather than gradual abolition of slavery – drew on women's perspective as outsiders to the endless debates and compromises involved in the parliamentary process, suffragists' less critical stance towards empire can be linked to their desire to become insiders of this imperial parliament. Despite such shifts, the substantial continuities between the discourses of abolitionism and feminism outlined above suggest that female anti-slavery provided an important foundation of 'imperial feminism'.

The triple discourse of anti-slavery in early feminist tracts

If female anti-slavery provided one ground for the development of 'imperial feminism', the discourse of anti-slavery in early feminist tracts provided a second. Rereading early feminist tracts of the 1790–1869 period I was struck by the way in which, while overwhelmingly preoccupied with the position of white middle-class women in Britain, they critiqued British women's oppression with reference to three different forms of slavery existing outside Britain: black chattel slavery in Britain's West Indian colonies and North America; the slavish position of women in 'savage' societies; and the enslavement of women in the harem under 'Oriental despotism'. While separate elements of this anti-slavery feminist discourse have already been identified by literary scholars such as Moira Ferguson and Joyce Zonana, no integrated picture of the discourse as a whole has emerged, and its *centrality* to early arguments for female emancipation has not been highlighted.[20] Through highlighting this 'triple discourse' of anti-slavery in a succession of key early feminist tracts I hope to illuminate the way in which feminist and colonial discourses were intertwined in emerging modern Western feminist thought in Britain in the period between 1790 and 1869.

Catherine Macaulay's *Letters on Education* (1790) is a somewhat neglected founding feminist text, but is of importance both in its own right and for its influence on Mary Wollstonecraft's more famous writings. Macaulay, in common with many other writers in the Enlightenment tradition, is concerned to place her comments on European society within a comparative framework, and acknowledges that there were some positive aspects to non-European societies.[21] Macaulay also asserts 'the natural equality of man', in keeping with her anti-slavery stance and political radicalism, and attacks those who claim the natural superiority of Europeans over Asians or Africans. While believing that 'most European states have at this day an apparent superiority in government, in arts, and in arms' she argues that this is an accident of history, and that European history also shows periods of achievement followed by periods of decline.[22] When it comes to the position of women, however, Macaulay sees nothing positive in non-Western societies. She states that 'the situation of women in modern Europe ..., when compared with that condition of abject slavery in which they have always been held in the east, may be considered as brilliant', thus locating Europe as the site of progress towards female emancipation, while simultaneously acknowledging that 'if we withhold comparison ... we shall have no great reason to boast of our privileges'.[23] The image of the unchangingly oppressive East also appears in Macaulay's condemnation of the inferior state of female education in Europe, which she describes as resulting from 'a prejudice, which ought ever to have been confined to the regions of the east, because it accords with the state of slavery to which female nature in that part of the world has been ever subjected'.[24] Her presentation of female subjection as anomalous to Western society is reinforced by her critique of Rousseau's views on female education, which she characterises as Eastern,[25] and contrasts with her own programme of female education in these terms: 'I intend to breed my pupils up to act a rational part in the world, and not to fill up a niche in the seraglio of a sultan.'[26] Macaulay thus promotes feminism as Western progress away from a negatively imagined East.

Mary Wollstonecraft's *A Vindication of the Rights of Woman* (1792)

[167]

is similarly preoccupied with the problem of female education and with developing an effective critique of Rousseau's views on the issue. She is sympathetic with Rousseau's disillusionment with current European society.[27] She disagrees, however, with what she interprets as Rousseau's belief that 'a state of nature is preferable to civilisation, in all its possible perfection'.[28] She argues that he was mistaken to attribute existing ills in European societies to 'the consequence of civilization' rather than 'the vestiges of barbarism'.[29] Her position is that 'the perfection of man' should be sought 'in the establishment of true civilization' rather than a 'ferocious flight back to the night of sensual ignorance'.[30] She sees evidence of this past 'night of sensual ignorance' in existing 'savage' African and 'despotic' Oriental societies, both of which she describes as oppressive to women. In African societies polygamy 'blasts every domestic virtue' and is associated with belief that 'woman must be inferior to man, and made for him'.[31] In critiquing Western women's 'immoderate fondness of dress, for pleasure, and for sway' she mobilises a triple discourse of anti-slavery. First, she compares them to African savages, whom she sees as 'uncivilized beings' who lack 'cultivation of mind' and are thus governed by their passions and are unable to think abstractly or to adhere to principle.[32] Second, she compares them to Eastern women 'immured in seraglios and watched with a jealous eye' and 'educated only to excite emotions in men'.[33] Finally, she compares them to colonial slaves, whose subjection to severe restraint is the result of 'prejudices that brutalise them' and which deny them the exercise of reason in order 'to sweeten the cup of man'.[34] Her point is that in order to become virtuous citizens, European women should be educated to become rational human beings like their menfolk; in the process, she implies, they will become less like African 'savages', 'Orientals' and colonial slaves.

A similar combination of opposition to colonial slavery with anti-savage and anti-Oriental discourse runs through Irish utopian socialist William Thompson's *Appeal of One Half of the Human Race* (1825), though here a much fuller comparison is made between the position of Western women and that of colonial slaves. Thompson's *Appeal* is an extended critique of the 'article on government' by James Mill, the leading disciple of Utilitarian philosopher Jeremy Bentham. Thompson points out that Mill, in explicitly excluding women from his call for men to have the right to represent their own interests,[35] had constructed a system of liberty built on continued 'political, civil, and therefore the social and domestic, slavery' of one half of the human race.[36] Writing soon after the launch of the British anti-slavery campaign, Thompson goes on to make extensive comparisons between the position of the British wife and that of Africans under colonial slavery, condemning 'the law-supported, literally existing slavery of wives',[37] and likening the marriage contract to slave-codes.[38] He calls on women to 'awake, arise, shake off these fetters',[39] and to 'make the most certain step towards the regeneration of degraded humanity' by freeing the world of both colonial and female slavery: 'opening a free course for justice and benevolence, for intellectual and social enjoyments, by no colour, by no sex restrained'.[40]

In attacking Mill, Thompson contributed not only to British attacks on colonial slavery but also to the circulation of negative stereotypes of non-Western societies. Mill is condemned by Thompson for having acted 'in true Eastern style' when he explicitly excluded women from his distribution of rights.[41] In addition, Thompson draws two specific comparisons between the position of British and Eastern wives. First, British women suffer from a double standard of sexual morality whereby women are punished for adultery whereas men's attachments may be 'as extensive and public as those of any Eastern despot'.[42] Second, when her husband dies, a wife is left in poverty, but, when his wife dies, a husband can simply select 'the next willing victim trained like the self-immolating widow of Hindostan'.[43] This was a reference to the practice of *sati*, the burning of widows on the funeral pyres of their husbands, which was the subject of intense debate in the time when Thompson was writing, and was eventually legally abolished by the British in 1829.[44]

The extended comparison with colonial slavery and the set of references to Oriental despotism are framed in Thompson's text by a discourse of savagery and civilisation, which appears both in the introductory letter to Anna Wheeler and in the concluding section. In the introduction, Mill's arguments are described as anachronistic to civilised Western societies – as 'the inroad of barbarism, under the guise of philosophy, into the nineteenth century' – and the present marriage code is condemned as a 'disgrace to civilisation' which 'represents the remnants of the barbarous customs of our ignorant ancestors'.[45] In conclusion, Thompson argues that while the 'favorable tendencies of civilisation' had 'mitigated the abuses of savage strength despotically used by man over woman', Mill was seeking to reverse this progressive trend.[46] This called into question Britain's claim to be 'the most enlightened' and civilised country in the world.[47] In his concluding sentence Thompson argues that female equality is essential to the social progress of both men and women.[48]

A similar presentation of female emancipation as the end product of Western social progress is evident in the writings of another feminist who was influenced by Utilitarian philosophy, the Scottish writer Marion Reid. In the introduction to her *A Plea for Woman* (1843) she argues that it was an auspicious time to call attention to women's 'degraded rank', describing the present age as one of progressive breaking with 'oppressive and tyrannical' social institutions previously revered as 'precedent and ancient custom'.[49] While Thompson compares present British society with its own barbarous past, Reid implies that societies at different stages in progress from savagery to civilisation co-exist in the present, and could be distinguished by comparing their treatment of woman:

> It is well known that, among savage nations, she is the menial slave of her lord; in barbarous states, she is alternately his slave and his plaything; while in lands like our own, which have made considerable progress in civilisation, though she has won herself many privileges, she is still very far from being allowed legal and social equality.[50]

In her call for the sexes to be 'allowed to advance side by side' Reid thus places feminism as the next stage in the progressive advancement of (Western) civilisation. In her concluding remarks she argues that woman 'advances refinement and civilisation, and is, in turn, advanced by them'.[51]

Harriet Taylor's essay 'The enfranchisement of women', which appeared in the *Westminster Review* in 1851, was written at a time when the interests of many British radicals were focused on developments in the abolitionist and feminist movements in the United States. Taylor highlights the contradiction between the principles of the American Declaration of Independence and the practice of excluding both women and black people from rights, and stresses that it is fitting that men associated with the extirpation of 'the aristocracy of colour' should be among the originators of 'the first collective protest against the aristocracy of sex'. Sex she describes as 'a distinction as accidental as that of colour, and fully as irrelevant to all questions of government'.[52]

Placing the treatment of women as inferiors as the relic of former ages' 'worship of custom', she situates it as an anachronism among modern Europeans and Americans, who supposedly pride themselves on having progressed beyond past knowledge and habits.[53] She goes on to link human progress to improvements in the treatment of women in a narrative which is a fuller statement of Reid's arguments. Using the examples of the Australian 'savage' and the American Indian she states: 'In the beginning, and among tribes which are still in a primitive condition, women were and are the slaves of men for purposes of toil.' Then, 'in a state somewhat more advanced, such as in Asia, women were and are the slaves of men for purposes of sensuality'. In Europe, however, progressive 'improvement in the moral sentiments

of mankind' has rendered women the companions of men.[54] Nevertheless, marriage remains a companionship between unequals.[55] Female
emancipation should be promoted as part of 'human improvement in
the widest sense'.[56]

In the process of representing female inequality as inappropriate in
modern Europe, Taylor draws on and reinforces stereotypical images
of Eastern women as passive and oppressed, of Eastern societies as
despotic and of Africans as servile savages. She describes 'what is com-
monly called affection in married life' as no more than the feelings
that 'often exist between a sultan and his favourites, between a master
and his servants'.[57] The fact that some British women do not desire
their emancipation does not mean that they should not get it: Asiatic
women accept their seclusion and veiling, Asians do not desire political liberty, the 'savages of the forest' do not want civilisation – but the
fact that habits of submission make people servile-minded 'does not
prove that either of those things is undesirable for them, or that they
will not, at some future time, enjoy it'.[58]

Taylor's views influenced those of her husband, John Stuart Mill.
His 'The subjection of women', first drafted in 1861, but not published
until 1869, can be seen as the culmination of eighty years of development in liberal thinking on the question of women's rights, and it is
strongly shaped by the discourses on black slavery, savagery, and Oriental despotism which inform the earlier feminist texts.

Mill begins by describing the 'legal subordination of one sex to the
other' as 'one of the chief hindrances to human improvement', as a
barbarism rooted in the past which ought to be replaced by 'a principle
of perfect equality'.[59] Early human society was characterised by the
slavery of both men and women. While male slavery has been abolished in Christian Europe, that of the female sex 'has been gradually
changed into a milder form of dependence'. This dependence was 'the
primitive state of slavery lasting on' and, despite 'successive mitiga-
tions and modifications' associated with general social improvement,
it 'has not lost the taint of its brutal origin'.[60] In 'the primitive condition of humanity', as revealed by the study of history or of 'the living
representatives of ages long past', the 'law of superior strength' was the
rule of life, but the ancient republics had commenced the 'regeneration of human nature' and the 'most advanced nations of the world'
had now abandoned the law of the strongest except when it came to
women's position.[61] This history of progress towards emancipation, as
in earlier feminist texts, sites the West as the locus of progress.

Like Thompson, Mill compared slaves' lack of legal rights with
British women's lack of legal rights.[62] He adds a new discourse of
modernity: the 'peculiar character of the modern world' was that

[171]

'human beings are no longer born to their place in life'. To create a fully modern society, he implies, we ought 'not to ordain that to be born a girl instead of a boy, any more than to be born black instead of white, or a commoner instead of a nobleman, shall decide the person's position through all life'.[63] Following the abolition of slavery, Mill argues, the social subordination of women is an anachronistic relic of traditional society in the midst of a modern society: it 'stands out an isolated fact in modern social institutions; a solitary breach of what has become their fundamental law, a single relic of an old world of thought and practice'; it is a practice in 'radical opposition' to 'the progressive movement which is the boast of the modern world'.

Mill's opposing of tradition to modernity is linked to the opposition he sets up between paganism and Christianity. Maintaining the social subordination of women, he argues, is equivalent to retaining a pagan shrine as the centre of worship in an otherwise Christian Britain: 'as if a gigantic dolmen, or a vast temple of Jupiter Olympus, occupied the site of St Paul's and received daily worship, while the surrounding Christian churches were only resorted to on fasts and festivals'.[64] This association of the oppression of women with non-Christian religions is later made more explicitly. Dealing with objections to women's emancipation based on the biblical passage in which St Paul urges women to submit to their husbands, he argues that the apostle was simply accepting the social institutions of his time rather than providing a timeless Christian prescription for human conduct. Christianity, Mill claims, does not fix forms of government and society and, as a result, 'it has been the religion of the progressive portion of mankind, and Islamism, Brahminism, etc., have been those of the stationary portions; or rather … of the declining portions.'[65]

This sense of female subordination as uncharacteristic of Christianity is reinforced by Mill's references to the Oriental harem, references to which – as in earlier feminist texts – rely for their effect on the reader rejecting Oriental society as a suitable model for the West. Thus he argues that if men wish to keep their wives subordinate they should educate them in no more than the skills of an odalisque or a domestic servant.[66] He asserts that women, lacking direct power, may exert an unhealthy influence in their households, like a sultan's favourite slave.[67] He describes men's selfishness as deriving from their feelings of 'sublime and sultan-like' superiority over their wives.[68] Finally, like Taylor, he claims that a lack of complaints from women does not render their situation less unjust: the same thing may be said of the women in an Oriental harem, who despise the freedoms of European women.[69]

Mill points out that 'every step in improvement has been so invariably accompanied by a step made in raising the social position of women, that historians and philosophers have been led to adopt their elevation or debasement as on the whole the surest test and most correct measure of the civilisation of a people or an age'. He suggests that complete equality would thus seem the expected result of the progress of human history, in which 'the condition of women has been approaching nearer to equality with men'.[70]

From anti-slavery to 'imperial feminism'

A developing 'triple discourse' of anti-slavery can thus be discerned in key founding texts of British feminism published between 1790 and 1869 and composed by writers both male and female, and variously of English, Scottish and Irish descent. Rather than simply describe the condition of women in Britain early feminists drew comparisons with colonial slavery, African polygamy and Oriental harems – conjuring up a series of vivid, disturbing images based on other texts with which the educated reader was assumed to be familiar: anti-slavery tracts, travellers' accounts of Africa, and the stories of the Arabian Nights. In the process an evolving set of images of extra-European societies, coupled with a contrasting picture of European societies, was circulated. Such images became an integral part of British feminist discourse, constructing feminism as intrinsically modern and Western in character.

In all these texts both the enslavement of blacks by whites and the enslavement of women by men are represented as anomalous and anachronistic in Western societies, which are defined as progressive and free in nature. Once achieved, black emancipation becomes the marker of Britain's status as the most progressive Western nation. Female emancipation is presented as the final step along the road to the creation of a fully enlightened society. Feminism, like anti-slavery, is the culmination of the progress of Western civilisation. In contrast, the subordination of women is represented as characteristic of, and part of the unchanging despotic nature of, Eastern societies, and as a mark of the backward and benighted state of savage societies in Africa and elsewhere. Female subordination in the West is an anachronistic relic of savagery or an alien Oriental element. This discourse reinforced the stereotypical Western view of Eastern countries as despotic, sensuous and corrupt by characterising them as keeping women as the sexual slaves of sultans in the harem, and it represented the societies of the indigenous inhabitants of Africa, America and Australia as living relics of the age of savagery.

All the feminist texts drew on Enlightenment responses to non-European societies. What G. S. Rousseau and Roy Porter have labelled 'Enlightenment exoticism' developed in response to increasing

European exploration, colonisation and control over non-European societies. While Enlightenment philosophers' attitudes varied to both colonisation and to the merits of the new societies encountered, they shared the project of attempting to reconstruct the history of the world through the identification of stages of social progress from savagery to civilisation. In the process 'the peoples and stages of civilisation of the European past were readily mapped onto the tribes contemporaries encountered in Africa or America', with such contemporary societies seen as living relics of the savage era.[71]

The tracts, while exhibiting a striking general continuity in discourse, also show shifts in its precise form over time. Macaulay and Wollstonecraft, writing in the 1790s, are willing to suggest that some aspects of European civilisation are not an advance on the situation in savage or Eastern societies, reflecting the unresolved debate among Enlightenment thinkers over the relative merits of different societies. Thompson, writing in 1825, positions the subordination of British women as a remnant of the barbarous customs of the British past rather than comparing them to contemporary 'savage' societies. A more explicit and unequivocally negative view of non-European societies is discernible in the Victorian tracts. Reid, writing in 1843, situates female subordination both in relation to Britain's past and in relation to a scale of women's current treatment ranging from that in 'savage' and 'barbarous' nations to more civilised Britain. Taylor in 1851 stresses the early and progressive improvement of women's position in Europe and moves beyond Reid's vague references to 'savage' or 'barbarous' societies to a more geographically situated narrative linking the remote European past with the current situation in Australian and American Indian savage societies, and placing Asian societies in an intermediate stage, above the savage but below the European. Finally Mill, reflecting both his own personal history of involvement in the administration of British India and wider imperial preoccupations in the aftermath of the Indian Rebellion of 1857, develops a discourse of modernity versus tradition which is linked to a discourse of Christianity versus paganism/Hinduism/Islam.

This leads into the question of shifts in the texts in the form taken by what Zonona has labelled 'feminist orientalism'.[72] By this she means the feminist contribution to what Said has defined as Orientalism: both 'a style of thought based upon an ontological and epistemological distinction made between "the Orient" and ... "the Occident" and a discourse that developed in the context of French and British imperial expansion from the late eighteenth century onwards as 'a Western style for dominating, restructuring, and having authority over the Orient'.[73] Feminist texts share with other Orientalist discourse a dominant association of the East with the harem, an association which, as Rana Kabbani has pointed out, conjured up images of both sexuality and despotism.[74] However, to this discourse concerning Arab and Islamic culture is later added a discourse around Hinduism and India, first appearing in Thompson in 1825 and more extensively developed in Mill in 1869. Here we have what Lata Mani describes as 'colonial discourse' on India: the 'mode of understanding Indian society that emerged alongside colonial rule' and was linked to 'the requirements of an expanding colonial power in need of systematic and unambiguous modes of governance'.[75] Thompson, who refers negatively to *sati*, was writing at a time of increasing British intervention in 'traditional' Indian practices, particularly as related to women, in the name of modernisation and progress.[76] Interestingly, it was the issue of *sati* which prompted the first recorded group of female petitions to parliament in 1829, as part of a successful national campaign 'for abolishing the practice of burning widows on the funeral piles of their husbands'.[77] Presented one year before women's first mass petitioning for the abolition of colonial slavery, the *sati* petitions arguably set a precedent for female intervention in colonial policy-making on behalf of colonised women, and were a forerunner of feminist interventions in the condition of Indian women in the period from 1865 onwards. The 1820s interventions in Indian practices were promoted both by evangelical Christian missionaries and by Utilitarians such as J. S. Mill's father, James Mill, who saw legal reform as a key means of improving the level of civilisation in India by the removal of 'barbarous' Hindu religious practices.[78] John Stuart Mill himself was an official of the East India Company from 1823 until 1858, and, like his father, condemned Eastern societies as despotisms, which needed beneficent British control and reform in order to advance. Breaking with his father in including British women in his calls for self-representation, and in using the criterion of liberty rather than utility to measure human progress, he nevertheless adhered to his father's belief that India could, in its present state of civilisation, only be governed by enlightened British despotism, without any Indian input.[79]

The nature of the analogy with African slavery also shifts over time, in response to successive developments in the abolition movement. In the early texts black slavery is represented as a blot on British civilisation on a par with female subordination; later the triumph of British abolitionism was seen as setting the stage for female emancipation. The slavery of women became the sole anomaly needing to be purged from the cradle of liberty.

Such continuities and shifts in the triple discourse of anti-slavery in early feminist tracts warrant much fuller contextualisation than has

been possible here: we need to avoid the ahistorical over-generalisa-
tions of some colonial discourse analysis by setting the production of
these tracts in the context of the complex history of the British
Empire, of changes in the nature of feminism itself, and of the shifting
intellectual and political discourses of the Enlightenment, Utilitarian-
ism, utopian socialism and liberalism. Nevertheless, I think that it is
possible to conclude on the basis of the evidence presented here that
feminist propagandists from 1790 onwards helped consolidate the
sense of Western superiority which came to underpin Victorian
notions of Britain's imperial civilising mission. Disapproval of all
forms of slavery was linked to a critique of non-European societies,
both African 'savage' and Oriental 'despotic'. Just as Western European
women would gain nothing from reverting to a state of nature so, the
writers imply, enslaved blacks would not benefit from being returned
to African savagery and Indian women suffering under *sati* could only
benefit from British intervention. Anti-slavery discourse in these early
feminist tracts thus opens the way for the spread of West European
models of civilised society under British imperialism, with the interests of Indian women and African savages represented by benevolent
British rulers, while simultaneously offering to British women a very
different fate: the opportunity to represent themselves.

'Imperial feminism', as it emerged with the development of the
organised women's movement between the 1860s and 1914, resolved
the tension between female anti-slavery campaigning, which had
drawn a sharp *distinction* between the privileges of white British
women and the sufferings of enslaved black women, and early feminist tracts, which had stressed the *similarities* between the position of
white middle-class women and black slaves, Eastern harem dwellers
and African 'savages' (while holding on to the image of Western society as generally superior). While John Stuart Mill did not explicitly
link his imperialist concerns for the government of India with his feminist concerns for the position of women in Britain, women's suffrage
campaigners of 1865–1914 did. Within their 'imperial feminist' framework, as Antoinette Burton has pointed out, it was possible for campaigners to expose the oppression of women in the West while
simultaneously representing Western women as liberated in comparison to their victimised sisters in Africa or India. British women would
be the first women in the world to be emancipated; having won their
own freedom, they would lead their victimised non-European sisters
out of patriarchal oppression under the mantle of empire.

The validity of this 'imperial feminism' as 'the only legitimate feminism' was subject to challenge from an early date, as black and Indian
women creatively appropriated aspects of Western feminism, and

developed their own movements for emancipation, confounding Western women's representations of their passivity.[80] In the process they found some allies among white women, beginning with women such as Annie Besant and Margaret Cousins, who supported both emerging Indian nationalism and the nascent Indian women's movement at the turn of the century.[81] Nevertheless, a century later, difficulties in moving Western feminism towards an anti-racist and anti-imperialist position persist: perhaps a better understanding of the roots of 'imperial feminism' may contribute to meeting the challenge. A full appreciation of the ways in which the projects of Western feminism and imperialism were intertwined will, however, involve a more extended investigation than has been possible here of how British feminists drew on and contributed to debates about the nature of non-Western and colonised societies, and of how a range of women campaigners developed a 'mission' to women in such societies in the context of Britain's imperial expansion.

Notes

1 V. Amos and P. Parmar, 'Challenging imperial feminism', *Feminist Review*, 17 (1984), 3–19.
2 For an updated and modified version of the original article see: C. T. Mohanty, 'Under Western eyes: feminist scholarship and colonial discourse', in C. T. Mohanty, A. Russo and L. Torres (eds), *Third World Women and the Politics of Feminism* (Bloomington, Indiana University Press, 1991), pp. 51–80.
3 V. Ware, *Beyond the Pale: White Women, Racism and History* (London, Verso, 1992), pp. 228–9.
4 Ware, *Beyond the Pale*.
5 M. Ferguson, *Subject to Others: British Women Writers and Colonial Slavery, 1670–1834* (London, Routledge, 1992).
6 C. Midgley, *Women Against Slavery: The British Campaigns, 1780–1870* (London, Routledge, 1992); C. Midgley, 'Anti-slavery and feminism in nineteenth-century Britain', *Gender and History*, 3:3 (1993), 343–62.
7 A. Burton, *Burdens of History: British Feminists, Indian Women, and Imperial Culture, 1865–1915* (Chapel Hill, University of North Carolina Press, 1994), p. 2.
8 L. Bland, *Banishing the Beast: English Feminism and Sexual Morality, 1885–1914* (London, Penguin, 1995); see especially pp. 71–85, 231–5, 304.
9 J. Rendall, *The Origins of Modern Feminism: Women in Britain, France and the United States, 1780–1860* (Basingstoke, Macmillan, 1985).
10 See T. Holt, *The Problem of Freedom: Race, Labor, and Politics in Jamaica and Britain, 1832–1938* (Baltimore, Johns Hopkins University Press, 1992).
11 B. G. Hersch, *The Slavery of Sex: Feminist-Abolitionists in America* (Urbana, University of Illinois Press, 1978); J. F. Yellin, *Women and Sisters: Antislavery Feminists in American Culture* (New Haven, Yale University Press, 1989).
12 C. Bolt, for example, in her Introduction to *The Women's Movements in the United States and Britain from the 1790s to the 1920s* (Hemel Hempstead, Harvester Wheatsheaf, 1993), states (p. 11): 'I consider that the community, benevolent and reform endeavours of American women of colour warrant a separate treatment, in recognition of the equal significance of race and gender for such women.'
13 Midgley, 'Anti-slavery and feminism in Britain'.
14 A. Burton, 'The white woman's burden: British feminists and "the Indian woman",

1865–1915', in N. Chaudhuri and M. Strobel, *Western Women and Imperialism: Complicity and Resistance* (Bloomington, Indiana University Press, 1992), p. 139.

15 The following comparison is based on research published in Midgley, *Women Against Slavery* and 'Anti-slavery and feminism in Britain', and in Burton, *Burdens of History* and 'The white woman's burden'.

16 Birmingham women's 1830 'Address to the Queen' recorded as entry for 23 December 1830 in 'Minute Book of the Ladies Society for the Relief of Negro Slaves' (ms. in Birmingham Central Library).

17 'Appeal from British ladies to the West India planters' (1825), recorded in Lucy Townsend's 'Scrap book on negro slaves', p. 127 (ms. in Rhodes House Library, Oxford); Josephine Butler, editorial in *The Storm Bell*, June 1898, p. 59, as quoted in Burton, 'The white woman's burden', p. 144.

18 'Appeal from British ladies'; Elizabeth Andrew, 'Report of the delegates', *The Dawn*, July 1885, as quoted in Burton, 'The white woman's burden', p. 144; Mrs Bayle Bernard, 'The position of women in India', *Englishwoman's Review*, July 1868, as quoted in *ibid.*, p. 146.

19 Petition of the female members of New Road Chapel in Oxford, quoted in *Appendix to the Votes and Proceedings of the House of Commons, Session 1830–1*, p. 78.

20 M. Ferguson (*Subject to Others* and 'Mary Wollstonecraft and the problematic of slavery', in *Colonialism and Gender Relations from Mary Wollstonecraft to Jamaica Kincaid* (1993), chap. 2, pp. 8–33) highlights the 'usage of colonial slavery as a reference point for female subjugation' from Wollstonecraft onwards but ignores the fact that many references to slavery by feminist writers – including Wollstonecraft herself – were not to colonial slavery but rather to the enslavement of women in 'savage' and 'Oriental' societies. J. Zonana ('The sultan and the slave: feminist orientalism and the structure of *Jane Eyre*', *Signs*, 18:3 (1993), 592–617) focuses exclusively on references to the Orient. Historians' studies of early British feminism (notably Rendall, *The Origins*) do not emphasise the discourse of anti-slavery.

21 C. Macaulay Graham, *Letters on Education. With Observations on Religious and Metaphysical Subjects* (London, C. Dilly, 1790), pp. 24, 258, 297.

22 *Ibid.*, pp. 257–8.

23 *Ibid.*, p. 210.

24 *Ibid.*, pp. 48–9.

25 *Ibid.*, p. 213.

26 *Ibid.*, p. 220.

27 M. Wollstonecraft, *A Vindication of the Rights of Woman*, ed. C. H. Poston (New York, W. W. Norton, [2nd edn, 1792] 1975), pp. 13, 60.

28 *Ibid.*, p. 14. Note that modern scholars would see this as a common eighteenth-century misinterpretation of Rousseau – see for example P. Gay, *The Enlightenment: An Interpretation. The Science of Freedom* (New York, W. W. Norton, [1969] 1977), pp. 538–9.

29 Wollstonecraft, *A Vindication*, p. 15.

30 *Ibid.*, p. 19.

31 *Ibid.*, p. 70.

32 *Ibid.*, p. 187.

33 *Ibid.*, pp. 188, 117.

34 *Ibid.*, p. 144–5.

35 William Thompson, *An Appeal on Behalf of One Half of the Human Race, Women, Against the Pretensions of the Other Half, Men, to Retain Them in Civil and Domestic Slavery* (London, 1825), p. 7.

36 *Ibid.*, p. 18.

37 *Ibid.*, p. 43. See also pp. 42, 66–7.

38 *Ibid.*, pp. 55–63.

39 *Ibid.*, p. 194.

40 *Ibid.*, p. 213.

41 *Ibid.*, p. 17.

42 *Ibid.*, p. 84.

43 *Ibid.*, p. 92.
44 L. Mani, 'Contentious traditions: the debate on *sati* in colonial India', in K. Sangar and S. Vaid (eds), *Recasting Women: Essays in Indian Colonial History* (New Brunswick, Rutgers University Press, [1989] 1990), pp. 88–126.
45 Thompson, *Appeal*, pp. ix, xiii.
46 *Ibid.*, pp. 184–5.
47 *Ibid.*, p. 195.
48 *Ibid.*, p. 213.
49 M. Reid, *A Plea for Woman* (Edinburgh, Polygon, [1843] 1988), pp. 1–4.
50 *Ibid.*, p. 2.
51 *Ibid.*, p. 92.
52 H. Taylor Mill, 'The enfranchisement of women' [*Westminster Review*, July 1851], in J. S. Mill and H. Taylor Mill, *Essays on Sex Equality*, ed. A. S. Rossi (Chicago, University of Chicago Press, 1970), pp. 95–6.
53 *Ibid.*, p. 98.
54 *Ibid.*, pp. 108–9.
55 *Ibid.*, pp. 110, 117.
56 *Ibid.*, p. 120.
57 *Ibid.*, p. 115.
58 *Ibid.*, p. 117.
59 J. S. Mill, 'The subjection of women' [1869], in Mill and Taylor Mill, *Essays*, ed. Rossi, pp. 125–6.
60 *Ibid.*, p. 130.
61 *Ibid.*, pp. 131–3.
62 *Ibid.*, pp. 158–61.
63 *Ibid.*, pp. 142–5.
64 *Ibid.*, pp. 146–7.
65 *Ibid.*, p. 177.
66 *Ibid.*, p. 156.
67 *Ibid.*, p. 168.
68 *Ibid.*, p. 219.
69 *Ibid.*, p. 214.
70 *Ibid.*, pp. 147–8.
71 G. S. Rousseau and R. Porter, 'Introduction: approaching enlightenment exoticism', in G. S. Rousseau and R. Porter (eds), *Exoticism in the Enlightenment* (Manchester, Manchester University Press, 1990), p. 9. For the Enlightenment origins of the idea of progress see J. B. Bury, *The Idea of Progress* (New York, Dover Publications, [1932] 1987).
72 Zonana, 'The sultan and the slave'.
73 E. W. Said, *Orientalism* (Harmonsworth, Penguin, [1978] 1985), pp. 2–3.
74 R. Kabbani, *Europe's Myths of Orient* (London, Pandora Press, [1986] 1988), pp. 18, 28.
75 Mani, 'Contentious traditions', pp. 90, 91.
76 *Ibid.*, p. 118.
77 *Journal of the House of Commons*, vol. 84 (London, House of Commons, 1829), entries for 13 February, 2 April, 3 June, 19 June 1929.
78 Eric Stokes, *The English Utilitarians and India* (Delhi, Oxford University Press, [1959] 1982), especially pp. 48–80.
79 *Ibid.*, especially pp. 241–98, 321.
80 See, for example, the following collections of essays: Sangari and Vaid (eds), *Recasting Women*; Mohanty (ed.), *Third World Women*; C. Johnson-Odim and M. Strobel, *Expanding the Boundaries of Women's History: Essays on Women in the Third World* (Bloomington, Indiana University Press, 1992).
81 N. Paxton, 'Complicity and resistance in the writings of Flora Annie Steel and Annie Besant', in Chaudhuri and Strobel (eds), *Western Women and Imperialism*, pp. 158–76; B. Ramusack, 'Cultural missionaries, maternal imperialists, feminist allies: British women activists in India, 1865–1945', in *ibid.*, pp. 119–36.

CHAPTER EIGHT

Going a-Trolloping:
imperial man travels the Empire

Catherine Hall

The imaginations of nineteenth-century Englishmen and women were filled with images of empire. The mid-Victorian world was chock-a-block with the material artefacts of empire – the sugar, the tea, the coffee, the cocoa, the tobacco, to name only the most obvious. But there were also the imaginative products of the colonial encounter – the novels, the paintings of military exploits, the travellers' tales and missionary stories, the new theories of ethnographers. Middle-class periodicals regularly discussed colonial questions, the burgeoning popular press delighted in tales of adventure from the many outbacks, travelling exhibitions included 'Red Indians' and Africans. The House of Commons may have emptied when some colonial issues were raised but empire was part of the everyday life of the English, part of their imaginative landscape, part of their sense of themselves, part of their mapping of the globe. To be English was to be white, Anglo-Saxon, and a master-race, masters indeed of a quarter of the world's population. Englishmen could dream of ruling 'natives' in India, making fortunes in the goldfields of Australia or the diamond mines of South Africa, converting 'heathens' in the Caribbean. The Empire offered the English adventures beyond 'the old country', forms of authority which they might not be able to achieve at home, visions of 'native' sexuality. Empire, it can be argued, was indeed constitutive of English masculinities in the mid nineteenth century. Dreams of empire were not only the imaginative food with which England collectively put itself to sleep at nights, as Martin Green has argued, but provided a frame for England itself, a way of knowing what it meant to be English, and to be an Englishman.[1] Metropolitan men occupied these dreams differently from women, for the Empire offered different opportunities to the two sexes. While men could travel the Empire with impunity in the mid nineteenth century, as officials, soldiers and sailors, missionaries, adventurers and explorers, travel writers and

[180]

men of commerce, women occupied these 'other' lands more circum-spectly, though, as much recent work has shown, white women's pres-ence in the Empire was exceedingly significant.[2] This chapter is concerned with one of these imperial men, one of the most famous fic-tion writers of his time, Anthony Trollope.

Anthony Trollope, 'the best loved and most widely read of the great Victorian novelists',[3] was one of the many who set that frame, who wrote in the knowledge of empire and who articulated for the English a way of being an imperial people. To Englishmen, as his readers, he offered some of the pleasures and dangers of colonial masculinities and the imagined safeties of an Englishman's identity. In 1858 Trollope set off on a trip to the West Indies for his employers, the Post Office. Before he left he arranged a contract with Chapman and Hall for a book about his journey which he wrote while he was away, a pattern that he was to repeat with his later travel writings. The book, titled *The West Indies and the Spanish Main*, was published on his return and was an immediate success, going into a sixth edition by the following year as well as being published in the United States. Trollope regarded it ret-rospectively 'as the best book that has come from my pen. It is short, and, I think I may venture to say, amusing, useful, and true.' Trollope wrote as he travelled, never made any notes or did any preparation, aiming to reproduce 'that which the eye of the writer has seen and his ear heard', 'the exact truth as I saw it'.[4] Some readers in Britain may have believed what they read but readers in the West Indies were less impressed by this claim to have truthfully represented their societies. 'Going a-Trolloping' passed into the Jamaican vernacular as a syn-onym for travelling commentators who knew not what they saw.[5]

'Going a-Trolloping' became part of Trollope's life. Since the family finances had been rescued by his mother's famous, or infamous, work, *Domestic Manners of the Americans*, published in 1832, the Trollopes had seen writing as an essential part of the family income. Frances Trollope went on to publish numerous novels; her eldest son Tom wrote six travel books on Europe. By the time Anthony wrote *The West Indies* he had published three unsuccessful novels about Ireland and had started on his Barsetshire Chronicles. By the 1860s and early 1870s he was at the peak of his power and popularity and travel writ-ing was an important extra source of pleasure, interest and indeed profit. In 1861 he went to Canada and the United States for it had 'been the ambition of my literary life to write a book about the United States', an ambition no doubt related to his mother's literary triumph.[6] *North America* was published in 1862. In 1871 he set out with his wife Rose to visit their son Frederic who was sheep farming in Australia. He visited all the colonies of Australia as well as New Zealand, and the book chronicling this came out a year later. In 1878 he went to South Africa and again published a most successful account, four editions of which, together with an abridged version, were produced in the following year.

Trollope's childhood had been lonely and unhappy, as he describes at length in his *Autobiography*. His family had gone through financial and emotional difficulties. His miserable boyhood, the 'disgrace' of his schooldays, left him with feelings of inadequacy combined with a longing for acceptance and popularity.[7] At nineteen he was appointed to a clerkship in the Post Office and worked in London until 1841, when he volunteered to go to Ireland as a surveyor's clerk. 'From the day on which I set foot in Ireland,' he recollected, 'who has had a happier life than mine?'[8] There he enjoyed a better income and found a wife, Rose Heseltine. It was Rose's love and support, as housewife and mother as well as reader, which made it possible for him to have two working lives, as civil servant and as writer.

Ireland, for Trollope, was associated with independence, with greatly increased happiness and with the beginning of his writing career. In Ireland he was able to discover and occupy his Englishness, through his recognition of difference. His sense of self as a man, not achieved as a young clerk in London, was reached in another place and was predicated on his judgement of the Irish, who were not like him, and yet with whom he was able to live 'altogether a very jolly life'.[9] The pleasures of instructing and improving others, the easy sociability, the expressiveness and constant talk, together with the hunt which he came to love and the life associated with horses and dogs, all these constituted Irish charm for him, a charm which was linked to an already established and racialised discourse of Irishness in England.[10] The Irish, whose character he had the 'means of studying', were 'good-humoured, clever ... perverse, irrational, and but little bound by the love of truth'.[11]

The social acceptance which he found in Ireland gave him the confidence to articulate a new identity as a man and to find a writing voice. This may have sensitised him to the ways in which other places could provide space for new masculinities. In 1859 he moved permanently back to England, thinking it the right place for a literary life. In his adulthood it seems that he worked hard to make people like him. His sense of inadequacy as a boy and young man and his longing to be accepted may have been compensated for with an over-anxiety 'to secure the goodwill and agreement of all with whom he came in contact'.[12] What became his popularity, his acceptability to all, was premised on his capacity to make people laugh, the sense of comfort and security which he exuded, combined with a rough vigour and energy, which those who met him remarked on and which his readers were able to absorb from his writing.

Trollope's characteristics could be described as peculiarly English. Indeed his quintessential Englishness is commented on again and again by contemporaries. 'Standing with his back to the fire, with his hands clasped behind him and his feet planted somewhat apart,' commented one, 'the appearance of Anthony Trollope, as I recall him now, was that of a thorough Englishman in a thoroughly English attitude.'[13] To another, Trollope was 'typically English', full of 'solid common sense, tending rather to commonplace sense'.[14] This 'solid common sense' was a characteristic of the man and his writing. As Henry James remarked, 'with Trollope we were always safe'. Similarly George Eliot commented on the 'good bracing air' which Trollope's novels evoked for her. His books were 'filled with belief in goodness', they were like 'pleasant public gardens, where people go for amusement and, whether they think of it or not, get health as well'.[15] Thomas Carlyle was less kind. In his caustic and cruel way he summed Trollope up as 'irredeemably imbedded [sic] in commonplace'.[16]

Trollope was safe and English: humorous as to the foibles of his own people; a particular lover of the hunt; a clubman (the Athenaeum and Garrick); a safely married man who loved to flirt but was a profound believer in marriage, family, and 'proper' relations between the sexes; a Church of England man who disliked enthusiasm or extremism of any kind, fascinated by class difference but with no sympathy for class politics, a believer in the superiority of the Anglo-Saxon race. He was kind, untroubling, interested in the daily round of politics without being political, producing happy endings for his novels, believing in Church, family and nation in ways which confirmed complacency rather than producing unsettled states of mind. These were some of the values of that 'best loved and most widely read of the Victorian novelists'.

Trollope's travel writing might make us rethink that notion of the 'pleasant public garden' of his mind. For it is in his travel writing that he spoke clearly on questions of 'race', with a voice that disturbs the safe and kindly image so often associated with him.

Trollope on racial difference

Trollope's travel writing, and indeed his travels, were focused on the Empire. He was fascinated by the colonies and particularly those colonies which were primarily peopled by Anglo-Saxons. But he was convinced that the Empire did not matter enough to the English and he wanted to spread colonial knowledge in readable and accessible ways. For Trollope the Empire was central to Englishness, part of what was special about the Anglo-Saxon race. Trollope's writing about the Empire, now forgotten, needs to be placed next to the Barsetshire Chronicles, the Palliser novels and even *The Small House at Allington* – former British prime minister John Major's favourite. For this most popular writer reveals something of the ways in which a particular preoccupation with the details and complexities of certain aspects of English social, political and domestic life can sit alongside a set of assumptions about other societies, 'races' and peoples. Trollope's amiable Englishness is embedded in an imagined map of the Empire which surfaces periodically in the novels, through the preoccupations with Ireland, a Jamaican orphan, an anti-Semitic portrait, but which acts more generally to secure a set of feelings about what England is and what English people are like. This chapter, unlike most writing on Trollope, focuses on his travel books rather than his fiction (the forty-seven novels). I aim to illuminate the ways in which Trollope's commonsensical account of some of the 'races' and peoples of the Empire gives us access not only to the racialised and gendered thinking of one key Victorian organic intellectual but more generally to the ways in which a popular novelist could articulate an imperial imagination.

Racial difference was part of the everyday life of Victorian men and women. Trollope's mapping of imperial places and peoples, embedded in familiar language and images, brought Maori 'cannibals', Jamaican 'Quashees' and energetic white Australian settlers right into the parlour. Difference was domesticated and binary divisions between black and white apparently secured in the colonising mind. The English were reassured that it was their country's right to rule. The sites of empire were represented by that quintessential English good fellow, Anthony Trollope, in ways that English readers could take great pleasure in, for here was their favourite fictional writer transporting them to Australia, Canada or the West Indies. Here also were the serious debates of the political economists and social critics translated into the popular form of the personal travelogue with vignettes on hotel accommodation, forms of transport and natural wonders, set alongside short disquisitions on matters social and political and entertaining anecdotes of 'other' peoples.

A crucial feature of colonial discourse, as Said was the first to remark, is the way in which it depends on fixity in its construction of 'others'.[17] But Trollope's confidence as to his right to provide a cartography of peoples, fixing them in his popular texts as they were constantly being fixed also in family magazines, newspapers, missionary sermons, novels and the plethora of other sites of cultural representation, contained also always within it the anxiety as to whether those peoples were really fully in place. Might Maori 'cannibals' really eat British soldiers? Might there be something more than a joke here? Were England and the Anglo-Saxon 'race' quite as secure as they seemed, given the 'Indian Mutiny' of 1857, the Maori Wars of the early 1860s, and the Jamaican rebellion of 1865? Trollope's work did something to quieten those anxieties and reassure his readers that all was indeed in place.

His writing on empire is part of the tradition which emerged from the rethinking in the wake of the traumatic loss of the American colonies. The end of the Napoleonic Wars saw a great increase in the population of British dominions, a stronger army and navy and an increase in economic power. By 1820 it is estimated that Britain ruled 26 per cent of the world's population.[18] The consensus on colonial policy deriving from the political economy of the late eighteenth century, emphasising above all the expense and burden of the colonies, began to unravel. The political economists became convinced of the economic importance of the colonies and Herman Merivale undertook for them the systematic analysis of colonisation. The Merivales were family friends of the Trollopes and Herman's brother was Trollope's oldest friend, indeed his son was named after him. There are many signs of Merivale's influence on his friend. Trollope was not an original thinker; rather he was a populariser working with elements of different intellectual and political traditions and translating them into common sense. Thus Merivale's definition of 'colony' as 'a territory of which the soil is entirely or principally owned by settlers from the mother country' becomes Trollope's own. Only the white settler colonies, therefore, were 'real' colonies. These were to be clearly distinguished from military outposts and from 'colonies of exploitation', which were primarily used as sites for the production of staples for Europe. Similarly, Merivale's view of the spirit of England as intimately linked with the colonial project was one that Trollope became deeply attached to, and his trope of colonial development as an infant's growth from dependence to independence was constantly reiterated by Trollope. Furthermore, the racial hierarchy from South Africans to Polynesians which Merivale mapped out gave Trollope food for thought.

The influence of a very different thinker, Thomas Carlyle, on Trollope has been much more generally recognised. Both at the time of the publication of *The West Indies* and since, those who were sympathetic to the emancipated West Indian islands have been very critical of Trollope's account, linking it with Carlyle's vituperative article of 1849, 'Occasional discourse on the Negro Question'. Carlyle's thinking marked an articulation of authoritarian conservatism (inflected with radicalism) to expansion overseas. For Carlyle, reflecting on mechanisation, poverty and social disorder in the 1830s, emigration was one possible positive response. The non-European world in his imagination was a 'vacant earth' calling to be tilled by white European man. Colonisation, for Carlyle, was initially the key to a better world, and it was thought of as an extension of Europe, a seeding of the self.

By mid-century the terrain of debates over empire had significantly shifted as the humanitarianism of the 1830s and early 1840s, associated primarily with abolitionism and the protection of Aboriginal peoples, was weakened. During the 1830s and 1840s Jamaica figured in the English mind as the place of slavery and the centrepiece of 'the great experiment of emancipation', as the abolitionists liked to think of it. The visions of enthusiastic anti-slavery supporters, of a prosperous island peopled by industrious Christian black men and women, living in well ordered families and communities, had suffered setbacks by the mid-1840s, when the debates over the abolition of protective sugar duties in Britain brought the West Indian islands briefly back into the political scene. By then the decline of King Sugar was all too apparent and Jamaica once again was represented as a site of trouble and distress[19] – a mood captured in its ugliest manifestation in Carlyle's pamphlet, which returned to a pro-planter, pro-slavery argument insisting that emancipation had been a failure and that black men would not work without coercion.[20]

In his mapping of particular parts of the Empire, Trollope was always reflecting on the differences between 'them' and 'us'. 'I wish to write of men and their manners and welfare, rather than of rivers and boundaries', he remarked in his book on the Antipodes.[21] His journey was to do with the mapping of peoples. While Darwin painstakingly constructed his theory of evolution from his discoveries on the voyage of the *Beagle*, Trollope engaged in a different kind of cartography, one which filled the sites of empire with men and women whom he characterised as in different stages of development, all observed with an ethnocentric eye. Wherever an Englishman is on the globe, wrote Trollope, 'he always thinks himself superior to other men around him'; he was certainly no exception to his own rule.[22] His mapping of empire gives us access to one Victorian man's vision of the imperial landscape, presented as common sense.

His first encounter with difference, as we have seen, was in Ireland and his first three novels were set in Ireland, his first series of articles on the famine. He was training himself in careful description of other societies and peoples, explaining them to the English. He was learning the imaginative capacity to engage with other societies and to capture something of that 'otherness' for consumption at home. His particular strength was to become the ability to provide colonial knowledge in a new register, one which entertained as well as informed. His journey to the West Indies took place in 1858, the year after the 'Indian Mutiny'. Throughout 1857 and 1858 the daily press was packed with reports from India, of the courage of the British troops in the face of 'barbarism', of the 'massacre' of 'innocent women and children' by Hindu 'savages', of the heroism of martyrs such as the pious Havelock. This was a time at which racial thinking was hardening fast. When *The West Indies* appeared in 1858 it both reflected and was constitutive of that hardening. Trollope's encounter with the West Indies was his first with a predominantly black society and this was a stirring experience for a white man. Like all English travellers he went there with a set of expectations as to what it would be like, shaped by the ways in which the islands had been represented in England. The book was speedily taken up by *The Times*, a fact which Trollope himself saw as crucial to its success.[23] In the book he provided an account of the relations between 'races' that made clear to his readers that black people needed 'civilising' and reminded them that violence and force were not always the order of the day. India provided one model of colonial relations, the West Indies another. The fear in the West Indies was not of bloodshed and revolution, but black people still needed to be ruled.

By 1859 Trollope had encountered the Irish, white but different; West Indian planters, again white but different; emancipated negroes, a race apart; and Cuban slaves who were 'sleek and fat and large, like well-preserved brewers' horses' in his estimation.[24] In 1861 his trip to North America meant that he met American negroes, both free and enslaved, North American Indians, and the white settlers of Canada and the United States. His mapping of empire was becoming more complicated. By 1871, when he and Rose went to Australia to visit their son Frederic, the Australian colonies had been established as sites of settlement for respectable British people for some time, a land full of promise for the Anglo-Saxon 'race'. New Zealand presented rather more problems. The Maori Wars in the early 1860s had only been won by the British with great difficulties – vicious fighting continued into the early 1870s – and this had seriously disturbed British ideas about colonial order.

Trollope's final imperial journey, to South Africa, also took place at a strategic moment in British relations with South Africa. The Transvaal had recently been annexed, which Trollope supported after considerable doubts. He was insistent, however, that the British should not annex Orange Free State. He chronicled a new revolt by Kreli and saw the significance of the diamond fields. He was critical of the British stereotype of the Boers and of the ways in which South African black people had been represented in Britain. Influenced by the liberal Bishop Colenso he was somewhat sympathetic to the Zulus and indeed argued in 1879 that the Zulu War had been provoked by the unreasonable demands of the British High Commissioner Sir Bartle Frere.[25] Trollope's admiration for the Zulus, his conviction that South African black people would learn to labour and that the country was one for black men, unsuitable for white settlers, all put him at odds with the imperial expansionism that was to triumph in the late 1880s.

Trollope's mapping of the peoples of the Empire became a central project of his travel books. Australian Aborigines, New Zealand Maoris, North American 'Red Indians', West Indian negroes and South African 'Kafirs' and 'Hottentots', all were placed by his pen. His account of the West Indies focused particularly on Jamaica, the island which had long been the particular object of English surveillance. His narrative, linked to a tradition of pro-planter writing, constructed an imagined antagonist, the missionary or philanthropist, whose vision of negro piety and gratitude to his white benefactors was the stock-in-trade of anti-slavery publications. Trollope attacked this stereotype and left his readers in no doubt as to his certainty of the inferiority of the negro to the Anglo-Saxon race. 'Nothing was so melancholy' as Jamaica was to him, a country 'in its decadence', a truly melancholy sight.[26] Labour, the great civiliser, had not been able to get to work on its subjects in this island, mainly because of the plentiful supplies of food. 'He *is* a man', wrote Trollope on the negro, playing directly on anti-slavery rhetoric, 'and, if you will, a brother; but he is the very idlest brother.' 'The negro's phase of humanity differs much from that which is common to us', he confidently asserted and drew up a series of comparisons which marked the black man off from the white, as in 'the lower sphere of life'. If left to themselves West Indian negroes would slip back into barbarism. 'The first desire of man in a state of civilisation is for property ... Without a desire for property, man could make no progress.'[27] Trollope, in his ignorance, writing from the plantations, saw no evidence of this desire. Negroes must be forced to work, precisely the argument which Carlyle had made.[28] Trollope did not despair, however, of the future of the West Indian islands. The hope in Jamaica, as he saw it, lay with the coloured class, who he thought were going to be the 'ascendant race'.[29] The British should let Jamaica go, they had left their sign in blood. Englishmen, he argued, had needed the wild and savage energy of their vandal forefathers; similarly the mix in the coloured race would allow them to combine negro

[188]

strength with European intellect, and this mixed again with the Asian willingness to work, for South Asians had come into the West Indian islands in significant numbers as indentured labour. Jamaica had a future, one that was made possible by the mixing of races, anathema to many of the scientific racists such as Robert Knox, whose ideas were becoming increasingly influential.

Trollope's visit to the United States during the Civil War concentrated his mind on the question of slavery as it did the minds of the British public. This was perhaps his most Carlylean moment. He refused to damn slavery and argued that the difference between the races was that 'the tropics can produce, but the men from the North shall sow and reap and garner and enjoy'. Slavery had always existed, it had improved Africans, and Kentucky slaves were better off than English labourers. Yet, despite his sympathies with the South he firmly believed that the future lay with the North.

Trollope's encounter with Aboriginal people was shaped by the discourse of the inevitability of racial progression and the necessary disappearance of 'savage' peoples, a discourse which was long established in England. Aboriginal people were 'savages of the lowest kind', they wore no clothes, practised infanticide and sometimes cannibalism, they had made no progress for centuries, their extermination was inevitable. Maoris, on the other hand, were the 'most civilised' of the 'savages'. They were an active people, 'almost equal in strength and weight to Englishmen'. They possessed houses, weapons, tools, they owned tribal property, they cooked food and administered justice, they even treated their wives well, the ultimate sign for an Englishman of being assured a place in a civilised society. Courage was for them a virtue and their passion was revenge. Maoris were for Trollope 'a gallant people' who 'nearly had the gifts which would have enabled us to mix with them on equal terms'. But they were 'savages' at heart and would melt away in the face of the encounter with the colonisers.[30]

Crucial to Trollope's hierarchical schema of the 'races' were the relative capacities of different peoples to learn to labour. It was this which marked off those who could survive from those who could not. 'I like men who are energetic and stand up for themselves and their own properties', he wrote – white men, Australian colonists, who had the same concept of property as he himself did. To be independent was, for Trollope, the essence of white manhood and the best kind of independence was that which was earned. Travelling in South Africa twenty years after his visit to the West Indies he had a very different response to the Africans he encountered in their native land. South Africa made it possible for him to imagine a country in which black men would work. 'The white man has to be master and the black man servant', he argued, but this must be done justly and with no slavery or forced labour. To his mind South Africa was not like the other colonies for he saw every sign that the 'Kafir' was going to stay and survive. Yet white settlers had to prove their mastery. 'Kafirs' had to be brought into order, ruled and taught to earn their bread. The Irish provided a point of comparison for him with the 'Kafirs', a sign that the apparently straightforward binary division between black and white could be utilised at some times and not others.[31]

The best example for Trollope of labour as the great civiliser was the Kimberley diamond mines. 'I know no other spot on which the work of civilising a savage is being carried on with such a signal success', he reflected. Here black men had become orderly and disciplined, they were working regular hours with meal breaks, they were spending the money they earned and learning the pleasures of consumption – all this was much more effective to his mind than any work which the missionaries could do.[32]

Trollope's mapping of the 'races' was linked with a vision of empire, which drew on both the liberal political economy of a figure such as Merivale and the enraged conservatism of Carlyle. It emerged as a distinctive form of anti-imperialism, combined with a deep enthusiasm for particular aspects of colonial life. He was not in favour of Britain expanding its areas of control, or of keeping colonies as dependent territories. Ireland, however, was not a colony, it was a part of the self. The key colonies for him were what have come to be called the white settler colonies – Australia, New Zealand, South Africa, Canada and indeed the United States. The US still figured for him as a colony, indeed the most successful of the colonies, for colonies 'are the lands in which our cousins, the descendants of our forefathers, are living and still speaking our language'.[33] Colonisation was for him part of a providential and natural plan, whereby the more succesful races spread out, made fertile lands which had not been fertile and established new offshoots of the 'mother country'. This process he regularly likened to reproduction: the mother bore her children who gradually grew up and should become independent. A 'true British colony' must be self-governing whereas dependent territories of different kinds could be governed from the centre: 'Military depots must be governed from home. Sugar islands which are in fact not inhabited by white men but by negroes and half-castes, may be governed from home' – but white societies, the children, could rule themselves.[34] Indeed, he wanted the 'mother country' to stop thinking about 'her own power and glory' in relation to the colonies and to think instead of their welfare, just as a good parent should.[35] The familial imagery naturalised the power relations between the metropolis and colonial settlement and represented them as benevolent and domestic. That colonies, like children, should become independent, was to Trollope a much stronger claim to greatness than ruling dependencies over which the sun never set. Some colonies now offered better lives particularly for labouring people, places where men and women who worked with their hands could find better homes, higher wages, more education and indeed more freedom than could be found in the 'Old Country'. 'To have founded such colonies', commented Trollope, 'is the greatest blessing which we have above other nations.'[36]

Trollope on the gender order

In Trollope's imperial analysis, labour was one civiliser; family was the other. For him, like most middle-class men of the mid-Victorian period, familial and domestic order was at the heart of social order. A good society was one in which the classes, the 'races' and the sexes knew their place and stayed in it. The sense of timeless propriety that was attached to such notions belies the drastic reorganisation of relations between these groups that was part and parcel of industrialisation, urbanisation and colonisation. The emergence of a language of class was an index of the need for new ways of defining relations between workers and employers. The language of separate spheres became a way of talking about a new sexual division of labour within middle-class and then respectable working-class families. The language of racial hierarchy was a way of codifying relations between the English and their ethnic 'others', whether Celts in Manchester, Jews in London, Aborigines in Australia or Maoris in New Zealand. Both class and racial forms of belonging were always gendered in Victorian thought, albeit in many different ways. For Trollope a clear gender order with bread-winning husband and father and domesticated wife and mother was a necessary base for a good colonial life. The character of frontier societies meant that aspects of North America and Australia fitted very well with this notion of the idealised family, secure in its homestead. Jamaica, on the other hand, which was not of course a proper colony but a dependency to be ruled, where the missionaries had tried to build just such a dream of regulated families and households, demonstrated through its sexual incontinence its fundamentally decadent character.

Trollope's own experience of a father who did not succeed by any of the indices of middle-class society, and a mother who had to rescue the family finances by becoming a writer when she was over fifty, left him marked with a deeply conventional view of the sexual division of labour. Like so many who knew the precariousness of middle-class life

he needed order and stability. His powerful mother was complemented by a loving and dutiful wife who copied out his drafts, ran his
house, and bore his children.[37] In his later years his orphaned niece,
Florence Bland, became his secretary and helper.[38] While Anthony
went 'a-Trolloping' Rose mostly stayed at home. 'The necessity of the
supremacy of man [over women]', he wrote in 1879, 'is as certain to me
as the eternity of the soul. There are other matters on which one fights
as on subjects which are in doubt, – universal suffrage, ballot, public
education, and the like – but not, I think, on those two.' This assertion
of the 'natural' relations between the sexes was necessary because of
the challenge of feminism in the 1850s and 1860s. His meetings with
the Ladies of Langham Place and his encounter with American feminists – particularly Kate Field, with whom he had an intense and
painful relationship – stirred up questions for him about the proper
relations between the sexes.[39]

As a male writer of fiction his manhood was constantly at risk on
the feminised site of the novel, particularly since so much of his writing was focused on romance and domestic life. In his travel writing
that interest in manners, in dress and in emotionality could be offset
with a commentary on economic and political life – of a sort which
women were not supposed, in his view, to be able to make. Women
who ventured out of their sphere were troubling to Trollope, perhaps
partly because of his own vulnerability as a writer. He was sufficiently
troubled by his encounter with the women of the United States to
devote an entire chapter of *North America* to the 'Rights of Women'.
He was not sympathetic to political rights for women but he did recognise that in certain circumstances women had to work, however undesirable this was. He wanted women to be raised from 'hardening
tasks'. In England it had taken centuries to be able to effect this. The
aim of a woman should be to marry and that of her husband to support
her. 'Work is a grand thing', he argued,

> the grandest thing we have; but work is not picturesque, graceful, and in
> itself alluring. It sucks the sap out of men's bones and bends their backs,
> and sometimes breaks their hearts; but though it be so I for one would
> not wish to throw any heavier share of it onto a woman's shoulders.

'The grandest thing we have', the capacity to labour and to profit from
labour, was something for men. 'The best right a woman has is the
right to a husband', he insisted, for 'women are the nursing mothers of
mankind', his hopes for them that they would be 'soft, tender and virtuous'. This dream of the tender virtue of women was challenged by
the 'odious behaviour', as he saw it, of some women in the United
States, who 'are always talking of their rights; but seem to have a most

indifferent idea of their duties'. He was repulsed at the ways in which women in New York dragged their crinolines behind them, knocking into people and behaving as if no one else was there. In streetcars he had 'entertained ... that sort of feeling for an American woman which the close vicinity of an unclean animal produces'.[40] These were strong words, expressive of something much more violent than disapproval. When women stepped out of their place they lost their femininity, became another species.

The split that Glendinning points to in her biography, between Trollope's desire for a dutiful and ever present wife and the excitement and challenge of the independent and resourceful mother who had abandoned him, was perhaps re-enacted in his relationship with Kate Field and in his hostile response to public forms of feminism. He was excited by the prospect of independent women but castigated them for not knowing their place. He wrote to Kate Field, who persisted in lecturing in public, that she had signally failed to understand his objections. 'Oratory', he argued, 'is connected deeply with forensic, parliamentary, and pulpit pursuits for which women are unfitted because they are wanted elsewhere; – because in such pursuits a man is taken from his home and because she is wanted at home.'[41] His apparently confident assertion of the necessity of the 'supremacy of man over woman' was thus disrupted by his fascination with feminism and his preoccupation in his 1860s novels with the newly public presence and claims of women. The problem was that some women did not seem to accept that the most important aspect of life was marriage. This left him arguing that sexual frustration was at the root of feminist discontents for he was convinced that:

> Humanity has been at work for the last thousand years and more to relieve women from work, in order – to put the matter roughly – that man might earn the bread and women guard and distribute it ... that lesson comes direct from nature, – or, in other words, from the wisdom of an all-wise and all-good Creator. ... What we do not want is to assimilate men and women.[42]

This lecture was delivered up and down the country in 1868, a public riposte from a leading literary man to feminists in general, and to Emily Davies in particular who had cited Trollope in her book as saying, 'We like our women to be timid.'[43] Too much assertiveness, he suggested, would be a dangerous thing. A proper marriage was the key to personal and social harmony.

His encounter with a number of white, coloured and black West Indian women on his first long journey on his own was exciting. He enjoyed flirtation, though he was shocked by the extent to which white creole women in the West Indies carried it, and the female creole characters in his fiction are characterised as rampant flirts.[44] The period before marriage, as he saw it, was a time when women could exercise their power – a period which he explored extensively in his novels about English women. But that power must be properly contained – by men. An upsetting of this gender order was a sign of racial depravity. Black women, who do not appear in his fiction, were both exciting and disturbing to him. His first encounter with a black West Indian woman was on the island of St Thomas:

> as I put my foot on the tropical soil for the first time, a lady handed me a rose, saying, 'That's for love, dear'. I took it, and said that it should be for love. She was beautifully, nay, elegantly dressed. Her broad-brimmed hat was as graceful as are those of Ryde or Brighton. The well-starched skirts of her muslin dress gave to her upright figure that look of easily compressible bulk, which, let 'Punch' do what it will, has become so sightly to our eyes. Pink gloves were on her hands. ... What was it to me that she was as black as my boot, or that she had come to look after the ship's washing?[45]

But of course it was a great deal to him that she 'was as black as my boot' and that she had come to do the washing, for both class and racial boundaries were potentially transgressed. His reference to *Punch* evoked the ugly stereotype of the African woman with her large buttocks, pressing her sexuality on the white male viewer. Her pink gloves were mimicking a real lady, for hands were a crucial site of classed femininity;[46] and though she was a washerwoman who would carry the signs of her trade on her hands, her clothes could have passed in Brighton.

The black women of Jamaica he soon 'learned to think pretty, in spite of their twisted locks of wool, and to like the ring of their laughter, though it is not exactly silver-sounding'. They were stylish in their dress, never 'shame-faced', had good figures and knew how to make the best of them. 'She has a natural skill in dress, and will be seen with a boddice fitted to her as though it had been made and laced in Paris.' At the same time, though their costumes on Sundays were 'perfectly marvellous', some of their efforts after 'dignity of costume' he pronounced to be 'ineffably ludicrous'. Trollope's preoccupation with mimicry, with the impossibility of black women, or indeed men, ever being more than imitative, like monkeys, is striking. Take this vignette, one which was repeated in *The Times*:

> One Sunday evening, far away in the country, as I was riding with a gentleman, the proprietor of the estate around us, I saw a young girl walking home from church. She was arrayed from head to foot in

virgin white. Her gloves were on, and her parasol was up. Her hat also was white, and so was the lace, and so were the bugles which adorned it. She walked with a stately dignity that was worthy of such a costume, and worthy also of higher grandeur; for behind her walked an attendant nymph, carrying the beauty's prayer-book – on her head. ... When we came up to her, she turned towards us and curtsied. She curtsied, for she recognized her 'massa'; but she curtsied with great dignity, for she recognized also her own finery. The girl behind with the prayer-book made the ordinary obeisance ... 'Who on earth is that princess?' said I. 'They are two sisters who both work at my mill', said my friend. 'Next Sunday they will change places. Polly will have the parasol and the hat, and Jenny will carry the prayer-book on her head behind her.'

Black women, in other words, could only ever dress up in borrowed finery and pretend to be what they were not.[47]

Relations with women of other 'races' were never about marriage and, indeed, Trollope's interest in women of other 'races' was extremely limited. It was marriage which made men safe as well as women, and the dangers of bachelordom was another of his fictional themes. Families were at the heart of social order: English homes had the potential to be 'neat and nice', life in the Australian bush was 'decent and moral' for settlers needed wives, but the 'nomad tribe' of Australia, the travelling shearers with no ties, were a regrettable phenomenon and New York with its independent women was a site of danger and disorder.[48] Within the family a proper sexual division of labour was essential. While women should be soft, tender and virtuous, men were to be above all manly, and manliness meant independence, a commonplace among the middle and respectable working classes.[49]

Trollope's hopes for the colonies were intimately associated with manly virtues and independence. Colonial masculinity provided a new and vigorous offshoot, one that might feed and revive the 'Old Country'. His own son took that route. Fred, re-presented as Harry Heathcote in his novel of Australian bush life, was the quintessential rough and ready but steady, hard-working, skilful and determined young man. Australia was a place for sons in a way that Jamaica never could be. Trollope found that he liked Jamaican white men: 'A better fellow cannot be found anywhere.' They were hospitable, affable, generous, not generally hard-working. They fished, shot, ate and drank and looked after their estates. They assumed that negroes were born to be servants and that coloured men were uppity, assumptions that Trollope shared.[50] Jamaica could never be 'home' for them in the way that the white settler colonies with their supposedly fast-disappearing native 'races' could be, for the sugar islands remained in a state of dependence on the life blood of the mother country, could never become independent white states.

In contrast Trollope not only liked but also respected the energy and initiative of Australian, New Zealand and North American men. The life for artisans, he was convinced, was much better than in England. As long as emigrants were not idle and did not drink they could make 'modest competencies'. It was possible to work, save and buy a decent piece of land – become independent. At the same time he believed that England continued to offer a level of culture which could not yet be achieved in these white settler colonies. There was insufficient education, young men grew up too quickly, and there was too much equality. Though the absence of deference appealed to him in some ways it troubled him in others. But none of this substantially altered his judgement that 'such manhood among the masses of the people' was 'the highest sign of prosperity which a country can give'.[51] The Australians returned the compliment. As the *Sydney Morning Herald* commented on his book, some had been offended by the 'manly outspoken frankness' of that 'most popular of modern English novelists', 'the manly stirling character which so faithfully represents to us colonists all that we feel bound to associate with the name of Englishmen'.[52] Manliness, it seemed, was a quintessentially Anglo-Saxon virtue which could straddle the Empire and find new vigour in the colonies.

That new vigour gave the colonies, and the United States, an energy which was exciting to Trollope and which occasionally was allowed to highlight some of those aspects of England or indeed the British Isles which might not be entirely praiseworthy. In the western states of the United States he was impressed by the 'manly dignity' of the men, 'He is his own master, standing on his own threshold.' Intelligence, energy and endurance were his virtues. Indeed, such a man could claim superiority 'to the race from whence he had sprung in England or in Ireland' – for his honest industry contrasted with the corruption of the London financial market, for example, which Trollope satirised in *The Way We Live Now*. In this sense Trollope's colonial discourse did contain some seeds which unsettled the certainties of English ethnocentrism and complacency. There was something healthier about these white colonies than England; the same could not quite be said for South Africa, for the black population was too dominant there to make it a comfortable place for many white people. 'The working Englishman ... prefers a country in which he shall not have to compete with a black man', he wrote.[53] 'Good fellows' in England, or Jamaica or Ireland, might after all have their limitations.

The Irish instance is interesting for Trollope was fond of aspects of the Irish, sometimes in a patronising spirit – their docility and passivity – and sometimes in a more generous but nevertheless racialising way – their warmth and kindliness. Irish expressiveness he found moving. 'O my reader,' he inquired,

> have you ever seen a railway train taking its departure from an Irish station, with a freight of Irish emigrants? If so you know how the hair is torn, and how the hands are clapped, and how the low moanings gradually swell into notes of loud lamentation ... It means this: that those who are separated, not only love each other, but are anxious to tell each other that they so love.[54]

Such public expression of feeling was, of course, rarely found among the English. On his return from North America he stopped in Ireland for a few days. 'It has been my fate', he noted, 'to have so close an intimacy with Ireland, that when I meet an Irishman abroad, I always recognise in him more of a kinsman than I do in an Englishman.' But he was shocked by the beggars, both men and women, who importuned him the moment he stepped ashore. 'I myself am fond of Irish beggars. It is an acquired taste, – which came upon me as does that for smoked whiskey, or Limerick tobacco.' In the new country, he reflected, where he had of course met many Irish, there was no begging.

> The Irishman when he expatriates himself to one of those American States loses much of that affectionate, confiding, master-worshipping nature which makes him so good a fellow when at home. But he becomes more of a man. He assumes a dignity which he never has known before. He learns to regard his labour as his own property. That which he earns he takes without thanks, but he desires to take now more than he earns. To me personally he has become much less pleasant than he was. But to himself –![55]

The implication is that he has indeed become a man, with dignity and independence.

The 'Old Country' had its limitations. It might encourage good fellowship, warmth and comfort, but it might limit the growth of its sons. The Empire could offer new possibilities for the white men of the future – possibilities which could secure a 'Greater Britain' in which Anglo-Saxon men, linked through blood and culture, could ensure the continued development of the 'race'. This was the white brotherhood which Trollope celebrated in his travel writing – a white brotherhood whose power and prestige were embedded in assumptions about the inferiority of both women and native peoples. Such a vision was part of the everyday culture of Victorian readers.

Notes

I am grateful to the Nuffield Foundation for the fellowship which I held in 1995–96 which enabled me to work on Trollope. Thanks to Gail Lewis and Cora Kaplan for their comments on this essay.

1　Martin Green, *Dreams of Adventure, Deeds of Empire* (London, Routledge and Kegan Paul, 1980), p. 3.
2　See the relevant chapters in this collection.
3　This citation appears on the dustjacket of Victoria Glendinning's recent biography, *Anthony Trollope* (London, Hutchinson, 1992).
4　Anthony Trollope, *Autobiography*, 2 vols (London, William Blackwood and Sons, 1883), vol. 1, pp. 172–4.
5　Lord Sidney Olivier, *The Myth of Governor Eyre* (London, Hogarth Press, 1933), pp. 41–4.
6　Anthony Trollope, *North America*, 2 vols (London, Chapman and Hall, 1862), vol. 1, p. 1.
7　Trollope, *Autobiography*, vol. 1, p. 23.
8　*Ibid.*, p. 80.
9　*Ibid.*, p. 86.
10　Mary J. Hickman, *Religion, Class and Identity: The State, the Catholic Church and the Education of the Irish in Britain* (Aldershot, Avebury, 1995). See particularly chapter 2.
11　Trollope, *Autobiography*, vol. 1, p. 86.
12　The words are Julian Hawthorne's, son of Nathaniel, quoted in Michael Sadleir, *Trollope: A Commentary* (London, Constable, 1927), pp. 333–5.
13　Mabel E. Wotton, quoted in R. C. Terry (ed.), *Trollope: Interviews and Recollections* (London, Macmillan, 1987), p. 167.
14　James Bryce, quoted in Terry, *Trollope*, p. 168.
15　Quoted in *ibid.*, p. 138.
16　Quoted in Glendinning, *Trollope*, p. 303.
17　Edward Said, *Orientalism* (New York, Pantheon, 1978).
18　C. A. Bayly, *Imperial Meridian: The British Empire and the World 1780–1830* (London, Longman, 1989), p. 3.
19　For more detail on the Jamaican background see the relevant essays in Catherine Hall, *White, Male and Middle Class: Explorations in Feminism and History* (Cambridge, Polity, 1992).
20　Thomas Carlyle, 'Occasional discourse on the Negro Question', *Fraser's Magazine*, 41 (January 1850).
21　Anthony Trollope, *Australia and New Zealand*, 2 vols (London, Chapman and Hall, 1873), vol. 1, p. 29.
22　Anthony Trollope, *South Africa*, 2 vols (London, Chapman and Hall, 1878), vol. 2, p. 17.
23　Trollope, *Autobiography*, vol. 1, p. 175.
24　Anthony Trollope, *The West Indies and the Spanish Main* (London, Chapman and Hall, 1859), p. 134.
25　N. John Hall (ed.), *The Trollope Critics* (London, Macmillan, 1981), p. 434.
26　Trollope, 'Miss Sarah Jack, of Spanish Town, Jamaica', first published 1860, reprinted in Anthony Trollope, *The Complete Short Stories in Five Volumes*, vol. 3, Tourists and Colonials (London, The Trollope Society, n.d.), p. 1.
27　Trollope, *The West Indies*, pp. 56, 58, 60, 62, 66.
28　*Ibid.*, pp. 59–60, 62, 65.
29　*Ibid.*, pp. 74, 80.
30　Trollope, *Australia and New Zealand*, vol. 2, pp. 303, 315, 401, 413, 422, 488.
31　Trollope, *South Africa*, vol. 1, pp. 8–9, 18–19, 52, 178.
32　Trollope, *South Africa*, vol. 2, p. 188.
33　Trollope, *South Africa*, vol. 1, p. 1.

34 Trollope, *Australia and New Zealand*, vol. 1, p. 18.
35 *Ibid.*, p. 22.
36 *Ibid.*, p. 18.
37 Trollope, *Autobiography*, vol. 1, p. 137.
38 Terry, *Trollope*, p. 97.
39 Glendinning, *Trollope*, pp. 284, 480.
40 Trollope, *North America*, vol. 1, pp. 1–2, 394, 408, 400, 300, 281.
41 Sadleir, *Trollope*, p. 286.
42 Anthony Trollope, 'The higher education of women', in *Four Lectures* (London, Constable and Co., 1938), p. 73.
43 Cited in Glendinning, *Trollope*, p. 328.
44 See Anthony Trollope, *Ralph the Heir* (Harmondsworth, Penguin, 1993); 'Miss Sarah Jack, of Spanish Town, Jamaica'.
45 Trollope, *The West Indies*, p. 8.
46 See Leonore Davidoff on Munby's preoccupation with hands: 'Class and gender in Victorian England: the case of Hannah Cullwick and A. J. Munby', in *Worlds Between: Historical Perspectives on Gender and Class* (Cambridge, Polity, 1995).
47 Trollope, *The West Indies*, pp. 69–70.
48 Trollope, *Australia and New Zealand*, vol. 1, p. 308.
49 Leonore Davidoff and Catherine Hall, *Family Fortunes: Men and Women of the English Middle Class 1780–1850* (London, Hutchinson, 1987); Keith McClelland, 'Some thoughts on masculinity and the "representative artisan" in Britain, 1850–1880', *Gender and History*, 1:2 (1989).
50 Trollope, *The West Indies*, p. 89.
51 Trollope, *Australia and New Zealand*, vol. 1, pp. 181, 474, 480; vol. 2, p. 500.
52 Quoted in Marcie Muir, *Anthony Trollope in Australia*, (Adelaide, Wakefield Press, 1949), p. 97.
53 Trollope, *South Africa*, vol. 1, p. 58.
54 Anthony Trollope, *Castle Richmond*, 3 vols (London, Chapman and Hall, 1860), vol. 3, pp. 60–1.
55 Trollope, *North America*, vol. 2, pp. 464–5.

CHAPTER NINE

'Britain's conscience on Africa':[1] white women, race and imperial politics in inter-war Britain

Barbara Bush

The inter-war period saw the expansion and consolidation of British imperialism in Africa and by the end of the 1930s Africa arguably occupied 'a more intimate place' in British affairs than India.[2] Simultaneously, developments in black consciousness and the post-war conception of a liberal Empire ensured that the 'colour problem', race relations and colonial exploitation emerged as central issues. But there was another, equally important, element in these developments: the involvement of white women in both African affairs and the 'race problem'. While such women often followed male agendas (liberal or socialist) in analysis of the colonial problem, they were influential in their own right in spearheading new debates and engaging in pressure group activism. As 'the boundary makers of Empire',[3] white women were closer than men to the gendered and racialised margins of imperial culture and this impacted on the nature of their activism, their relations with both white and black men and their own identities as white women.

Since the movement for the abolition of slavery in the nineteenth century white women had become more conscious of their own gender oppression and identity as white women through active involvement in the 'black cause'. With the rise of both feminism and the 'New' Empire at the end of the nineteenth century, such analogies developed a more powerful resonance as expressed in the writings, for instance, of the South African socialist feminist Olive Schreiner.[4] There is now a developing literature that addresses the links between gender, race and empire pioneered in studies by Midgley (1992), Strobel and Chaudhuri (1992), Burton (1994) and Ware (1992). However, these address primarily pre-1914 developments and, with the exception of Helen Calloway's study of white women in Nigeria, there has been more emphasis on India than Africa.[5] Ware's book does highlight some aspects of gender relations within the post-World War One Empire and stresses interconnections between British histories of black people and women, but the inter-war period remains under-researched.

As the high point of British imperialism in Africa, but also a time of turbulent social and political developments in Britain and its African hinterland, this period constituted a distinctive era in the shaping of imperial race and gender relations. Women from the lowest to the highest classes broke through racial boundaries and engaged in sexual relationships with black men, a development which posed a threat to the very foundations of white supremacy. The gendered order of impe-rial rule was also threatened on the periphery by women breaching the masculine culture of the Colonial African Service (CAS) as wives, trav-ellers, academics and CAS employees. In tandem with these develop-ments, women also became more prominent in activism on race and imperial issues. Such activism was generated by the expansion and refinement of colonial administration in Africa, segregationist policies in the Union of South Africa, the development of colonial nationalism and the ideological conflict between liberalism and communism, a potent political cocktail in which race in Britain and Africa became a prime ingredient. In the imperial centre, black and white political activism pressured the British government to introduce colonial reforms and to consider ways of improving race relations to forestall the development of a more radical anti-imperialism that could threaten the whole fabric of empire.

Stimulus to these developments was provided by the expanding 'black presence' in Britain and the vibrant political climate of the 1930s which generated new debates around race, class and imperial-ism. It was fashionable during the inter-war years for liberally edu-cated middle-class women, emboldened by their recent political emancipation, to take up worthy political causes. In the serious 1930s even women who would have been frivolous socialites became 'polit-ical groupies' of the left or right. The unflagging commitment of indi-vidual women placed race and African issues more firmly on the political agenda in Britain but at the same time white women's involvement with black men generated new moral panics in racist and liberal discourses. Both black and white gender identities were thus redefined as the imperial and patriarchal certainties of the Victorian era were challenged by anti-colonialism, socialism and feminism.

Very little has been published on anti-colonial activism, with the exception of Stephen Howe's *Anti-Colonialism in British Politics: The Left and the End of Empire* (1994), and the gender dimension of such activism remains neglected. To bridge this gap in current research, this chapter addresses several key questions. Who were the white women activists and why and how did they become involved? What was their relationship with black men and women? How did white women progress debates about race and colonialism and interact with imperial politics? What influence did such activism have on shaping white women's identities and redefining imperialist culture? 'Activism' is defined here as activities within a broad political spectrum, including pro-imperialist, that impacted on imperial politics and discourses. The first section of the chapter addresses the African context that defined the issues around which activism developed. The second section examines women who were more directly involved in left-wing or liberal pressure group activities in Britain, highlighting individuals such as Nancy Cunard, Winifred Holtby and Sylvia Pankhurst. This is followed by an evaluation of relationships between white women and black men in progressing debate over the 'colour problem' in Britain and the Empire. The discussion thus opens up wider issues relating to women's gendered identities and political activism in the imperial context, highlighting the contrasts and similarities between the different types of women who became drawn to race and imperial issues and locating developments in the inter-war period in the longer-term perspective.

Defining the issues: the African hinterland

Inter-war activism in Britain can only be interpreted in relation to a continuous and complex interchange of ideas between Britain and Africa, white activists and imperial 'experts', and black activists in the African diaspora, the 'black Atlantic' spanning Africa, Britain and the black Americas.[6] Africa was fundamental to understanding the 'race problem', which was increasingly seen as the major problem of the twentieth century.[7] Racist representations of Africa at the most primitive base of the human pyramid of civilisation still strongly pervaded British culture, and racist literature perpetuated crude nineteenth-century 'scientific' racism. Such images were popularised through advertising, cinema, theatre, novels and travelogues and negatively impacted on the growing black population in Britain as well as reinforcing imperial identities.[8]

White women, as travellers and residents in Africa, contributed to these racial discourses, which had to adapt to the development of race consciousness. The inter-war years saw a new genre of travel writing by independent, 'emancipated' women. *Episodes from the Road to Timbuktu* (1927) and other travelogues by Lady Dorothy Mills are typical of this genre. Published by Duckworth's School Library, they speak authoritatively of the potential of the native 'mentally, socially and dangerously' and the 'vexed black problem' colonial authorities faced. As a wealthy traveller Mills could afford to indulge in an increasingly popular exoticism of Africa evident in the vogue for African dance and art indulged in by wealthy women of all political persuasions, including the radical Nancy Cunard with her 'trademark' African ivory bangles immortalised in Man Ray's photographic portrait.[9] Mill could be classed as 'pop anthropologist': like Cunard she was a tough, drinking, smoking, 'emancipated' upper-middle-class woman. Her own emancipation, however, did not prompt her to sympathy for black rights as it did in the case of Cunard and Holtby. For her Africa was solely the emotional appeal of 'uncivilised' African dancing and music and the animal-like beauty of 'savages'.[10] Other female writers on Africa like Elspeth Huxley and Karen Blixen were less exoticist but arguably equally racist in boasting an 'intimate' knowledge of, and 'maternalistic' concern for, the 'natives' with whom they had close contact as expatriate residents.[11]

Women with first-hand experience of Africa generated political interest in Britain through publishing pamphlets and books, giving lectures, engaging in pressure group activities and, in the case of Margery Perham, becoming a leading authority on Africa and an accomplished BBC broadcaster. Developments which gave Africa increasing prominence included the implementation of 'scientific colonialism' backed up by anthropological study of African societies, the entrenchment of white settler power, particularly in South Africa, the institutionalisation of the 'colour bar', and the exploitative nature of the colonial economy. Such developments stimulated African race and political consciousness and fuelled debates about African progress to modernity versus protection of 'traditional' cultures. During the inter-war years a number of 'exceptionally able' academic women including Margery Perham, Elspeth Huxley, Rita Hinden, Lucy Mair (who broke into the all-male discipline of African anthropology) and Odette Keun were thus drawn to the African scene. Through masculine eyes this represented a 'disproportionate' number of women experts and an 'abstention of masculine intellect' that was apparent until the post-World War Two era, when the African colonies became central to Britain's post-war reconstruction.[12]

The inter-war liberal ideal of progressive and enlightened imperialism premised on improving 'race relations' was arguably particularly appealing to the sympathetic 'feminine nature' of women colonial experts. Perham reputedly had a 'passionate concern' for progress towards racial equality and 'a strong consciousness of race' although her 'candid' descriptions of Africans were not always complimentary and she remained essentially conservative in her politics. She attributed her 'intuitive reaction' to Africa as 'an artist and a traveller' to her 'early fascination' with the race problem.[13] Her interest in Africa was aroused when she visited her married sister in Somalia in 1921 at the age of twenty-four. The visit fulfilled her 'romantic' childhood dreams inspired by Rider Haggard and afterwards she devoted herself to the study of the government of the 'native races'.[14]

Both Margery Perham and Winifred Holtby matured into African affairs through visits to South Africa in the 1920s.[15] South Africa was at the heart of imperial politics as Afrikaner nationalism asserted itself, eclipsing British liberalism: the ongoing threat to African rights channelled 'pan-liberal' activism between South Africa and Britain and this broadened into general concern over the 'race and colonial question' in Africa. Perham became one of the foremost experts of the 'progressive' school of colonial administration, with its emphasis on education and development, and was close to influential imperialists such as Frederick Lugard. She travelled extensively in Africa and became a lecturer on native administration at Oxford, where she had a strong influence on generations of British and colonial students. Perham criticised the 'purists' who wished to preserve an exoticised and static 'traditional' African culture, and in *Ten Africans* (1936) she pleaded for the recognition of the achievements of individual educated (male) Africans.[16] She flirted with mildly liberal ideas but, in the eyes of more acerbic male critics of colonial rule, was opportunistic, disdainful and condescending to blacks, retaining a 'naive faith' in the benevolence of the Colonial Office and allegedly seeing only the good side of British administration in Africa.[17] However, she undoubtedly encountered prejudices from colonial officials in the field and male academics, reflecting, perhaps, an element of sour grapes because she had the ear of the powerful in a way that eluded them.

Perham was strongly aware of the gender dimension of her involvement in African affairs; 'I have always played the woman', she acknowledged in her diaries. Described as exceptionally 'striking, attractive and athletic' with 'an outstanding brain', she made use of her femininity and personal 'magnetism' to influence men and gain their patronage in advancing her career.[18] Despite her intellect and eminence she retained a romanticised view of imperial masculinity, epitomised in her depiction of the colonial officer, Dane, the 'man of action' and civilised integrity in her novel about Africa, *Major Dane's Garden* (1925). It was powerful male patrons who launched her into African studies in sponsoring her Rhodes Trust world tour in 1930 to study 'the administration of the coloured races'. However, she was torn by conflicts between her intellect and her 'natural mission in life'. Like Holtby, she never married and her diaries reveal an underlying dissatisfaction with her own achievements which failed to 'fulfil her femininity'.[19]

As a major publicist and analyst on African affairs Perham had an important impact on imperial politics in Britain, where her activities intermeshed with those of more radical women campaigners against colonialism through her membership of pressure groups like the London Group on African Affairs (LGAA) and the League of Coloured Peoples (LCP). Her views were indeed enlightened in an era when attitudes to colonial administration in Africa were shaped by a deeply entrenched racist ideology which influenced both popular images of Africa and the practical policies of colonial administrators. Progressive women imperialists were arguably less patronising and more genuinely committed to the ideal of racial equality for Africans than their male counterparts, who still emphasised Africans' lack of history and culture, their child-like mentality and the need for long-term 'guidance' of Africans under white tutelage. While the African hinterland provided the context for female activism, however, it was London, the junction-box of empire, that became the centre of political activity, both pro- and anti-imperialist.

'A passion of pity': white female anti-imperialist activism in inter-war Britain

After World War One there were two distinct strands of minority activism directed towards the problems of colonialism in Africa. The first derived from the older anti-slavery tradition of championing the weaker races and protecting them from imperialist exploitation. It was represented by the work of the male-dominated Aborigine Protection Society (APS) and was regarded as conservative and cautious by more radical activists. The second strand comprised the newer radical anti-imperialism inspired by the British liberal J. A. Hobson in *Imperialism: A Study* (1902) and Marxist theories developed in Lenin's *Imperialism: The Highest Stage of Capitalism* (1917). This clarification of the link between capitalism and imperialism, combined with the increasing popularity of socialism, opened up new discourses on empire. While the mainstream Labour movement activists generally colluded in the conventional imperial discourses, a minority became vocal critics. The most radical anti-imperialism was articulated by the small Communist Party (CPGB) and 'fellow travellers', regarded as the 'enemy within' by all but the most radical of the non-revolutionary left.[20] Women had an increasingly strong voice within this broad political spectrum and were disproportionately represented in groups involved in 'African work'.

Three broad strands of female political activism can be discerned. First, there were the 'humanitarians', Quakers like Ruth Fry and Anna Melissa Graves who continued the abolitionist commitment to the protection and defence of 'weaker' peoples and were motivated by 'sympathetic benevolence' towards the underdog, altruism, duty and a Quaker belief of 'God in all men'.[21] Second, there were the non-revolutionary or 'ethical' socialists, like Winifred Holtby, Vera Brittain, Diana Stock and the Labour MP Ellen Wilkinson, who regularly raised questions on Africa in the House of Commons before 1931.[22] This group embraced Fabian socialists such as Rita Hinden, who became a leading policy analyst on Africa during World War Two when the Labour Party and its Fabian 'think tank' were far more influential on government policy on Africa.[23] Third, there were the women of the more radical or revolutionary left: Eleanor Burns, who wrote on Africa,[24] and Sylvia Pankhurst. Nancy Cunard, whose unorthodox lifestyle and transgression of inter-racial taboos was inseparable from her identification with the black cause, may also be included in this category. In addition to these white female activists there were also a handful of black women activists resident in Britain in the 1930s, the most notable being Una Marson, Eslanda Goode Robeson and Amy Ashwood Garvey.

Women activists, liberal, Labour or left-wing, were part of a 'political generation' profoundly influenced by World War One and empowered by pre-war feminism and the exhilaration of their own political emancipation. They were 'modern women', politicised by the ideological schisms created by the Russian revolution and inspired by the ideals of the League of Nations on international peace and development. There were strong overlaps in liberal ideals, political influences and social networks between the Quaker humanitarians and 'ethical' socialists. As the numerically larger and more socially acceptable constituency of female activism, they contributed significantly to the surge in middle-class activism on African and black issues that was a response to the development of black consciousness. Younger women activists worked closely with black male activists. For such women blacks were equals, not simply victims, and they saw themselves as less patronising than the older generation of liberals. The 'politically correct' of the 1930s, they were active in other causes of the day, including Spain, Indian nationalism and anti-fascism (causes that also attracted left-wing women) and were arguably the role model for female involvement in the third-world pressure groups of the post-World War Two period.

Linked to developments in Africa, there were important issues within Britain that also stimulated this female activism. Britain was the political heart of the English-speaking 'black empire' and this resulted not only in an increase in the numbers of black residents but also the spread of a diasporic black consciousness through pan-

Africanism and Garveyite black nationalism. With the 'race riots' in Britain and elsewhere in 1919 a stronger concern over the 'colour problem' emerged that continued throughout the period.[25] This growth of black unrest was complicated by the perceived 'Bolshevik' threat to the colonies and developed into an ideological struggle for the 'hearts and minds' of the African intelligentsia. Thus a major preoccupation of liberal and more moderate socialist activists, male and female, was to 'guide' this emergent black consciousness along a gradualist, non-revolutionary path.[26] In the 1930s this also came higher on the agenda of more establishment liberals like Margery Perham.

Among the non-revolutionary socialist activists, the novelist and feminist Winifred Holtby is undoubtedly the most outstanding woman in terms of connections and influence. Her involvement in Africa stems from a lecturing tour of South Africa for the League of Nations Union in 1926, when she made contact with British liberals in Johannesburg, who were committed to 'multiracialism' (improving relations between the races through collaboration with educated blacks and pressure for moderate reforms). These activists were also concerned to counteract the communist influence in the Industrial and Commercial Workers' Union (ICU), the first black trade unions formed by Clemens Kadalie in 1920; Holtby was able to meet Kadalie and other 'Zulu Bolshevists' and was thus converted to the native cause.[27] Perham also had an interest in the ICU and on her tour of South Africa in 1929 met an ICU leader in Durban whom she respected but could not 'like' as a white person. Unlike Holtby, she was too linked to the establishment to embrace such a cause.[28]

British liberals had been involved with the South African 'native problem' since pre-war days but Holtby's visit generated an upsurge of new interest. On her return to England she set out to canvass the support of the British labour movement for the ICU and to publicise the 'terrible' conditions in Johannesburg that had also made an impact on Margery Perham. According to her close friend Vera Brittain, she was concerned over the developing cleavage between blacks and even liberal whites in South Africa which allowed a 'crude ... undiluted ... brand of vehement communism' to impose itself on native ignorance.[29] In response to these issues, in 1927 Holtby instigated the formation of an 'Africa group' which by 1934 was known as the 'Friends of Africa'. The new group was associated with the Socialist League and the Independent Labour Party (ILP) and adopted an openly political perspective. It also had contacts with the left-wing publishers Gollancz and the newly formed National Council for Civil Liberties, which also attracted women activists and took a keen interest in black civil rights in Africa and Britain. The linchpin of the 'Friends' was

Holtby, who, as a journalist with influential contacts, was able to pub-licise and co-ordinate British links with South Africa. The group also raised funds to sponsor a Scottish trade unionist, William Ballinger, to go out to South Africa to act as an 'adviser' to the ICU and steer it away from communism.

The 'Friends of Africa' saw themselves as more radical than the male-dominated LGAA, the main pressure group on Africa in the inter-war years. Although the two groups did co-operate on certain important issues, the LGAA remained essentially conservative, main-taining close establishment links. Even Perham, a member of the LGAA, threatened to throw her lot in with the 'radicals' in 1934 when the organisation failed to take a stronger critical stance on develop-ments in South Africa.[30] Like that of the LGAA, the work of the 'Friends' was centred almost exclusively on South Africa and in prac-tical terms failed to reverse the growing repression or promote better conditions for natives. However, it did widen and deepen the 'pan-lib-eral link' between Britain and South Africa and its members used their middle-class networks to gain a wider profile for African issues in gen-eral before they rose higher on the official agenda after 1935.

The energies of women like Holtby, however, were not restricted solely to campaigning on African issues. They were also actively chan-nelled into multiracial initiatives to combat racial discrimination in Britain. In contrast to the experiences of black colonial seamen resi-dent in Britain, the racism experienced by educated blacks was muted by contact with liberals, and thus their responses to whites were com-plex and ambivalent. Black students and the avant-garde London set mixed together in inter-racial 'Harlem style' West End night clubs which created a false illusion of equality.[31] The more conservative pro-fessional class and the popular black American entertainers, like Paul Robeson, were invited to inter-racial garden parties, tennis club teas and similar events organised by well-intentioned liberals. There was also a small circle of ILP activists including Reginald Reynolds, his wife, Ethel Mannin, and, of course, Holtby, whose doors were 'always open to black and white alike'. Black intellectuals like C. L. R James and George Padmore were welcomed in the left-wing literary circles satirised in Mannin's novel, *Comrade O Comrade* (published in 1945 but written during the 1930s).[32] At one of Holtby's parties in 1934, attended by Una Marson, her cousin Daisy Pickering and a 'talented West Indian writer', Eric Walrond, 'the colour question, miscegenation ... and race prejudice' were 'turned inside out'.[33]

However, the cosy multiracialism of the Holtby clique provided only a cosmetic alternative to the racism all blacks experienced in mainstream British society. Eric Walrond believed that blacks in the colonies tended to see Britain through a 'romantic and illusory' veil. He argued that there was a 'peculiar negro problem … complex and varied' in London and other major centres with black populations and that, given their vast black empire, the British were 'surprisingly inexpert' in race relations. Una Marson, a Jamaican writer who lived in England for ten years from 1932 to 1942, was enraged by the racist insults which she had to endure in addition to sexist attitudes from both black and white men as one of the rare black women trying to make a name for herself in literary circles. No official segregation existed but blacks were not welcome in certain districts and university students were subtly discouraged from settling in Britain. Other contemporary accounts also testified to the widespread discrimination in housing, hotels, nursing and other professions.[34]

In response to such problems, a long-term Jamaican resident, Dr Harold Moody, founded the multiracialist League of Coloured Peoples in 1931, of which the energetic Una Marson became secretary in 1932. Sympathetic white women were keen to join the organisation[35] and its magazine, *The Keys*, had a readership which included progressive pro-colonialists like Margery Perham (an LCP member). It reflected a wide range of race and colonial issues topical in the 1930s and contributors included black radicals such as C. L. R. James as well as white conservatives like Dame Catherine Furse of the World Bureau of Guides and Scouts. The LCP also held annual conferences reflecting the growing diasporic awareness on race issues, with delegates from the West Indies, Africa, Australia and the United States; guest speakers included the ubiquitous Holtby. As with her 'Africa work', Holtby threw herself enthusiastically into multiracial initiatives in Britain and counted resident blacks in her circle of friends.[36]

Holtby's approach to the race and colonial questions of the day was less patronising than many, particularly that of the cautious liberal males involved in the 'welfare of Africans' in Britain. Her commitment and selflessness were acknowledged by African students, whom she helped financially, and a close male colleague described her as the 'stoutest warrior of all' and a constant source of inspiration to others working in the black cause.[37] She was one of the few white women activists who seems to have had a genuine friendship with a black woman in Una Marson. They shared an interest in feminism as well as race issues and Una was reputedly shaken by her sudden death and the loss of her valued support.[38] Holtby also knew Eslanda Goode Robeson although their relationship was much cooler, possibly because of Robeson's increasing commitment to communism and suspicion of 'woolly' socialists. Eslanda Robeson was also a formidable woman in her own right, an anthropologist who carried out field work in Uganda in 1936, visited South Africa and published her own *African Journey* (1946). She did not need Holtby's sympathetic white patronage, however well-intentioned it may have been.

What motivated Holtby and other sympathetic middle-class women to take up the black cause? Lady Rhondda, a close friend of Holtby and editor of the feminist periodical *Time and Tide*, felt that at times Winifred may have exhibited 'an unwholesome pity complex'. Yet men with whom they collaborated intimated that their feminine qualities were invaluable to the cause. Norman Leys, who was an unflagging critic of colonial rule in Kenya, believed that it was highly fortuitous 'at a period of the struggle for the Liberation of Africans' that Holtby possessed qualities 'exactly fitted to make that struggle a success'. 'I shouldn't wonder if the fact that you are a woman may help to turn the scale', he wrote in a letter to Holtby.[39] A degree of emotional sublimation may also have been involved in Holtby's activism: friends saw her as a 'martyr' to the cause and in her satirical novel, *Mandoa, Mandoa! A Comedy of Irrelevance* (1933), the main female character, Jean Stanbury, 'bound to a life of duty and self sacrifice' and foregoing marriage for 'independence and work for the native', was arguably modelled upon herself.

Indeed the martydom element may have been exclusively linked to female activism. For the dedicated few, work for the native cause often resulted in ill health and/or personal hardship. On hearing in 1933 of Holtby's illness, Margaret Hodgson, an activist from a respectable Scottish working-class background and a resident of South Africa who lectured at Witwatersrand University, commented on how 'misfortune seems to dog [our] African work' and, prophetically perhaps, warned Holtby not to sacrifice herself to it. For other women involvement in the native cause may have masked an arid emotional life. A senior schoolmistress in Pretoria was described to Holtby by her South African-based friend Jean MacWilliam as 'working hard for the natives' as a form of solace for a 'very unhappy marriage'. Holtby had an elusive and unsatisfactory relationship but never married; her life was dedicated to helping the ill and needy and her friends and relatives as well as Africans.[40]

After her premature death in autumn 1935, and without her optimism and energies, the 'Friends of Africa' lost impetus. Interest in South Africa declined and activists 'in the field', like Margaret Hodgson, became increasingly disillusioned and cynical. After 1935 attention turned increasingly to West Africa, now seen as the locus of the 'African renaissance'. Holtby and other earnest women had pioneered pressure group activities on Africa with zeal and dedication but by the mid-1930s they had been superseded by the less emotive male

'Africanists' who had first-hand experience of African conditions and became the 'experts' on development problems. As unrest in Africa intensified, African issues were placed higher on the official political agenda and thus became a more respectable concern for men, although Perham remained a foremost African expert through to independence.

On balance Holtby, like other liberal and 'ethical socialist' women, could be described as politically naive with a tendency to woolly idealism. She was, however, rightly critical of the more conservative and paternalistic liberal humanitarians involved in native welfare (many of whom were strong-minded men) whom she satirised in *Mandoa*. Intended as 'political comment', this novel was described by Vera Brittain as a 'ruthless satire' on British imperialism. It was a fictitious account of the European impact on Mandoa, a fictitious African kingdom loosely akin to Ethiopia. Holtby was irritated when literary critics described it as a piece of fun, for she saw herself as a serious socialist and anti-imperialist.[41] In reality she advocated little that challenged the wider structures of British imperialism, but she did have valuable influence in middle-class networks that helped publicise Africa, the 'Cinderella' cause.

Like Perham, Holtby was very much a product of her 'good' background. She had a private income which facilitated her entry into establishment circles where she could promote the black cause. Female critics of colonialism were thus still privileged as 'colonisers', benefiting, for instance, from share holdings in South Africa, which calls into question the degree to which even the most committed of the white left could bridge the ontological gulf between coloniser and colonised.[42] Despite Holtby's 'radical' ideas, her relations with blacks never transcended the bounds of political or moral respectability and she remained committed to the 'higher ideals' of empire. It is here that the main contrasts can be made with women activists who adopted a more left-wing perspective, like Nancy Cunard, the politicised heiress to the Cunard fortune and an avant-garde poet. Cunard was particularly critical of the fact that in the multiracial social circles of London, individual blacks were only accepted as equals because they conformed to white standards, were 'cultured' and educated, politically moderate and dissociated from the mass of blacks in Britain and the colonies. For individuals, such patronage was highly seductive, but arguably perpetuated racist conceptions of the 'otherness' of Africa.

In the 1930s Cunard was in the vanguard of a cultural movement to redress the denigration of African history and culture and the desire of whites to reform the world in their own 'dreary and decadent image', only recognising black achievements based on having attained 'honorary white' status. Her *Negro Anthology* (1934), heavily influenced by black cultural movements like the Harlem Renaissance, was compiled to challenge such ethnocentrism and covered the whole of Africa and the African diaspora. Contributors included black writers and activists and British and French anthropologists and avant-garde writers. This unique and path-breaking anthology was strongly anti-imperialist and designed to counteract race prejudice, embracing contributions on 'Negro' history, art and culture as well as political themes.[43]

Central to the compilation of Cunard's *Negro Anthology* was the campaign to free the Scottsboro boys. The Scottsboro boys were nine young blacks (the youngest was fourteen) who were charged with rape of a white girl in Scottsboro, Alabama, in 1932. The threat of lynching was ever present and the case became internationally famous, rousing liberal and left opinion on both sides of the Atlantic which arguably saved the defendants from execution. In 1932 the communist-influenced League Against Imperialism and the Negro Workers Association co-operated to form a Scottsboro Defence Committee. For activists involved in Africa, the Scottsboro affair was intimately linked to a wider international problem of racism and white supremacy. White women were strongly represented on the campaign committee with Mrs Carmel Haden Guest as co-chair and Eleanor Rathbone and Naomi Mitchison, the writer, as vice-presidents; Jomo Kenyatta (the future Kenyan nationalist leader who was a student in England at the time) and Mrs Gladys White were joint secretaries. More moderate organisations like the LCP were also represented on the committee, which organised speeches, demonstrations and protests and helped co-ordinate a 'world wide petition'. The campaign also brought white women into rare contact with black female activism when Mrs Ada Wright, mother of one of the defendants, addressed a large meeting outside Shoreditch Town Hall, London, in June 1932.[44]

Despite some collaboration over the Scottsboro affair, white liberals were suspicious of communist involvement. They were also alarmed at the way issues like the Scottsboro affair stimulated race consciousness throughout Africa and the African diaspora, inspiring feelings of black racial solidarity and a greater awareness of the international dimension of racism and its link with colonialism. These developments constituted a left-wing challenge to liberal multiracialism. After 1935 with the emergence of a more radical pan-Africanism, black activists increasingly rejected white liberal patronage, male or female, and attacked the multiracialism so readily espoused by 'Uncle Toms' like Harold Moody, warning of liberal duplicity. The turning point for many black activists was the failure of Britain to act on the

Italian invasion of Ethiopia (Abyssinia), the last 'free' African kingdom, in 1935.

In response to the invasion, black activists in Britain co-operated in setting up a new 'umbrella' organisation, the International Association of the Friends of Abyssinia (IAFA). It was described as an 'All Negro Organisation' whose aim was 'to assist ... in the maintenance of the territorial integrity of Abyssinia and to alert the British public to the threat of fascism'. Executive members included young African nationalists in Britain, like Jomo Kenyatta, Amy Ashwood Garvey and Una Marson. Marson became intimately involved in the Ethiopian cause and in 1935 resigned as secretary of the LCP. In 1936 she became the private secretary of the Emperor Haile Selassie, now an exile in England, and accompanied him to Geneva when he went to plead his case before the League of Nations. The work of the IAFA was supported by the Abyssinian Association, formed in 1937 by white left-wing sympathisers, and the *New Times and Ethiopian News*, launched and edited by Sylvia Pankhurst, long involved with black activists in campaigns against racism. The *New Times* began as a newsletter on events in Ethiopia but developed into an anti-imperialist and anti-fascist publication, deeply critical of the League of Nations. It supported self-determination for all blacks, race and class equality and opposed 'all racial propaganda' in education, cinemas and the media. Sylvia Pankhurst ultimately went to live in Ethiopia.[45] Margery Perham was also 'fiercely concerned' about the invasion and it arguably stimulated her own critical reappraisal of colonialism. In her book *The Government of Ethiopia* (1948), she publicly advocated the Ethiopian cause. However, she was 'bitterly attacked' by Pankhurst in the *New Times* as insufficiently critical of the British role in Ethiopia and Perham was convinced that it was Pankhurst's influence with Haile Selassie that prevented her from visiting the country.[46]

Ultimately this alliance between white activists and black radicals could not be sustained and in May 1937 young, male African nationalists based in London formed the International Africa Service Bureau for the Defence of Africans and Peoples of African Descent (IASB). Yet the IASB still encouraged the support of sympathetic whites, particularly women like Nancy Cunard, Sylvia Pankhurst, Mary Downes and Dorothy Woodman (Union of Democratic Control) who were allowed associate, as opposed to 'active', membership. Black men were still prepared to accept white support but only if it was not directed to manipulating or directing black movements and here white women proved more acceptable than white male activists used to being 'in control' and less able to work in a subordinate capacity. In retrospect, the 1945 Pan-African Congress acknowledged 'certain white women and men on the Left' who had championed the black cause and denounced racism and colonialism when it was not 'fashionable'.[47]

While white women readily espoused black men's causes, black women remained marginal to their conceptions of race equality. The black discourses on nationalism and pan-Africanism that helped shape their political activism were highly gendered and reflected only the black male perspective. This lends support to bell hooks's and other black feminists' contention that white women only identify with black men's causes, undermining any closer identification of white and black feminist issues.[48] With the exception of Holtby, few activists expressed any interest in, or understanding of, black women's problems. In the inter-war period there was not even the 'maternalist' identification of 'female issues' characteristic of pre-war 'imperial feminism' that linked moral reform of empire with concern for female colonial 'others'.[49] Feminism was generally lower on the agenda after the enfranchisement of women and, as has been illustrated here, female activism was channelled into other pressing political issues. However, the 'special relationship' white women had with black male activists was arguably still based on an identification of oppressions that reached back to the anti-slavery campaigns. Like Olive Schreiner, Winifred Holtby perceived a 'close relationship' between racial and sexual oppression and for Jewish women activists this link became acutely relevant with the rise of fascism.[50]

The complex psycho-sexual relations between white women and black men were rooted in conceptions of black and white masculinities which have been integral to the power relations of imperialism and institutionalised racism. Put simply, white men could assert power over white (and black) women but, with the exception of sexual power, black men were subordinate to white women in race/class terms. McClintock and others have argued that racist discourse 'feminised' black men and located them on the margins of the civilisation and progress that defined white male identities. Both white women and black men were associated with degenerate characteristics that positioned them below white men in the racial and cultural hierarchies of imperialism. But the masculine conception of progress also embraced educated white women and 'civilised' black men, whereas black women were rendered invisible and outside modern time.[51]

White women activists arguably developed an empathetic relationship with black men and felt able to interact with them in a more 'egalitarian' way than with white men. Commenting on this 'special relationship', the pan-African activist Ras Makonnen, a British Guianan resident in England in the 1930s, asserted that black activists did not need to seek out white women's help, for they would simply come round and ask what was to be done. In his opinion such dedication to the black cause was an expression of equal rights, for 'one way of rejecting the oppression of [white] men was to associate with blacks'.[52] But this scope for social interaction between black men and white women blurred the dangerous borders that underpinned the gendered and racialised order of British society, and it is here that white women activists differed most from their male counterparts. While the majority of white women activists did not overtly breach sex/race taboos, the minority who did added a new dimension to race and imperial politics in inter-war Britain.

'Black man, white ladyship': inter-racial sex and the politics of imperialism

The dangers of trans-racial sex between white women and black men of all classes became an obsession among white males as the black male presence in Europe increased. This was first articulated by the liberal anti-colonialist Edmund Morel, who championed the rights of natives in Africa, but was opposed to the presence of French Senegalese soldiers on the Rhine in 1918. He warned of 'The Black Scourge in Europe', arguing that the temperate climate 'enhanced black men's sexuality' and posed a threat to white women. Similarly, a writer on the 'race problem', Basil Matthews, warned that passionate love scenes in cinemas degraded white women in African eyes, whereas Lord Sidney Olivier, a progressive Governor of Jamaica, opposed unions between black men and white women on the grounds that Europeans were the most 'advanced' in intellectual development and it was bad to breed 'backwards'. Such attitudes are also evident among the male liberals involved in charitable work amongst the poor black community in British ports. As Cedric Dover, a Marxist Eurasian biologist writing in the 1930s, noted, this 'bourgeois obsession' with inter-racial sex ('miscegenation' in racist discourse) and its resultant 'half-caste' population was reflected in a plethora of literature on the subject which insidiously supported biological theories of white racial superiority.[53]

The sexual element in racism thus remained strong despite the new liberal 'race relations' discourse. Such racism was reinforced through the media, education and popular entertainment. According to the black nationalist Marcus Garvey, the media were preoccupied with white women's strange fascination with black men who reputedly 'gathered in cafés' and seemed to do 'no honest work'. He contrasted this to the lack of coverage of the 'frequent moral abuse' of African and

Indian women by colonial whites.[54] In the colonies there was tight policing of white female sexuality and it was black women who represented the dangerous borders in sexual liaisons with white men. This was reversed in Britain where trans-racial sex and the black threat to white Britain became firmly linked in the popular consciousness. When Little carried out his pioneer study of blacks in Britain in the 1940s he noted that, in the question of colour prejudice, intermarriage was of 'paramount' importance.[55]

While strong taboos existed in colonial Africa against relationships between white women and black men, in Britain women of all classes reputedly 'consorted' with blacks. For educated blacks relationships with white women were bound up with struggles over power and status. Margery Perham, who had contact with West African students at the West African Students' Union hostel in London, argued that blacks entered into liaisons with white women as the 'supreme ... compensation' for the 'severe racial humiliation' they suffered in Britain. For black male activists this sexual assertion was a 'revolutionary act' employed by blacks and Indians to 'get their own back in Europe'. But they also criticised the 'gigolos' and 'Europeanised missionary boys' who capitalised on rich white women's 'fascination' with black sex ('sexual imperialism') merely for 'prestige value'.[56] These complex dynamics are summed up eloquently by Ras Makonnen:

> All this made us very careful in associating with white women: otherwise you could have terrible things said of them and yourself. Sometimes if you were walking down Piccadilly with a white girl some white drunk would shout 'white bastard' at her. Some people would immediately identify this white woman who was walking with you as someone loose, because no outstanding woman would be seen with a nigger. So against your will you took up a defensive attitude, and managed to let the woman be a little in front of you. ... One had the same tactics with older women who felt you were a missionary boy, and would take you into coffee shops with some sort of pretentious English smile. Here one could see the great injustice being done, often unconsciously, by many of these fine women who were dedicated to establish Negro rights.[57]

Race, gender and sexuality became fiercely contested terrains linked to imperial power relations. Thus women who were merely friendly with black men risked moral censure. This risk was enhanced by the fashion in avant-garde circles in London and Paris for black boyfriends. As 'forbidden fruit' black sex was tempting and became linked in the inter-war years to a passion for black music and dance, a return to the primeval.[58] In Paris 'all the chic Parisiennes ... consorted with Negroes' and a similar situation existed in London, where even aristocratic women of empire like Edwina Mountbatten created scandal

[216]

through allegedly becoming involved in 'compromising situations' with 'coloured men'.[59] Evelyn Waugh in *Decline and Fall* (1928) and Holtby in *Mandoa* both satirised this fad, portraying women involved in such liaisons (Margot Beste Chetwynde and Felicity Cardover respectively) as scheming, shallow and decadent characters for whom black men were simply a short-lived whim. But whereas Holtby attacked racist attitudes and was sympathetic to the Mandoan official Cardover tried to seduce, Waugh openly ridiculed Beste Chetwynde's flashily dressed black American boyfriend, insinuating the 'uncontrollable passions and animal nature' of blacks.

Shortly after Waugh's novel was published Nancy Cunard's controversial liaison with Henry Crowder (a black American composer) was luridly exposed in the popular press, resulting in Cunard's social ostracism and estrangement from her socialite mother, Emerald. Cunard's left-wing associations combined with her sexual peccadilloes and passion for jazz music and African exotica made her an easy target for caricature as an archetypal 'nigger lover'. One of her mother's high-society friends, Margot Asquith, quipped on enquiring about Nancy, 'what is it now, drink, drugs or niggers?' and Sir Thomas Beecham, another Cunard family friend, reputedly wanted Nancy 'tarred and feathered'. When Cunard visited London with Crowder, the couple faced open discrimination in hotels.[60] Although she was a somewhat difficult and temperamental person, her concern with Africa was motivated by political commitment and she was one of the few well-heeled British women to have any contact with working-class blacks. She wrote a spirited defence of her relationship with Crowder, *Black Man, White Ladyship: An Anniversary* (1931), in which she made a fierce attack on prejudiced attitudes, and black activists like Nnamdi Azikiwe, the Nigerian nationalist, have testified to her unswerving support for the black cause.[61]

Other women were also 'viciously attacked' in the media and the socialite Doris Garland Anderson, who was married to a black American 'celebrity', bitterly criticised the 'smart set' who treated black men like toys, and devalued genuine relationships. Her book *Nigger Lover* (1937), which dealt with the problems faced by inter-racial couples, was 'strongly recommended' by the LCP.[62] Although it was relations between white working-class women and poorer black men resident in Britain that were the main focus of the moral panics over racial degeneration, upper-class women's relationships with black men were used to trivialise the serious political issue of race. Similarly, the 'sexual imperialism' of some hedonistic rich women muddied the more genuine commitment of many white women to black causes. This was testified to by Makonnen, who praised the many 'devoted' women like Holtby, Ethel Manning and Diana Stock (a WEA activist and editor of the ILP's *New Leader* in the 1930s) who were 'above scandal' and gave practical help and support to black causes. He maintained that the best helpers were 'the typical English type of devoted girl from LSE or Cambridge' like Stock.[63] Black male activists thus made a clear distinction between the attitudes of British men and women and remarked that their stay in Britain would have been 'almost intolerable' without the 'sympathy, kindness and assistance' of British women as 'landladies and organisers'.[64]

Summary

In an area which intertwines race prejudice and colonialism, and which is complicated by gender relations between white women and white and black men, no hard and fast conclusions can be drawn. There were significant differences and similarities between the women who were influential in shaping discourses on empire and race in the inter-war years. All the women discussed above were over-whelmingly middle or upper class and products of the post-World War One 'mood of the times' and contemporary discourses on politics and imperialism. As 'modern' women they were part of a 'new world order' that replaced the braggadocio imperialism of the pre-war era with more liberal conceptions of commonwealth premised on progressive development towards self-determination and racial quality for colonial peoples. This ethos permeated the approach of 'imperialists' like Perham as much as that of the 'anti-imperialists' like Holtby, and distinguishes her from pre-war women imperialists like Flora Shaw. However, whereas the 'establishment' experts directed their activism towards popularisation of progressive and developmental conceptions of Britain's African empire, the pressure group activists helped to bring a more critical perspective on race and imperial issues on to the agenda of the 'chattering classes' of the 1930s.

A number of points of contrast with the pre-war period have also emerged in this chapter. Post-war women activists worked more closely with men as colleagues and were responsible for important political initiatives. This contrasts with earlier female involvement with the 'black cause', when men primarily determined the discourses on both race and imperial issues and the nature of both black and white femininity. In establishment circles there was arguably a greater recognition of women's academic expertise on imperial issues. Another important contrast with the pre-war period relates to feminist discourses. Although some activists like Holtby were self-defined feminists they tended to compartmentalise their 'African work' from their feminist activities and their preoccupations differed substantially from those of the maternalist 'imperial feminists' who occupied themselves with the 'female' empire, including the welfare of native women. With rare exceptions, post-war women activists interpreted 'race' and imperial problems within a generalised socialist 'meta-theory' or in relation to contemporary academic writings on race and imperialism from both right and left. This reflects the way in which emancipated women had embraced the male-defined shibboleths of Western modernity. They thus had few links with black women and little interest in feminist issues in Africa. Establishment 'experts' like Perham could by no stretch of the imagination be described as feminists except from the liberal perspective of seeing themselves as successful in a man's world.

Where gender remained significant was in a feminine sympathy for and identification with the most oppressed 'underdog' that can be traced back to the abolitionist women of the early nineteenth century. From the white and black male perspective, inter-war activists had 'special feminine qualities' of sympathy and intuition that made their contribution unique. But such women's close social contact with black men also raised controversial questions about their attraction to black men. The inter-war period witnessed a rejection of nineteenth-century respectability and rich 'emancipated women' could flaunt convention through engaging in unpopular political causes: the ultimate act of rebellion was to 'consort' with black men. This was used to discredit certain women and the causes they championed. Despite class and political differences, women activists were all affected by the shifting discourses on race, empire and sexuality.

In conclusion, while there were threads of continuity between pre-war and post-war female activism on race and imperial issues, the female activism analysed here was deeply influenced by the new uncertainties of the inter-war years, the rapid development of race consciousness and colonial nationalism, and the related crisis of imperialism intensified by World War Two. More continuity can arguably be established with white female activism of the 1950s and 1960s, the era of decolonisation and *laissez-faire* colonial migration, than the pre-World War One era of confident 'imperial feminism'. As the focus of the 'race problem' moved from 'out there' in the Empire to the heart of British society, the new field of 'race relations' attracted a disproportionate number of women academics.[65] Pressure group activism was continued by women like Felicity Bolton, who worked tirelessly for the Movement for Colonial Freedom and Campaign Against Racial Discrimination in the 1950s and 1960s, and educated black men (but not women) continued to enjoy the patronage of sympathetic middle-class white women. Debates around race and sexuality also intensified after 1940 as the incidence of black man–white woman relationships increased.[66] Thus the inter-war years, the most neglected period in 'imperial history', were formative in the development of anti-imperialist and anti-racist activism: the activities of white women activists in Britain fused central debates about race, sex and imperial power that were to be placed more centrally on the political agenda in the post-war period. In turn these developments led to further redefinition of white women's identities, forged in relation to black male activism, black women and constructs of white imperial womanhood, a redefinition that has had ongoing resonance in the 'post-colonial' epoch.

Notes

1 Alison Smith and Mary Bull (eds), *Margery Perham and British Rule in Africa* (London, Frank Cass, 1991), Introduction, p. 1.
2 Malcolm Hailey, 'Nationalism in Africa', *Journal of the African Society*, 36 (April 1937), 140. Hailey was ex-Governor of the United Provinces in India.
3 Anne McClintock, *Imperial Leather: Race, Gender and Sexuality in the Colonial Contest* (London, Routledge, 1995), pp. 24–5.
4 See, for instance, her novel, *From Man to Man* (1926: repr. London, Virago, 1989); also of interest here is McClintock, 'Olive Schreiner: the limits of colonial feminism', *Imperial Leather*, Chapter 7.
5 Clare Midgley, *Women Against Slavery* (London, Routledge, 1992); Napur Chaudhuri and Margaret Strobel (eds), *Western Women and Imperialism: Complicity and Resistance* (Bloomington and Indianapolis, Indiana University Press, 1992); Antoinette Burton, *Burdens of History: British Feminists, Indian Women and Imperial Culture, 1865–1914* (Bloomington and Indianapolis, Indiana University Press, 1994); Vron Ware, *Beyond the Pale: White Women, Racism and History* (London, Verso, 1992); Helen Calloway, *Gender, Culture and Empire: European Women in Colonial Nigeria* (London, Macmillan, 1987).
6 Black activists' links are explored in Paul Gilroy, *The Black Atlantic: Modernity and Double Consciousness* (London, Verso, 1993).
7 See, for example, Magnus Hirschfield, *Racism* (trans. and ed. Eden and Cedar Paul, London, 1938), pp. 112–15.
8 An interesting overview of the durablity of racist images and their permeation into popular culture is provided in Jan Nederveen Pieterse, *White on Black: Images of Africa and Blacks in Western Popular Culture* (New Haven and London, Yale University Press, 1992).
9 See Daphne Fielding, *Emerald and Nancy: Lady Cunard and her Daughter* (London, 1968) for Man Ray's photo.
10 Lady Dorothy Mills, *The Golden Land: A Record of Travel in West Africa* (London, 1929), pp. 39, 71, 120–1.
11 Ngũgĩ wa Thiong'o, *Moving the Centre: The Struggle for Cultural Freedoms* (London, James Currey, 1994), pp. 113–15. For Huxley's 'maternalistic' concern for African women see her travelogue, *Four Guineas: A Journey Through West Africa* (London, Chatto and Windus, 1954).
12 Sir Ralph Furse, *Acuparious: Recollections of a Recruiting Officer* (London, 1962), pp. 305–7.
13 Cherry Gertzel, 'Perham's view of Africa' in Smith and Bull (eds), *Margery Perham*, pp. 31–4.

14 Biographical data from a BBC talk in the series 'The Time of My Life', Radio 4, 11 January 1972.
15 Smith and Bull (eds), *Margery Perham*, Introduction, p. 7; Vera Brittain, *Testament of Friendship: The Story of Winifred Holtby* (London, 1941), p. 11.
16 Margery Perham, *Ten Africans* (London, 1936), pp. x–xii.
17 William Macmillan Private Papers: personal information, interview between B. Bush and Mona Macmillan, 20 March 1982.
18 Anthony Kirk-Greene, 'Forging a relationship with the Colonial Service' in Smith and Bull (eds), *Margery Perham*, pp. 77–8.
19 Deborah Lavin, 'Margery Perham's initiation into African affairs' in Smith and Bull (eds), *Margery Perham*, p. 54.
20 Developments in this period are the focus of my forthcoming book, *Imperialism, Race and Resistance: Britain and Black Africa in the Inter-War Years* (London, Routledge, 1998).
21 Anna Melissa Graves, an American Quaker, was a strong critic of colonialism who travelled in West Africa and developed a close friendship with Gladys Casely-Hayford, a young Sierra Leonian creole who travelled and worked in Europe in the 1920s and studied at Ruskin College from 1931 to 1932. See Anna Melissa Graves (ed.), *Benvenuto Cellini Had No Prejudice Against Bronze: Letters from West Africans* (Baltimore, privately published, 1943), pp. 76–7, 90–1.
22 Barbara Bush, 'Britain and Black Africa in the inter war years: metropolitan responses to the growth of race and political consciousness in West and South Africa' (PhD Thesis, University of Sheffield, 1985).
23 Rita Hinden, *Plan for Africa: A Report Prepared for the Colonial Bureau of the Fabian Society* (London, George Allen and Unwin, 1941).
24 See, for example, *British Imperialism in West Africa* (London, L.R.D., Colonial Series, No. 4, 1927).
25 See Barbara Bush, 'Blacks in Britain: the 1930s', *History Today*, 31 (September 1981), 46–7.
26 See, for example, William MacMillan, *Warning from the West Indies: A Tract for Africa and the Empire* (London, 1936), and Rita Hinden (ed.), *Fabian Colonial Essays* (London, 1945).
27 Brittain, *Testament of Friendship*, pp. 131, 161.
28 Margery Perham, *African Apprenticeship: An Autobiographical Journey in Southern Africa, 1929* (London, 1974).
29 Holtby to Brittain, June 1926, 15.3.26, Holtby Papers, Hull City Libraries; Brittain, p. 184.
30 Correspondence between Holtby and Arthur Creech Jones, 18.12.32, Holtby Papers: Lavin in Smith and Bull (eds), *Margery Perham*, p. 55.
31 Nnamdi Azikiwe, *My Odyssey: An Autobiography* (London, 1970), p. 197. For a perspective on poorer blacks, see Laura Tabili, *'We Ask for British Justice': Workers and Racial Difference in Late Imperial Britain* (New York, Cornell UP, 1994).
32 Ethel Mannin, *Comrade O Comrade, or Low Down on the Left* (London, 1945), pp. 134–9; Ethel Mannin to B. Bush, 3.6.80.
33 Holtby to Brittain, 23.9.34, Holtby Papers.
34 Eric Walrond, 'The Negro in London', *The Black Man*, 1:11 (December 1935), 9–10; Erika Smilowitz, 'Una Marson: woman before her time', *Jamaica Journal* (May, 1983), 68; Harold Moody, 'Race prejudice', *The Keys*, 3:3 (January to March 1936), 29–30. For further information about Marson, see Delia Jarrett Macauley, 'Exemplary women' in Delia Jarrett Macauley (ed.), *Reconstructing Womanhood, Reconstructing Feminism* (London, Routledge, 1996).
35 See, for example, 'Why I joined the League of Coloured Peoples' by an Englishwoman (Rita Fleming Gyll), *The Keys*, 6:3 (January to March 1937), 48–50.
36 Brittain, *Testament of Friendship*, p. 41.
37 Leys to Holtby, 1.10.30, Holtby Papers.
38 Smilowitz, 'Una Marson', p. 69. Information about LCP membership and campaigning issues is from a survey of *The Keys*, 1932–1937.

39 Leys to Holtby, 1930, 10.4.34, Holtby Papers; Lady Rhondda cited in Britttain, *Testament of Friendship*, p. 110.
40 Personal correspondence, 1928, 1933, Holtby Papers; Holtby, *Mandoa, Mandoa! A Comedy of Irrelevance* (London, 1933), p. 252.
41 Holtby to Arthur Creech Jones, 29.8.33; Brittain, *Testament of Friendship*, p. 65.
42 This criticism of the European left is forcefully made in Albert Memmi's polemic, *The Coloniser and the Colonised* (London, Souvenir Press, 1974), pp. 34–7.
43 *Negro Anthology Made by Nancy Cunard, 1931 to 1933* (published by Nancy Cunard at Wishart and Co., London, 1934).
44 *'We Were Framed': The First Full Story of the Scottsboro Case* (London, Scottsboro Defence Committee, 4 Paton Street, WC1, June 1934), pp. 1–18; *The Keys*, 1:3 (January 1934), 42, 62.
45 J. M. Kenyatta, 'Hands off Abyssinia', *Labour Monthly*, 17:9 (September 1935), 532–6; 'Declaration of the Coloured People at Brussels', *New Times and Ethiopian News*, 19 (12 September 1936), 14; see also Barbara Winslow, *Sylvia Pankhurst* (London, UCL Press, 1996), for general biographical detail on Pankhurst.
46 Patricia Pugh, 'Margery Perham and her archive' in Smith and Bull (eds), *Margery Perham*, p. 113.
47 IASB Publicity Handout, 1937, Arthur Creech Jones Papers, Rhodes House, Oxford; *History of the Pan-African Congress* (reprint of the *Report of the 1945 Pan-African Congress*, first published, 1947; second edition, London, 1963), pp. 11–13.
48 bell hooks, *Ain't I A Woman? Black Women and Feminism* (London, Virago, 1982); see also Gloria T. Hall, Patricia Bell Scott and Barbara Smith (eds), *All the Women are White, All the Blacks are Men, But Some of Us Are Brave* (New York, Feminist Press, 1982).
49 Antoinette Burton, 'Rules of thumb: British history and imperial culture in nineteenth and twentieth century Britain', *Women's History Review*, 3:4 (Autumn 1994), 483–500.
50 Brittain, *Testament of Friendship*, p. 34.
51 McClintock, *Imperial Leather*, pp. 44–5.
52 Ras Makonnen, *Pan Africanism from Within* (as recorded and edited by Kenneth King, London, 1973), pp. 132, 146–8.
53 Robert C. Reinders, 'Racialism on the left: E. D. Morel and the 'Black Horror' on the Rhine', *International Review of Social History*, 13:3 (1968), 5, 6, 7–8; Basil Matthews, *The Clash of Colour: A Study in the Problem of Race* (London, 1924), p. 43; Sidney Olivier, *White Capital and Coloured Labour* (London, 1929), pp. 21, 37; Cedric Dover, *Half Caste* (London, 1937), pp. 14–16.
54 Garvey's critique of 'Coloured men who attract white girls', *News Chronicle*, 15.4.37; *The Black Man*, 2:6 (March to April 1937), 71–8.
55 Kenneth Little, *Negroes in Britain: A Study of Race Relations in English Society* (London, Tavistock, 1947–8), p. 245.
56 Margery Perham, *The Colonial Reckoning* (London, 1963), p. 28; Makonnen, *Pan Africanism from Within*, pp. 132, 147.
57 Makonnen, *Pan Africanism from Within*, p. 132.
58 See, for instance, J. A. Rogers, *Sex and Race: Negro–Caucasian Mixing in All Ages and All Lands*, 3 vols (New York, 1944), vol. 3, pp. 184–93, 203–4.
59 Nancy Cunard, *Black Man and White Ladyship: An Anniversary* (Toulouse, privately printed, 1931), pp. 2–3; Rogers, *Sex and Race*, pp. 214–17.
60 Cunard, *Black Man, White Ladyship*, pp. 10–13.
61 Azikiwe, *My Odyssey*, p. 192.
62 Doris Garland Anderson, *Nigger Lover* (London, 1937), pp. 245–7, and review in *The Keys*, 5:4 (April–June 1938), 92.
63 Makonnen, *Pan Africanism from Within*, p. 172.
64 E. Moore and S. R. Wood, 'What Moore and Wood think of the English', *The Black Man*, 1:7 (July 1936), 14–15. Moore and Wood were representatives of a Gold Coast delegation to Britain to publicise colonial grievances.
65 Shiela Patterson's *Dark Strangers: A Study of West Indians in London* (London,

Tavistock, 1963), for instance, was very much in the liberal multiracialist tradition of the inter-war period and was informed by her earlier research in the 'black empire'.

66 For middle-class female patronage of a Nigerian student (complicated by sexual desire) see Colin MacInnes's novel about black sub-culture in 1950s London, *City of Spades* (London, Alison and Busby, 1993; first published, 1958); for debates over race and sex in World War Two see Graham Smith, *When Jim Crow Meets John Bull* (London, Tauris, 1987). See also Richard Fries, 'A wild colonial lobbyist', Obituary, Felicity Bolton, *Guardian*, 8 July 1995.

INDEX

Note: 'n.' after a page reference indicates the number of a note on that page.